Black Lives

Published by Big White Shed, Nottingham, England
ISBN 978-1-9163105-5-1
Printed and bound by Booksfactory, EU
Cover and original artwork by Kim Thompson
Copyright © Big White Shed 2021
individual copyright remains with the authors

Developed by Nottingham Writers' Studio

Content Warning: A number of the stories in this anthology address issues that some may find difficult to read, such as violence, abuse, and medical practices. Reader discretion is advised.

This book is dedicated to Sophia Ramcharan who tragically passed before its publication. A director at Nottingham Writers' Studio, she was a fierce advocate for this anthology and the cause behind it. Her voice helped amplify Black Lives across the airwaves and without Sophia, this collection would be diminished; as are our lives without her. Rest in Peace.

Foreword

Many stories start with a mysterious death, but this anthology was sparked by a senseless murder. George Floyd was killed over a period of seven minutes and forty-two seconds by a man meant to protect him, despite multiple witnesses begging the killer to stop. The video is heart wrenching to watch with George dying, calling for his 'Mama.'

After seeing it, I wiped away tears, sadness giving way to impotent anger, because I was powerless to do anything. I am not a politician or a lawyer. I don't even like social media. What could I do about events that happened thousands of miles away on another continent?

Inequality though isn't just a state-side problem. A Black person is ten times more likely to be stopped and searched than any other race in the UK. If taken to court, they are twice as likely to receive a higher prison sentence than a white counterpart for the same crime. Racism can be seen in all walks of British life ranging from the supermarket all the way through to education, economic opportunities and home ownership.

A quarter of all children identify as being from an ethnic minority, yet only 1% of books feature a non-white main character. This number barely increases to 6% if you include the main cast. Additionally, writers of colour are only half as represented as white writers.

Knowing this I wondered about launching an anthology to help tackle this issue. Creating a new platform for non-Caucasian authors to spread their work while highlighting stories where a white person wasn't the main hero or protagonist.

I was extremely nervous when I put my idea of the 'George Floyd Short Story Competition' to the board of Nottingham Writers' Studio, but the project couldn't have found a warmer home. 'Black Lives' is the result of the efforts of over 150 writers who submitted their stories and numerous others working hard behind the scenes to bring this book to life.

Alan Walker, Chair of the Studio, was a true superman. Despite battling cancer, he arranged meetings, kept the project on track, and was a reader on several of the stories. Sophia Ramcharan was the voice of our media campaign and a dedicated reader who helped shape this anthology. Sadly, she passed away unexpectedly before it's publication. Her input cannot be over-stated on this project and she will be sorely missed.

Thom Seddon, while doing the hundreds of things necessary to keep the lights on at NWS, also found time to be our editor – something akin to agreeing to be a cat shepherd. However, it must be noted that as little editing as possible has been done to these stories, to ensure the words remain true to the authors who wrote them.

The equally hard-working Sophie Scott was also one of our main readers even though she had to split her time between the Studio and the Nottingham Refugee Forum. Thanks, must also go Tracey Hylton Burrows and Hannah Gascoyne, who both offered their time as preliminary readers, and insight as members of the board.

On behalf of the Studio, I'd like to thank Yvvette Edwards for being our inaugural judge, and always a pleasure to work with as she conquered the unenviable task of choosing the top three entries in the competition.

Last, but certainly not least, if it was the front cover that caused you to pick up this book (and why wouldn't it?) then look no further than Kim Thompson, our brilliant illustrator.

In closing, I'd also like to show my appreciation not just for the 27 exceptional talents who grace these pages, but for everyone who took their time to submit their work. This anthology would have been weaker for anyone of you not taking part.

If there is anyone who worked on the project but isn't mentioned here, then please accept my sincere thanks. The fault isn't in your great work, but my faulty memory.

Adam O'Connell
Vice Chair at NWS

Contents

A Letter From The Grave

Tyrone Takawira

Why does my skin colour offend you? Does my black not look like magic? Does it not remind you of culture? Of rhythm? Of soul? Black is not excellence? Black is not king? My melanin does not illuminate? It does not radiate? Am I not a star burning brightly in this universe? Or maybe you see dirt? The same dirt that lynched Negroes collapsed on. The same dirt that overflows with the blood of the innocent – the blood of my ancestors. Is my accent too 'ghetto'? Does it remind you of rumbling waters? The same waters that harbour dead bodies. And aging bones. Of rebellious slaves. My ancestors. Thrown overboard. For not conforming. Do you hate my hands? Are they too big? Is this why you arrest me? To keep me in shackles – like you did my ancestors? To keep me from forming fists? To keep me oppressed? To keep me chained to a system that does not benefit me? Are my lips too plump? Too full? Spilling demands of freedom. Spilling the cries of a people - demanding equality. Racism does not haunt you? Do you not see flashes of our pain, of our tormented faces, after you kill us? After you leave holes in Breonna Taylor? In Atatiana Jefferson? In us. Aren't you tired of carrying murder in your hands - like Louis Vuitton bags? Is systematic oppression fashionable? Aren't you tired of fingers that strum death - every time you pull the trigger? Aren't you tired of orchestrating evil - like rogue soldiers? Aren't you tired? Eight. Derek Chauvin killed me in eight minutes. My neck was the stool he knelt on. A metaphor. How 'black' is the steppingstone. How 'black' is bottom. How 'black' is not king - but peasant. Three. Three other officers stood. Watching. Applauding. Approving. My body started to breed death – turning vibrant skin to corpse. My body became a vessel, hallow insides where there once lived a man. A man with dreams. A man with children. A man who was loved. A man who was love. A man who was imperfect but human. I… I couldn't breathe. I. couldn't. breathe. Words ignored by men who swore to serve and protect. Words that have sparked a revolution. Words that depict the black experience. We can't breathe. We are suffocated by police brutality. By targets that zoom on our backs – because we exist. Because we 'look like' threats. We can't breathe. We are denied life by limiting social narratives. By a blemished history. By a past we haven't healed from. WE. CAN'T. BREATHE. And we will riot in the streets of Minneapolis until we can. Until buildings burn. Until statues fall. Until our voices are heard. Until the social contract is fixed. Until black no longer offends you. Until you see our magic. Until you see our culture. And rhythm. And soul. Until black is king. Until black becomes synonymous to excellence. Until you stop seeing dirt. Or lynched Negros. Or rumbling waters. Or slaves. Until our light is given right to burn. Until we illuminate. Not only the United States, but the universe.

The Worth of a Miracle

Vishwas R. Gaitonde

"Oh, do you know the muffin man,
The muffin man, the muffin man?
Oh, do you know the muffin man,
That lives on Drury Lane?"
-Children's Nursery Rhyme

The faceoff on the railway platform started with just two people, the yogi and the stationmaster, but then grew, first with half a dozen looking on, the crowd then swelling to well over a score. Some of them chimed in with their two *annas* worth, but when the stationmaster stood his ground and made it clear there would be no give and no take, the crowd grew restive. Their raised voices put the stationmaster on edge.

"Order! Order! What's this now, eh?"

The angry bellow made everybody, including the stationmaster, jump. It came from a little way down the platform but was loud enough to carry without losing its steam. Two military officers had emerged from the train and strode towards them. The taller, older man looked cross; he was the one who had yelled for order. The other man, looking like he had just graduated from high school, had a scraggly moustache that was mousier than his face and body. He was sweating, his eyes constantly flitting.

The grizzled old stationmaster sized them up in an instant.

The mousy officer was a newcomer just off the ship from England on his first assignment; the older officer hadn't been here too long either. They were travelling Second Class. But they were still military officers; they still carried clout.

"The yogi," said the stationmaster, jerking his chin in the yogi's direction, "wishes to ride the train without a ticket."

"Then why are you dawdling away until kingdom come, my man?" The older officer turned red. "Ask the bloke to leave the station double quick. If he or his gaggle don't like it, call the blasted police. There's police and army units here in Arcot, if you weren't aware of it, my man. What's your name?"

"Davies, sir. Derek Davies, Stationmaster, Arcot." The stationmaster glanced at the officers but did not hold his eye contact. These were definitely new arrivals. They would have ended up clerks or bellboys or shop assistants in London but when they got to the colonies wearing uniforms, they thought no end of themselves. They were the worst kind of trouble.

"Well, Davies, get on with it, my man, get on with it."

Davies addressed the mendicant yogi in halting Tamil, the local language. The yogi remained impassive but was impressive in his own way: saffron dhoti, a saffron scarf draped across the back of his neck, its tasselled ends hanging across his bare hairless chest. His garments were embellished with a necklace of plump brown *rudraksha* beads, an ornate shiny bronze armband shaped like a cobra with its hood outspread coiled tightly around his biceps, bright against his mahogany skin. His hair hung down halfway to his waist, some strands braided and others dangling loose, and his long beard was twisted, its salt-and-pepper shade complementing the sacred ash that streaked across his forehead in three smudged horizontal stripes, like a military insignia.

But if the yogi chose not to utter a word, the crowd more than made up for it. They were resentful, contemptuous, and annoyed — and every raucous syllable of their speech reflected it.

"Davies, why the dickens aren't the bloody natives leaving? It's your job to keep the station running smoothly."

Davies swallowed. His Adam's apple bobbed up and down as though a capricious Eve was jerking it like a yo-yo. The yogi, the crowd lectured, had renounced all material possessions and only worked for the good of society, so it was society's duty to now take care of him. The yogi was not asking to travel First Class although, in the name of God Almighty, he deserved that and more. Third Class was good enough for a true mendicant. Davies was about to tell them the yogi would never be allowed in First Class anyway, a right which only the British had. Then he thought the better of it as a parade of thoughts marched through his mind.

The First Class compartments were only for the rich and privileged, pink-skinned folk – for every white man turned pink after coming to India. The crowd knew about who could travel First Class better than they knew their own names. But not all of them — perhaps most of them — had any idea of exactly how luxuriously vulgar each carriage was. There were no corridors; the doors of each suite-carriage opened directly onto the platform. The interiors had plush carpeting, electric lights and fans, wooden panelling, berths sized for an emperor and bedding fit for an empress, bathrooms with showers, and even servants' quarters. Third Class, which the crowd demanded for their beloved ticketless yogi, consisted of carriages stinking of filth accumulated over weeks. They could only boast of hard wooden benches guaranteed to make every butt ache; no lights, fans, or even toilets.

On this train that chugged between Arcot and the Royapuram railway terminus in Madras, if people could 'hold on' for a few hours, they could survive the journey without requiring a visitation to the toilet. But that wasn't so on the long-distance trains that chugged between far-flung cities like Madras and Bombay and Calcutta and Karachi. Whenever the train halted at a station or even between stations waiting for a signal clearance, the third-class passengers ejected themselves helter-skelter from their hothouse carriages, squeezing their dignity along with their excreta out of their bared bottoms as they relieved themselves beside the tracks. The passengers in First and Second Class, sipping their fine wines, whisky, and gimlets, turned into titillated peeping Toms as they watched the shitting barbarians in delight and disdain, never realizing that the real barbarians were the geniuses in Mother England who designed such trains with cold and calculated inhumanity.

"Davies, stop daydreaming and execute your duty. I not only demand it, I positively order it in the name of Her Majesty, our most beloved Queen-Empress Victoria."

Davies, his reverie interrupted, swallowed again before blurting out, "With due respect, Sir, if we are to maintain good relations with the subjects we govern, we have to accommodate them some of the time. This train has Fourth Class. Can I —"

"No! A free ride? Never, not on this or any train of the British Imperial Railway. Especially for a ragamuffin man who lives in a shack on some dreary lane. That's an order, Davies."

That the officer cut in even before Davies completed his sentence unnerved him in more than one way. First, the impunity with which a military officer could order a civilian. Then, Fourth Class was the lowest of the low, just a box carriage with no seating. For the numbers of bodies squashed into it like pigs and cattle, there were a pathetically small number of rungs dangling from the roof, and nothing else to cling on to. Sweaty and smelly bodies slammed into each other as the train lurched and swerved, and people hugged, clutched, grasped, and clung onto each others' body parts when the jolts threw them off balance, which was just about every couple of minutes.

"I say, Sergeant Arbuthnot." The young mousy military man opened his mouth for the first time, speaking in a low, deferential whisper. "I say, Davies sure knows the local lingo. He understands what these buggers are saying and they understand him."

Arbuthnot froze, as though he had been slapped on the face. He mused for a few split seconds, then commented sotto voce, "Parsons, old man, lick my arse, wipe my arse, you've nailed it, snap, bang, wallop, and you've barely been in this shithole country. I clean missed it, old man. This Davies bugger, of course he's not one of us. He's one of *them*, he's a damn Anglo."

"Anglo?" Parsons looked as lost as he had felt when midway on the long ocean voyage between England and India.

"The shoddy product of a British daddy and an Indian mum. The sods who think they're one of us when they really belong to the other side.'

"Ah." Parsons nodded to Arbuthnot knowingly, and Arbuthnot looked pleased at the reaction. He called out to Davies, "First Class or Fourth Class or any class be damned, nobody travels without a ticket. Now then, are you going to kick out all these people back to the street — or will you not, because they're *your* people? A full half of their blood runs through your veins, doesn't it, *sir?*"

Davies turned bright red and then blanched. But Arbuthnot wasn't done yet.

"We're on our way to Madras," he said, with a sideways glance at Parsons, "to an important meeting with the Governor-General at Fort St. George. And if you don't handle this situation the right way, *sir*, and if the Governor-General asks us about our journey, why, we *might* just mention that a certain Mr. Davies stationed at Arcot flouted the rules of the Madras Presidency."

Parsons looked uncomfortable, and Davies' heart plummeted but was quickly buoyed by Arbuthnot's brashness. Threatening to report him to the Governor-General? Davies was sure that the meeting would consist of a large group of military personnel, with these two upstarts standing with their backs pressed to the wall at the rear of the room, unnoticed even by people with ranks far below Governor-General. But for his safety, Davies weighed each word before it left his mouth.

"Gentlemen — sirs, you'll be in Madras soon, but I will

have to forever deal with the locals in Arcot who will never forget any insult, real or imagined, to their holy man. A matter of law and order in the long term, sirs."

"They're *your* people so in the end it'll all blow over amicably," sneered Arbuthnot.

"There's no guarantee of that, sirs." Davies ignored the slur. "The yogi is highly respected."

"Tell him he'll be more respected if he follows the rules. Ticketless travel is against the law for everybody. Equality and all that, old chap. Talk to him"

"Sir, he knows no English."

The yogi abruptly stepped forward, thrusting himself from the sidelines as he faced the officers. His inscrutable gaze, calm demeanour, and grave silence slapped an intangible lustre onto his appearance, an aura which everybody seemed to sense. He spoke in a thin, cracking voice, "We shall meet again in Madras." Before anybody could say anything, he did a smart about-turn and marched briskly out of the station, the crowd parting on either side like the roiling blue waters of the Red Sea and then trailing behind him.

"Well, how about that!" Arbuthnot chuckled, and said to Davis. "Knows no English, eh?"

"A miracle!" Davies looked shaken. "He really doesn't know English."

"They fed you that lie, did they? Well, Davies, looks like you swallow whatever you're told," Arbuthnot shot back. "And that's a bad thing, Davies, a bad thing. People like you will be the downfall of the Empire."

"Perhaps he never formally studied English at school," put in Parsons, "but picked it up on the fly — enough to manage a sentence."

Arbuthnot threw a frigid glance Parson's way and then parodied the yogi, using a high falsetto, "'*Vee sall mitt uggyen in Madras*.' And just how will the holy madman get to Madras? Caw caw caw — fly there like a wretched crow?"

The engine suddenly shrieked out a loud toot with an accompanying puff of steam. The officers clambered back into their Second Class carriage without as much as a parting glance at Davies.

A little over the halfway point between Arcot and Madras, the train inexplicably ground to a complete stop. Despite the whirring fans, the heat extracted its toll from the passengers. The irate officers asked two of their carriage attendants to get out and hoof it to the engine to enquire what in Gawd's name was holding up the bloody train. What the attendants reported back in their pidgin English – that the engine had a smallish problem that twisted into biggish problem but was being expertly fixed by the bestest experts (not to worry, sahib) although, sadly, there were still floating problems that would not sink – made no sense to the officers, who despatched the attendants again on another much simpler errand: to scamper on the hot earth alongside the train to the restaurant car and fetch them chilled beer.

They had expected lukewarm beer – all the ice in the iceboxes would have melted – but the beer was surprisingly cold.

As they licked the froth and savoured each sip, they overlooked the passage of time and did not realize that the train was well behind schedule when it chugged into the Royapuram railway terminus in Madras.

As the officers walked down the platform, their attendants in tow carrying their suitcases, Parsons stopped in mid-stride.

"Sergeant Arbuthnot, sir, look! Do you see what I see?"

Arbuthnot followed Parsons' gaze at the passengers walking ahead of them. He was irritated at Parsons for speaking in riddles, and then he saw what had confounded his colleague. A little way ahead of them was a dark-skinned man clad in a saffron dhoti, his bare back covered with flowing salt and pepper hair, some strands braided and others hanging loose.

As though sensing that other eyes were observing him, the man slowly turned, and his face flashed a wide grin their way. Many grins, for with the wrinkling of his brow, each stripe of ash on his forehead had turned into a grin if not an outright smirk. The yogi bowed, palms pressed together in the traditional Hindu greeting, then turned around and walked briskly out of the station, his cloth swishing against his legs, just as he had in Arcot.

"A miracle!" Parsons burst out, unknowingly echoing Davies. Arbuthnot looked unnerved too, but scrunched his face back to its normal stiff upper lip look.

"Miracles? Damn you, there are no such things outside of the Bible," he said, with contempt. "There's another explanation. A twin, maybe."

"Farfetched, if I may say so, Sergeant. A twin? Riding the

same train with us, wearing *exactly* the same clothes, complete with that ugly necklace and that cobra bracelet?"

"*Clothes?* The bugger was half-naked. And remember our train stopped? Somebody could have put the rascal into a buggy and driven him over so that he could sneak in. A goddamn stowaway."

"But how could anybody have known the train would stop? And where? Besides, no horse could pull a buggy that far in so short a time. No, sir – we've really seen a miracle."

"Snap out of it, Parsons. This country fries the brains of those who are new to it. You've fallen victim. Snap out of it. We're prey to their deviousness. No miracles can occur in places that the good Lord has forsaken. Besides – okay, I'll humour you, let's just say this was a miracle. What of it? What's it worth, Parsons? What's its value? Just the few paltry rupees the bugger would have had to fork out for shitty Fourth Class on a short train journey. Not much of a miracle, is it?"

Parsons looked around to locate the yogi. He brimmed with questions but the yogi had vanished. He must have walked awfully fast to get out of the station so quickly. When Parsons and Arbuthnot were on the street, Arbuthnot glanced at his watch and gave a stricken cry.

"Bloody hell! Hell, by Gawd, we're *late.* The meeting starts in nine minutes. We'll never reach Fort St. George in time, the goddamn fort might as well be in London."

Parsons blanched. He'd have a big black mark on his record just as his military career in the Empire was beginning. He looked up at the sky, as though in appeal to divine Providence to do something, anything, to erase the blot. But there was no sign or signal of any kind; the dark clouds just floated above them, uncaring. The blinding glare of the sun that they had been subject to earlier in the day had been snuffed out without warning. There was a low, disgruntled rumble from up above the clouds. A crack of forked lightning signalled the start of hostilities. And it seemed to Parsons that the raindrops were like bullets, the first two striking both him and Arbuthnot with unerring aim.

Sometimes
Bethel Levien

2,923 days.

Sometimes I feel her being the bigger spoon when we sleep. Sometimes she almost cracks the bathroom mirror with her high-pitched attempts at Beyoncé's *Dangerously in Love*. Sometimes I find myself tutting and cursing at her for wetting up the floor after her steamy showers. Sometimes I smell whiffs of my perfume on her collar bones as she kisses me goodbye before heading out on a date with Jacob; or Michael, or Noah, or Raheem with the lob-sided glasses that she pretends not to notice because of his great taste in designer shoes that he fortnightly gifts her with. Sometimes I let her paint my nails, even though that isn't really my thing. And sometimes, despite my snacking on avocado-toast while she snacks on Pringles and Tangfastics, she genuinely believes she's fitter than me. That is until we go head-to-head on our morning runs where she suddenly insists that fitness is for the boring and the overly anxious. She had a point there. Sometimes we share headphones on our walks when running becomes pretentious. Sometimes we have karaoke sessions together. Sometimes along with the whistles of the trees, sometimes to the adlibs of Jill Scott. Sometimes to the beat of Nas. Sometimes to the sass of Solange…

"Do you believe in love?" Shannon's hazel eyes glistened against the morning's amber. Her smile was contagious. Warm like summer. Her skin was a soft caramel and the mole to the left of her nose looked none other than a beauty spot exemplifying her unique beauty. Her eyes were thin, like lines, almost. We knew that she was mixed race – Black and Asian – but we didn't know what countries exactly. She sure gave all the girls everywhere we went a reason to be envious, that's for sure. As each of her black curls bounced – each curl on a mission of their own – they threw daggers with tightened lips. She was the face of the two of us. I was the brains. Mum said we'd make the perfect combination if we were men-fighting-warriors. That'd often make us giggle. Until I realised the truth behind such a statement.

Mum didn't care that she wasn't like the rest of us. Physically or otherwise. It was simple. She was just a part of our family.

"What?" I asked, wiping my nose with a scrunched-up tissue I retrieved from my cave of a sleeve.

Shannon spun on the lamppost as we waited for the 279 towards Manor House. Her arm stretched wide as she held on tight. Her grip was so firm, it let out a squeak each time she spun. Her raw hand against the metal, embracing the feeling of happy. Happy, for no reason.

"You know dogs pee on that, right?"

"*Ew!*" she squealed, darting backward as though it was suddenly hot enough to sting. She then wiped her hands on her pink and white tweed skirt matching her blazer. "And you let me feel it up like that? Yuck."

I laughed.

"*Soooo,*" she teased, prodding at my shoulder with her index fingers. "You didn't answer my question, Miss Thing."

I looked at her expectedly. Though we were the same age, she was definitely the younger-spirited one. I often felt like I took care of her most of the time. She was a free spirit, like a Gemini or a Sagittarius. I was type A, sort of like a Capricorn.

"Love!" she yelled. Her eyebrows then began to bounce. "I said, have you ever been in *luurv?*"

"I mean..."

Her eyes widened.

"I don't know. I don't think so..." I trailed off.

She shrugged, unaffected by my response, or probably bored of the conversation. She refocused into her suitcase of a bag. It also matched her tweed outfit with its pink and white sheer colours. She began rummaging, huffing and flustering as a collection of noises and clacking came from her hasty movement.

"What're you looking for?" I leaned on one leg, my hands in the back of my jeans pockets.

"My gloss! I can't find it. Damn! It's limited edition Fenty! Do you know how much I paid for it? £38!"

God.

"Shan," I snorted. "Chill, its just—"

"Sofia, no. Not now," she interrupted with a sassy palm and a slither of the neck. I rolled my eyes, leaned against the bus shelter and slid my phone out of my denim-jacket pocket. It was 8:23AM. The bus was late. It was supposed to be here eight minutes ago. Damn, I couldn't be late. Not today. I needed to get her there on time. Xavier said

9:30AM. It was bad enough we were coming from North London heading south with all the rush hour traffic, but to be running late with Shannon was basically rubbing salt in the wound. Though, Shannon didn't care for time. She wasn't afraid to let people know she felt that way, either. Even if it *was* for one of the leading modelling agencies in the UK that I snuck her on the list for when I covered the lifestyle segment last month. Shannon was Shannon and people deserved her – not the other way around.

"Found it!" she yelled, followed by the pop of the lip-gloss stick being removed from its tube. "Here," she pushed it in my face. I shook my head. She shrugged and slid it back into her mess of a bag.

"The bus is late," I tutted.

She shrugged, widening her mouth to wipe the excess gloss from around her lips in her pocket mirror's reflection. I checked the bus app and it said the next bus wasn't coming for another twelve minutes. I was beginning to get annoyed at our delay, and Shannon's blasé attitude, so I decided to go to the shop to treat myself. Just the thought of a ready-made iced-mocha-coffee shot a smile to my face.

"Do you want anything? I'm getting an iced-coffee."

"Umm..." she pouted her lips in ponder, before a well-dressed man carrying a grey-leather briefcase approached Shannon. She dazzled at his sparkling white teeth, his dark swimming hair, and eyelash-filled doting eyes. He kissed her hand, telling her he simply *had* to stop to let her know of her fascinating beauty. *Like she didn't already know.* He was almost blinded by it, by the looks of it. I mean, he didn't seem to bother that she was texting somebody on her phone.

"You are a sight, hermosa," he said, a Spanish twang highlighting his accent as he rolled his R's. "Are you of the mixed of races?"

"Then what happened?" the detective asked, his partner scribbling down messy notes as sweat beaded his forehead from the summer's heat almost fogging the small room.

"Mum..." I turned to mum. Her eyes were weak but her face sat strong. Almost for the both of us. She cupped her hand on top of mine. Dad sat in the seat to the left of me. He too seemed as though he was trying to be strong. I guess we all were. We had to be.

"I-I don't know. I mean, she was there... she was..."

"Take your time," the detective smiled.

I rolled my eyes, the whites of them flooding my sockets as I huffed and walked away. Did she have to entertain *every* man that approached her? It happened everywhere we went. At school, in college, through university– hell, even at mum's birthday dinner that time. Of course, Mum let her. After all, Mum's dream for us was to get married so she can brag to her friends whose daughters were not married.

I often found myself reminding Mum that beauty was

something of minimal substance. That these men purely fetish over Shannon's beauty as opposed to genuinely taking interest in her as a person. She would then roll her eyes and do that thing where she assumed my shoulder had suddenly caught a chill as she'd comfort it with a rubbing palm and tell me I was pretty, too. I'd then remind her that I wasn't insecure before she'd abruptly interrupt me, kiss me anyway, and leave a whiff of *my* Chanel on *her* wrists in the air. I glared at myself for a while in the mirror that day, after she left. And then at the picture above my mirror of Shannon and I in a happy hug. Her caramel skin being the unexpected twist to my dark chocolate cup. The sweetness to my bitter. The softness deep, deep inside of my harsh exterior. *Was I insecure?*

I popped the plastic lid off of my iced coffee, peeled the foil lid back, placed the plastic lid back on and sucked through the cups hole as I walked out of the shop. I turned the corner to find Shannon gone. There it went, my tolerance. I huffed through puffed cheeks, angry, that she would actually do this again. And today of all days.

I noticed she'd sent me a text message, but I ignored it and phoned her instead. It went straight to voicemail. I left her a voicemail.

"I can't believe you're doing this again. You fucking selfish bitch. I snuck you onto that list to try and put you ahead and you throw that all away for a fucking man! Again! A man that you don't even *know*, Shannon, really? All the while, you have fucking Jacob who loves you to your core and you're doing this? Again? Noah, Michael, Raheem—you're an unbelievably selfish person, Shannon.

Don't ever ask me to do anything for you ever again, 'little sis'."

I stormed to the bus stop, throwing my phone in my bag this time. I could see the bus in the distance, so I held my arm out to signal for it to stop, taking a swig of my iced coffee. A gust of wind pushed me, I tumbled back. My oyster fell to the floor, so I crouched down to pick it up, which is when I noticed it. Shannon's unjustifiably priced lip-gloss. I picked it up, noticing it was full of scratches. I frowned.

Wasn't it new?

A vibrating sensation hummed between my pencil case and folders in my bag. It was Xavier. *Shit.*

"Hi X—"

"Morning sugar, are you guys on your way?"

"Um..."

"What? Don't play with me, Sofe. You know we're counting on your baby sister to come through and give it to us this morning, hunny!"

"Yeah. Right. Yes, of course," I scratched my forehead, slipping Shannon's lip-gloss into my bag. I stretched my arm out again, flagging the bus as it was almost at my stop. "I'm just, I um..."

"Okay, you're multi-tasking, *clearly*. But listen. I've put a few domestic violence case studies on your desk for when you get in. I want you to do some digging on percentages in groups – we want to build a comparison between women of colour and white women to see who is more prone to being victim."

"Okay. Yes, okay."

"Also, I've messaged you a few links..."

Messages. I thought. *She messaged me.*

"...and yesterday, but I didn't know whether to assess the details first—"

"Xavier, that's great. Erm. I will get on it on the ride over but the bus is here now. I have to go-"

"Bus?! I thought you were on your—"

I hung up the phone, shaking Xavier's sass off. I could deal with that later. I opened my messages, scrolled through Xavier's, and clicked on Shannon's.

"Well?" the detective asked, his eyebrows almost merging into one. "What did the text say, Sofia?"

My vision started to blur from the tears welling in my eyes. A sudden tightness pulled and tugged at my throat. I tried to swallow. Saliva, vomit, guilt, I don't know – all of it.

"Sofia?" the detective leaned forward. His partner, who seemed younger and as though this might've been his first case with the way he scribbled enthusiastically and licked his lips repeatedly, stopped writing.

"It didn't make any sense..." I blinked, clearing my vision as the tears fell and my shoulders shuddered as I sobbed. "I-I didn't know, I mean, I thought she was just doing what she normally did with guys who thought she was pretty and beautiful and– you know, letting them treat her and take her wherever while blowing me off in the meantime, I mean... I-I-I didn't –"

"Sofia, please," Dad rested a hand on my shoulder. This time my shoulders *were* cold. "What did the message say? What did Shannon say? *Please.*"

There it was again. Surfacing like a thick liquid layer, ready to boil over and drown me in my own throat – it was guilt. Trying to choke me, guilt.

"It said, 'don't'..." my face began to itch so I scratched my cheek. It was the salty wetness that caused the itch. The wetness of my salty tears. This hurt. I loved her like a sister. My adopted sister. She was my sister. And this hurt.

"You are doing so well, Sofia. Just speak when you can. We are here. With you, we are here," Mum squeezed my hand and smiled with her mouth. Though, not with her eyes.

"It said, 'don't leave'... 'news'... 'trafficking'... 'light girls'... 'don't'," I inhaled. "'Go'," I breathed out.

2,923 days.

...Sometimes Mum would smile at how short her prayers were for dinner because of her eagerness to dig in. Sometimes she'd fart with Dad, blame it on him, and he'd take the bait every time, finding it hilarious that such gruesome could come from something so perfect. Sometimes she'd bring me ice cream when she could just tell I was low. And sometimes she'd bring me carrots & brown sugar to bring me back up again. Sometimes she'd proofread articles for me when Xavier would throw his tantrums.

Sometimes she couldn't care less and would tell me to submit them anyway because, 'Fuck the rules! Live dangerously, like Beyoncé!' Because living dangerously in love is all we have. To love and to be happy, for no reason at all. To sing *Dangerously in Love*, even when you just want to be safely in like. And sometimes... well, sometimes, it all seems so real.

But then I wake up.

And I realise that it has been 2923 days since she's been gone. And sometimes I forget the exact number. Because most of the time she's all I can remember. Not the days that she's been gone. But her. Her smile. Her happy. Her life-ness. And so now I sing, and try to be happy, just like her... for no reason at all.

Mr. Freddie Mercury
Shahed Yousaf

Mr. Freddie Mercury had changed his name by deed poll. He was previously Michael Jackson and before that Sir Elton John. Most prisoners were identified by prison numbers which were printed on their ID cards and must be carried at all times. Mr. Mercury was not a number; he broke rules, fought, took drugs. He had served fifteen years for a three-year prison sentence and did not meet any of the criteria to show he was reformed and rehabilitated. It was an interminable cycle of bad behaviour and punishment. He was deemed a danger to himself and the public.

Imprisonment for Public Protection (IPP) sentences, like Mr. Mercury's, had been abolished by the European Court of Human Rights in 2012 as a human rights violation. The abolishment was not retrospective and Mr. Mercury and thousands of others like him languished in hopelessness. As a prison doctor all I could do was stitch his wounds. I was called to the Inpatient Unit, otherwise referred to as the hospital wing, to see him. Mr. Mercury was on a constant watch observation. An officer was monitoring him through the glass observation panel in the cell door. It was his job to make regular entries in the Assessment, Care in Custody, Teamwork (ACCT) document. The officer was known as Ginge; he was ex-services, always incredibly cheerful.

"What's up, Doc?" he asked as I approached.

"Another day in Paradise, mate! What is it this time, the

hands or the feet?" I asked.

"The spoon," Ginge said.

I feared the damage Mr. Mercury could do to himself with a spoon.

"Why does he do it, Doc?" Ginge asked.

"Can I see your hands?" I said.

Ginge held out his hands with some hesitation and I examined his nails.

"You and Mr. Mercury both bite your nails. The difference is that he is an auto-cannibal and he swallows his fingernails. He eats his hair, his fingers, his toes, and ears. Rapunzel syndrome can kill," I said.

Ginge withdrew his hands with a look of disgust.

"Why haven't you taken the spoon off him?" I asked Ginge.

"It was the Governor's decision."

I felt a tap on my shoulder and I turned to see Nurse Vicky standing beside me. Vicky was the Inpatient Unit manager and was quick to remind me that she was a mental health nurse and did not like blood. The glass in the observation panel had been smashed and our shoes crunched as we stepped closer to the door. We watched Mr. Mercury who, despite his long history of eating himself, was morbidly obese with great folds of fat bulging around his body. He was sitting on his bed, naked apart from his stained underwear. Both of his ears had been sliced off and he had missing fingers and toes. There was a deep gash on his left inner thigh and he was scraping the fat from his bloodied muscle with a plastic spoon and eating it. The blood trickled down his leg and congealed on the floor. He did not appear to be in any discomfort. Quite the opposite; he appeared to be in a trance.

"That poor man!" Vicky whispered with her hand over her mouth.

"It's so sad," I responded.

"Mr. Mercury is a hostage-taker, you can't go in alone," Ginge said.

I whispered thank you when an additional officer arrived and the door was unlocked.

"Good luck," Ginge said.

The door swung open and a wave of hot stench washed over me. I staggered back. It smelt like a butcher's shop; lard and blood. There was the unmistakeable odour of faeces. It was a sweltering summer day and yet the heating was on at maximum capacity. The prison's thermostat seemed to be controlled by someone who was either a sadist or shockingly negligent. The cells were roasting hot in summer and freezing cold in winter, so the prisoners were either at risk of heatstroke or pneumonia. There were so many layers of madness in a prison it was surprising more inmates did not lose their minds completely. With a population of over a thousand there were only seventy prisoners on ACCT documents.

"Hi Mr. Mercury, I'm Dr Y. Can I come in?" I asked as I stood in the doorway and breathed through my mouth.

"I said no Pakis and no Muslims!" Mr. Mercury yelled.

I was winded for a moment by the racist gut punch. Any difference in a prison could be exploited and weaponised; all races became slurs, women were called 'bitches' or 'lezzas' and men were accused of being gay. You had to have a thick skin to work in this environment. One of the reasons I chose prison medicine was because I wanted to toughen myself up. Prison taught me to fight.

I wondered why Mr. Mercury assumed I was a Muslim other than my brown skin tone. I did not have a beard or any other signifiers of my Islamic faith. I laughed it off, but the P-word stung. I had been called a 'black bastard' before, but I managed to sidestep the intended offence because I was unsure if I was considered black. Did Black in the political sense encompass all non-white people? Was the world divided neatly into the binaries of black and white? In my hierarchy of slurs, the N-word trumped all insults and had he called me that I would have terminated the consultation and asked a colleague to take over from me.

Vicky raised her voice to admonish him; "Mr. Mercury, the NHS will not tolerate intolerance. Is that clear?"

"Shut up, you fake plastic bitch!" he yelled.

"Don't forget this 'fake plastic bitch' gives you your medications! I am sick and tired of you insulting staff. This ends now. Do you understand?" she retorted.

He scoffed, blood trickling from his mouth. How could I be offended by someone like him?

"I am the only doctor working today. You can either see me or wait until tomorrow?" I said in a conciliatory tone.

"Whatever," Mr. Mercury said, and licked his spoon.

"Okay," I said half-heartedly and followed the officers into the cell, avoiding the large blood clots on the floor.

Prison was almost entirely grey. Grey cement floors, grey painted brick, grey tracksuits, and grey faces. All of the cells were approximately eight feet by ten feet. Mr. Mercury filled the room making it appear far smaller. His single bed was secured to the floor in the corner. There was no way someone of his size could fit in a single bed. There was no provision for double beds in prison. The majority of prisoners shared cells and slept in tiny bunkbeds. If a prisoner was grossly obese, like Mr. Mercury, they would be advised to put their thin mattress on the floor and sleep there, if there was space.

The room was stagnant with the reek of his unwashed body and infected ulcers. I wandered how I was going to get close enough to do his stitches. I tried to push the small window open to let some fresh air in but it was nailed shut. The perforated air vents on either side of the window had been painted over and they were blocked and redundant. The sun was shining outside and yet he kept his room dark by covering the windows with newspaper. He was illuminated from the overhead light which made his skin seem almost translucent. He reminded me of a painting by Francis Bacon.

Prisoners were encouraged to personalise their cells to make them homely on their limited budget of seven pounds a week. A bright collage of images was plastered to the wall beside his bed. Blu Tack and chewing gum were contraband in prison so the pictures had been secured in place with toothpaste. It leaked through the images like fresh bruises. The happy families and beautiful beach holidays had shadows eating into their hearts.

I looked closer and realised what I had assumed were personal photographs had been cut from magazines. He had superimposed photographs of his huge head onto the men's bodies in a heart-breaking collage of wishful thinking.

I had to turn away. His misery was leaking into me like the toothpaste on the pictures. I cleared my throat and tried to find something positive in this hellhole. He had a pile of books beside his bed; mostly novels by Stephen King and Dean Koontz.

"You like horror?" I asked.

"Can't you tell?" he replied, smiling to reveal dark gums and missing teeth. No horror story could compete with the terror of his existence.

"I used to like horror and fantasy too," I said quietly.

"Not anymore?" he asked.

I shook my head.

"Because of this place?" he asked.

"Yep," I replied.

Mr. Mercury had made excellent soap sculptures of teddy bears and skulls which surrounded him like a substitute family. He was very talented at carving. Beside the toilet stood a life-sized model of a brown puppy with its red tongue sticking out. The eyes were rendered in beautiful detail and I reached down to pat its head.

"Don't touch it!" he snapped.

I stepped back.

"I don't have paints," he said softening his tone.

It was only then that I noticed the brown dog smelt of poo

and the tongue was the colour of dry blood. I recoiled in disgust.

"It's a Poodle," he said, and laughed.

"That's sick," Ginge said.

"What do you expect? The officers don't let me have crayons and colouring pencils because I keep eating them and putting them inside my wounds. But the thing is nothing feels as good as hurting myself. I feel better as soon as I see the blood leave my body; it takes the pain with it," he said.

I had read his file and I was aware he began to bite himself when he went into care as a child. Self-harm was his oldest coping mechanism.

"Why did you pull out your stitches?" I asked, pointing to the open wound on his leg.

"I'm protesting," he replied, chewing on his own fat. "Because I am in pain and no one is helping me."

I explained his leg was hurting because he was putting a spoon into a wound. Pain was the body's defence mechanism against injury. A general rule of thumb was not to push past the pain barrier.

"I ate my thumb," he said, and showed me the stub where the distal phalanx was missing.

He wanted to have his dose of Tramadol increased. I explained he was on the maximum dose of 400mg in twenty-four hours. It would be unsafe to go beyond it because he could damage his liver and kidneys. He could develop problems with his breathing and slip into a coma and die.

He extended his spoon towards me. The blood-stained fat

wobbled on the spoon like a strawberry trifle.

"I'm a vegetarian," I lied.

He shrugged and licked his spoon clean.

"The psychiatrists are coming in tomorrow, Mr. Mercury, you can discuss your medications with them. Are you happy for me to put some fresh stitches in?" I asked.

"I can do my own stitches with a bit of metal and strips of blanket. It's getting more difficult because the scar tissue is tough. When I had MRSA the stitches fell out after two days. Maggots were crawling around in there. Then they turned into flies. I was their dad; The Lord of the Flies."

Ginge's colleague suddenly heaved and was sick on the floor. The colour had drained from his face and he looked as if he was going to faint, so I escorted him out of the cell for fresh air. Ginge covered the mess with toilet paper.

"I was in Helmand, Afghanistan. Nothing fazes me, Doc," Ginge said when I asked if he was okay, but I could see his face had become paler too. I needed to get the stitches in to Mr. Mercury's wound so we could all leave.

Returning to the room, I addressed Mr. Mercury. "It is probably best not to perform surgical procedures on yourself," I said and took the spoon from him.

Vicky arrived with a surgical trolley and a suture pack.

"Will you be my glamorous assistant Vicky?" I asked.

"My pleasure, Doc," she replied in her sing-song voice.

I gloved up and assessed the ten cm wound on his leg. It was fetid and I breathed in and out through my mouth. Although

40

Mr. Mercury had eaten the fat he had not cut away the overlying skin, and the wound edges had not curled and died. He was covered in scars and prison tattoos; wispy spiders, birds, and fish appeared to flit in and out of his putrid wounds. Most of his tattoos were in blue ink as if he had doodled on himself with a heavy hand. There was a list of female names on his arm, presumably ex-girlfriends, because lines were crossed through them. On the knuckles of one hand he had marked 0121 and on the other BRUM so there was no mistaking he was from my hometown of Birmingham.

I anticipated that soon after I put in the stitches he was likely to open them up again and insert pens, spoons, dirt, or faeces into the open sores. He had been prescribed protracted courses of antibiotics and was a case study in how to develop drug resistance. When he became septic he was transferred to hospital for intravenous antibiotics but the hospitals found him difficult to manage because he scared the other patients. He was abusive and swore at staff. He stole and swallowed jewellery, batteries, spoons, whatever he could find. He had perforated his bowels on numerous occasions. The hospital doctors wrote angry letters to the prison about what an awkward patient he was. We responded defensively to ensure his care was not compromised by his abrasive personality. He was banned from many of the local hospitals and he had to be taken to the edge of the county for emergency surgery. Sometimes he self-discharged himself and came back to the prison where he and his wounds festered.

Prison medicine occupied the grey zone between primary care, hospital care, mental health, and substance misuse.

It was often the place for people with nowhere else to go. The psychiatrists diagnosed Mr. Freddie Mercury with an emotionally unstable personality disorder (EUPD). This was previously known as bipolar personality disorder and was not to be confused with a bipolar affective disorder. A personality disorder was not classified as a mental illness and he was not eligible to be sectioned under the Mental Health Act or to be transferred to a mental health unit.

Our thoughts, feelings, and behaviour define our personality and Mr. Freddie Mercury's personality caused longstanding problems for him and the people in his life. He had difficulty navigating his intense emotions which fluctuated faster than he could manage. He acted impulsively. He reported feeling numb apart from when he was self-harming and he had been suicidal for years. It was our job to keep him alive despite his daily efforts to kill himself. He took multiple overdoses and had tied ligatures around his neck many times. He was a hugely complicated gentleman and sometimes it felt as if we were prolonging his death rather than giving him a real life.

I took swabs of all his dirty wounds to send to microbiology to see if he was growing any unusual bugs and then I cleaned his sores with saline. As I brought the edges of the leg injury together, I noticed the skin was overlaid with a huge Swastika tattoo.

"Well this is awkward," I said.

He sighed loudly.

"The swastika is Indian," I murmured, and he pulled away from me, slightly.

"Why don't you go back to your country and look after

your own people, Doc?" Mr. Mercury asked. His tone was not hostile. I had been asked this question before, usually by old middle-class people. It seemed obvious to them that because I was brown I could not be English and must be from somewhere else. It made me uncomfortable because I had never considered myself anything other than British.

My answer was rehearsed but heartfelt. "You are my people," I said.

His eyes flickered. For a moment I thought we saw each other as humans.

I injected the edges of the gash with Lidocaine to make them comfortably numb. After a few minutes I prodded with the needle to see if the anaesthetic had worked.

"Does it hurt?"

He shook his head.

"Okay, I can start putting the stitches in. Are you ready?"

"I need to put my song on, it relaxes me, reminds me of the good old days when I used to get high."

"Is it The Stranglers?" Ginge asked.

"No, it's 'Pass Out' by Tinie Tempah," Mr. Mercury said, missing the joke.

"So you are not a fan of Queen?" I asked as he fiddled with his CD player.

"No, why would I be? I hate that queer. I just like the name."

"Don't be nasty," I admonished.

He shrugged. His song began to play and I had to hold on

to his jumping leg. The singer's voice was whispery and confessional to start with, as if Mr. Tempah had awoken from a heavy night. Vikki and Ginge knew the words and began singing and dancing. I smiled at how ludicrous this entire situation was. I wondered what outsiders would think if they saw this. No one would believe it. Sometimes it was hard to tell the prisoners from the staff other than the uniforms; I think we all became slightly unhinged from working in this intensely strange environment.

I silently recited a prayer before I put in the first stitch. I started in the middle of the wound and pulled the stitch through the tough scar tissue with some difficulty. Forward knots, back knots, forward knots, back knots, and trying not to get them snagged on the forceps or his hair. When the song finished, Mr. Mercury played it again, and again, so the trance-like tune formed a trippy loop, forwards, backwards, forwards, backwards. I was staring down into a putrid wound and trying not to breathe in the stench. I was concentrating with such intensity the wound appeared to expand and contract before my dancing eyes. Mr. Mercury was a known drug user. I wondered if he was exuding some noxious substance in his sweat and I was getting high.

"It is not the stitch that bothers me, it is the skin and muscle being pulled back together that hurts. It must be quite satisfying fixing something that's broken?" he asked.

"It is," I said with relief that it was over. I wiped away the blood and cleaned his leg. The swastika had not been distorted and I covered it in a dressing. Vicky and I counted the needles, thread, forceps, and swabs to ensure we did not leave anything behind that could be used in self-harm or as a weapon. He was already on antibiotics and the sutures could come out in five to seven days; if he did not take them out sooner. Vicky said she would assess him later. I implored him not to pull out the stitches I had worked so hard to place.

"You did a good job, Doc," he said, avoiding eye contact. It was the closest thing to a thank you. However difficult someone was I always tried to find something to like about them. I noticed his eyes were aquamarine with flecks of gold; like a tropical ocean in one of the images beside his bed. I felt a pang of sadness.

"You're welcome," I said, and I reached over and patted his clammy shoulder.

As I walked away to wash my hands I tried to comprehend what I had just witnessed.

"You're a brave man Doc," Vicky said.

"How can we stop him harming himself?" I asked.

"They have tried everything to work with him over the years and nothing has worked. If you read his history, you can see he has 'Shit Life Syndrome' – he never stood a chance."

I surveyed the chaos of the Inpatient unit. It was a long white corridor and had over a dozen cells on both sides. It reminded me of the scene from the film *Silence of the Lambs* where Agent Starling first meets Hannibal Lector. The locked doors had a small observation panel at eye level and I was aware of being watched by unseen eyes. Many of the panels had been smashed and arms reached out through the broken glass. The din of screaming and banging doors was deafening. There was an overpowering smell of stale urine and faeces which indicated that some of the prisoners were on a dirty protest, either covering themselves or their environments in their own mess. Biohazard screens surrounded the doors because sometimes men on dirty protests targeted passers-by with squeezy bottles of their effluent. Some of the inpatients were sexually disinhibited and wanted to make eye contact as they pleasured themselves. It became second nature to duck as we passed by and keep our eyes on the filthy floor to avoid slipping and falling.

For me the strongest sense of a prison was the vibration felt in the bone marrow when a heavy gate was slammed shut. It took time to acclimatise and no longer jump or shudder when my bones rattled. Maybe this was what they meant when they said prison got in your bones? Once you were used to this environment it was difficult to leave. The thought of going back to community GP with a list of 'normal' patients filled me with dread. I liked not knowing what each day in a prison would bring. I thrived in the chaos.

"This is a very strange place," I said.

"Oh yes," Vicky laughed. "Very strange people. And that's just the staff."

The Butterfly Jungle
Diriye Osman

Death is but an eternal blink. There are no paradisal gardens or grim hellscapes, no dances with the devil or trumpeting angels. You simply blink and your mind's eye - the wellspring of your cognition - loses sight of your selfhood forever.

But what about God, you ask, dear reader? Where does that leave Allah and Christ and Yahweh and Buddha and Krishna and-and-and? To my thinking, God in all His infinite glory is a manifestation of the magicality of our imaginations. When I, beloved reader, say that I see the God in you, it means that I see your power and poise and, most crucially, the quintessence of your humanity. I see your divinity, dear reader. I see you and I believe in you.

Once, in a moment of youthful arrogance, I asked my aabo and hooyo, "What is the source of your suffering? Doesn't it hurt you bone-deep to wear all the pain you've experienced at the hands of your people like a shroud? Couldn't you carry your sorrow lightly like a scented scarf?"

My aabo smiled sadly. "Pain - in all its inventively malevolent variations - doesn't know how to disguise itself. If you have tasted pain, it doesn't simply stick to your tongue. It seeps into your flesh; becomes encoded in your DNA until the day you die. Only then, as your cells collapse, does it truly cease to matter."

"That's one way of looking at it," said hooyo. "But Migil,

if you don't mind, I'll take it over from here for a spell. Reader, are you there? Yes, I see you now. Okay, I'm going to tell you a story that savages these sad bloke theories. Is you ready? I know you are, so here we go.

There was once a bundu Somali brother who grew up as a camel herder in the outer habada of Bosaaso, Somalia. This brother was a riggedy-raggedy ass motherfucker - sweet but simple in his black and white view of the world. He immigrated to London in his thirties and decided to become a taxi driver. Well, it was a job he could get. Bredrin was truly shocked by the city's splendour and guttural gloom. At night, he would schlep around Soho and drive around young femboys who would fondle each other and puke all over his cute little car. Man was pissed at the flagrant disrespect so he ditched the taxi driving business and became a Tesco delivery man. The hours were long, the pay was poor, and he was tired and lonesome. Homie longed for some loving. He wanted to sekkle and plant seeds. So he did what a lot of diasporic brothers do and sent for a young bride from the bush. Reader, are you ready for this gear change? I hope you are because I'm about to switch this shit up on you.

The young bride, a pretty likkle ting with a tight chocha worth writing choons about, rocked up to London, got hitched to this hustler, and prepared herself for a life of dull domesticity. Sis couldn't speak a word of English, and she found life in their South London council flat to be a claustrophobic contrast to the sea and warmth of Somalia.

One day, her husband, the poncey delivery man, hired an

Irish handyman to fix their house up and told his wife, our good sis, to make sure that the yard was finessed to perfection. Sista gyal reluctantly agreed. She didn't want to be left alone with a strange white man. Every day, after her husband left for work in the a.m., the handyman arrived, ready to get more than his fingers dirty. The handyman clocked the curvaceous thighs and booty of this beautiful black woman. Jungle fever hit the motherfucker mightily. He would sweat and turn the colour of a handmaid's cloak. I'm telling you, Offred didn't have shit on this Shitty Shitty Bang Bang. Our good sis scoped the handyman's hungry eyes and decided to skip the tedious games and instead serve him some finger-lickin' good lovin'.

Meanwhile Ms. Arnette, the elderly Bajan neighbour, grew puzzled by the howls that she heard coming from next door on the daily. She wondered if her neighbours had adopted a new cat or a strange breed of vixen. She wondered if the young wife of her kind neighbour was being raped by the bloodclaat whitey that came to their house every day, armed with paint cans and brushes. Ms. Arnette didn't call the police. Instead she picked up the steel baseball bat that she reserved exclusively for the non-existent robbers she feared would break into her clapped-out house and schlepped to her neighbours' yard. Ms. Arnette was not playing as she rang the buzzer. She was ready to klep the fuck out of this ponce for molesting this poor Muslim woman who had probably never seen dick in her life. Ms. Arnette was no fool. She knew about FGM. She had read all about it in *The Sun*. Those poor Somali girls. So oppressed. Well, she'd save one today, in Jesus' name, Amen.

She rang and rang and rang the buzzer until the door creaked open.

Out popped a visibly dishevelled sista gyal wearing a satin robe and smelling of sex and sweat and more sex. She was breathless and irritated with Ms. Arnette for fucking up her groove.

'Darling, you alright in there?' said Ms. Arnette, sussing out the situation and scandalised by this turn of events. 'I heard noises. Howling sounds, like someone was puttin' a hurtin' on you.

'Me ferry busy,' said sista gyal. 'Take care.' She slammed the door in poor Ms. Arnette's face. Poor Ms. Arnette who only wanted to save some silly Somali rube from rape. Incensed, Ms. Arnette hobbled back to her home, using her steel bat as a walking stick.

What was wrong with people, thought Ms. Arnette, once she was back in her home. *Why don't people want to be saved?* The way Ms. Arnette saw it, she was a messenger of the Almighty and his son, Jesus Christ, and it was her duty to do the right thing at all times. Ms. Arnette was so fastidious when it came to this purpose that she didn't even like farting in any room in her empty home except the bathroom, which everyone knew was the devil's sanctuary. She decided that this stoopid Somali girl should be punished for her transgression. If she didn't teach her a lesson, who would? Ms. Arnette poured herself a cup of tea and sat down on her sofa and waited. It was a cat-and-mouse ting now.

Two weeks of this ceaseless dicknotization coupled with wall-penetrating squeals and howls were enough to make Ms. Arnette hurl. When she couldn't take no more, she confronted the man of the house, our clueless delivery man, and spilled the juice.

Ms. Arnette told him that his missus was running game on him and he needed to stop being a mug. Our delivery man suspected foul play but not of this variety. He simply thought that the handyman he had hired was refusing to work. Vexed like a muthafucker, he confronted his wife, and for the first time in what felt like aeons, Ms. Arnette slept right that night.

Our beloved sista gyal denied-denied-denied this attack on her character. 'You think I'm a shakshuuko?' she shouted at her exhausted husband. 'You think I've come all the way from my beloved Bosaaso to shack up with a useless delivery man and his cadaan handyman. Spin me a new story, pal, cause this one is as old as my granny's knickers.'

'You're right, my love,' said the delivery man. 'I'm so sorry for doubting your dopeness. Please don't leave me. I'm so lonely.'

'No-one is leaving no-one,' said sista gyal. 'I'm your wife and Allah Almighty has blessed this marriage, so we'll ride this shit together till the wheels fall off.'

Fast forward to five months later and sista gyal was preggo-preggo. We're talking a pair of twins in the oven preggo and her husband was ecstatic. What he didn't know, however, was that sista gyal was knocked up with the Irish handyman's pickney. Contrary to what Ms. Arnette believed, sista gyal was sharper than a shank. She currently lived in Peckham but she wanted to upgrade to one of the fancier neighbourhoods like Mayfair or Chelsea. She hippity-hippity-hopped onto a bus and went to Westminster City Council's Housing Office and asked for a Somali interpreter. The housing officer granted her request and listened to her as she wept and wept and wept. They could see that she was heavily pregnant and felt incredible sympathy for her. She spoke of an abusive marriage laced with gas-lighting and much grimy mess. She spoke of an unwanted pregnancy that she could no longer abort. She spoke convincingly of an emotional and psychic pain that had been conjured from her expansive imagination. As per its statutory obligations, the council immediately put her into emergency accommodation and just before she gave birth, she settled her scammer ass into the swishiest little apartment in Mayfair. When she gave birth, she and her babies were given a first-rate social worker, who made sure that she was safe from that 'horrible, horrible' husband of hers.

Meanwhile, her 'horrible, horrible' husband, our likkle delivery man, toiled and toiled in his half-decorated home, worried that his wife and his babies had been kidnapped, not realising that sista gyal had used her body as a bribe in order to buy her freedom.

He saw her many years later, wearing the tightest jeans, nails done, hair did, getting into a cute powder-blue Mini Cooper in Sloane Square, where he was making a grocery delivery. She saw him, gave him a cryptic smile, slipped her Cavalli sunglasses on and got into her car, drove off and disappeared from his view forever."

"What is your point, hooyo?" I asked. "That scammers always know how to game the system? That if you pop your coochie, you end up with the world in your palms?"

"No, my lovely," said my mother, "I'm simply saying that life is not one extended depressive jag. There is joy to be had amidst the pain. We make art and we tell stories. That is what our people have been doing for millennia. This is how we live. Are you going to get hurt along the way? Damn skippy. But it's what you do with that pain that fortifies your character."

I couldn't tell my hooyo that sometimes storytelling wasn't enough to stem the bowel-to-core deep sadness; that loneliness often made my mind spin in the small hours, that the inability to move beyond one's anxieties felt like pushing against a standing stone, that the struggle to connect with others stung one's consciousness in ways that were startling and hallucinatory.

Oh, who am I kidding, beloved reader? Just spinning this yarn for you feels like a balm. I hope you feel comforted, knowing that we're constructing this tapestry together. So let's do this. Grab your tings, gorgeous one, and let's head over to my second job. What? You thought a brother could live on a part-time journalist's salary in London? Ha! That story is even funnier than my hooyo's souped-up, street folktales.

Neon Gumbo was a boutique located along Rye Lane in a snazzy new space called The Market, which was right next to my other gig in the Bussey Building. It was an upscale store specialising in customised clothing, jewellery, and funkadelic flyness from West African artists, designers, and tastemakers. If you wanted Ankara and kente-imprinted hoodies and leather jackets, you would feel finer than Fela Kuti here. If you wanted the freshest organic cosmetics from Nigeria, Mali, and Ghana, you could cop that from us. The joint was pure drip but the salary was sawa sawa tu: nothing to holler to your hooyo about, nothing that would allow my co-workers, two young queer art students called Ariel and Maimuna, to move out of their parents' houses. I was lucky enough to have my own place: a poxy but rent-controlled council flat down the road that I got a few years ago because I was a high priority patient in a psych ward at the time. Let me tell you, dear reader, that flat is one of the best things that has ever happened to me. I don't take it for granted that I have my own apartment in London at a time when homelessness in this merciless city is growing at a horrific rate.

But enough grimmage for now. Let me introduce you to my crew. Ariel is an Israeli bredda with bright green eyes and matching hair and nails who's always kitted out in *Calvin & Hobbes* gear that he designed himself since Bill Waterson, the characters' creator, has resisted the capitalistic seductiveness of merchandising for nearly four straight decades. (Side note: if you're Bill Waterson and you're reading this, please don't sue poor Ariel. The kid can barely afford food, let alone a decent solicitor).

Next up is Maimuna, a hijabi queen from Cameroon with skin like liquid silk and the mouth of a young Millie Jackson (reader, if you don't know good ole Millie, YouTube is your bestie). Maimuna - or Muna as she liked to be called - dressed modestly, didn't drink, but smoked enough dutch to resurrect Bob Marley. Maybe they puff-puff-passed together in a past life.

This time last year, both Ariel and Muna, who were studying together at Camberwell College of Art, identified as nonbinary. This year they were using regular, schmegular pronouns but now called themselves neosexuals. When I asked them what this meant,

Muna giggled sheepishly and said, "It's just something different, innit?"

"Yah," added Ariel, "Nonbinariness is so 2010s. We've evolved and created our own sexuality."

"Mazeltov," I said.

I didn't have it in me to tell them that neosexuality was not a new concept, especially amongst gender studies scholars. Especially when the only thing these kids were trying to do was find other ways of being, alternative modes of existing in this frightening era where your best friend and most fearsome foe was your phone, which had the capacity to sedate you with cute memes or catapult you into psychosis. These kids couldn't catch a break.

"Migil, someone came to see you today," said Muna. "This sexy Congolese trans brother. Said his name was Claude and that you knew him from the Butterfly Jungle. Is that some kinda code for a kinky sex club? Because if so, you have to take me there. I wouldn't mind pegging a hot bloke or three."

"I thought you were a lesbian," I blurted, before quickly realising my mistake.

"Neosexual," barked Muna, "God, there is nothing more traumatic than being misgendered."

"I'm really sorry, Muna," I said, "I didn't mean to misgender you."

"To be fair to Migil, you do see yourself as a lesbian sometimes," said Ariel, consoling Muna.

"I'm only a lesbian on the weekends when I'm at Pussy Palace and want to eat nothing but pum-pum," said Muna. "On weekdays, I'm a neosexual. We both agreed on this, Ari. We are neosexuals."

"I know, sweetie," said Ariel, giving her a hug. "I know."

"Forgive me for my binary thinking, Muna," I said.

"It's alright," said Muna, pulling away from Ariel. "It must be nice to live in such a bubble of sexual privilege."

"Muna, what are you bleating on about?" I said. "You're the one who can get men, women, and nonbinary folks to drop their pants and hop into bed with you. Darling, you have a superpower."

Muna perked up as she considered this notion. "You're right, Migil. I'm really blessed. Last night, I was being double-penetrated by this cis-het man and his wife and right before I nutted, I thought, how lucky am I to have such an insatiable appetite? I jizzed like a muthafucker just thinking about it and I still have the carpet burns from the session."

"Let me see, you sexy minx," said Ariel, unbuttoning Muna's jeans.

"I'm off to the stock room," I said, leaving them to continue their coital escapades.

"Migil, don't you want your pal Claude's number?" said Muna as she undressed. "Ari, pass him that green post-it."

Ariel ran to the counter, picked up the post-it and handed it to me before heading back to investigate Muna's sex bruises. I scanned the note briefly before going downstairs to the stock room.

Reader, come through and peep this semi-cute shit. Claude was my first inamorato. He was a sculpture of his own design, a statuesque god attuned to his own divine nature. I was twenty-one, he was forty and more flavoursome than a fat rascal served with cinnamon tea. Whenever he kissed me, he would leave traces of his cologne all over my collar bone, making me sweat until my mind melted. Just thinking about him sent me into a sex-funky spiral. I wanted to call him, lick his clit, make him scream-and-cream until we were both in a rhapsodic state. But something held a brother back.

I was broken and I didn't know how to restore my self-worth. Afraid that my anguish would ossify into a fear of others, I turned instead to the strange voices in my head for comfort, a Greek chorus that synthesised the same bromides on a schizoid loop: *You will be fine. You will survive this moment. You will, you will, you will…*

I didn't know if I could trust these voices or if I could trust my own instincts. This revelation made the terra incognita of my perceptions more treacherous. I worried that I would revert to my innate wildness: the feral, dangerous self that I had silenced with antipsychotics. This shadow self didn't have a sense of self-preservation or a single particle of dignity. This shadow self was my truest essence. Good god, how grimy. Let's bounce, beloved reader, before I unleash the dragon, Dru Hill-style (and trust me, that shit is messier than Joan Crawford and her wire clothes hangers in *Mommy Dearest*).

Many years ago, on the kind of humid-but-pissing-down-with-hail summer night that makes Londoners go loony, I was locked up in a loony bin, fanning myself with a copy of *Prozac Nation*. The edition I held in my hands was given to me by my adeer Anatoly, my father's husband. Adeer Anatoly used to be in the Russian military and before that he was a high school literature teacher. When he lived in Moscow, he was married to a sturdy Latvian sistren and they had a daughter my age. During his time in the army, he cooked all the meals that his comrades needed to survive the cold, including, but not limited to, liver and tripe baked in pots together with cereal, pelmeni (a dope dumpling-like treat), or jellied pork. His homies in the barracks fed well, and at night one or two of the twinky ones would creep into his bunk and bless him with a discreet blowjob. As soon as adeer Anatoly was discharged, he immigrated to London and never looked back.

Brotherman met my dad at Bootylicious, the gay hip-hop club, and before any member of my family knew wagwan, we were all dressed in kangas dancing to WizKid at their wedding in the Connaught Rooms in Holborn.

Don't get it twisted, reader. It's hard out here for two OGs with power-hungry personalities. From the beginning, my aabo and adeer were boxing on the daily in that very East African/Eastern European way of fisticuffs followed by days-long sessions of hard fucking and tantric play. They shared a house with my mother and her wife, who would both be listening to these blokes' shenanigans with simmering rage and envy.

"How are they still fucking twelve hours later?" said a genuinely flummoxed hooyo, which eventually led to her screeching,

"Will you cunts shut the fuck up?" before finally coming to me as a defeated woman and saying, "Migil, we need your entire supply of white lady pills. We have to be in a coma tonight whilst those two are knocking boots."

Luckily for my hooyo, things calmed down with my aabo and adeer's heat-seeking ways, and both breddas became more discreet with their dick-downs. They all somehow found a way, through much trial and error, to build a happy home on a foundation of kinship and respect. We all loved one another and found tremendous comfort in each other's company.

Adeer Anatoly, ever the enterprising gourmand, opened a food truck on Rye Lane, where he served his customers Jamaican cuisine (side note: I've seen super-hardboiled, separatist Rastafarians queuing up for servings of his slow-cooked curry goat). The food truck was called The Conquering Lion, which was named after my adeer's favourite Marley riddim. On weekends, my whole family chipped in as servers and business was soon sweeter than the cherry on a fruit cocktail.

The Conquering Lion was where I found myself after work one day, telling adeer Anatoly that Elizabeth Wurtzel, the author of *Prozac Nation*, the book he had given me when I was sectioned in the psychiatric ward all those years ago, had passed away.

"I'm so sorry," he said, serving a Guyanese sista a steaming plate of plantain, jerk chicken, and rice and peas. "What happened to her? Please don't tell me she committed suicide. That would just break my heart."

"No, she died of breast cancer."

"Oh man, what a tragedy," he sighed. "It's always a shame when someone like Wurtzel manages to not only survive something as soul-destroying as severe depression, but goes on to make a wonderful life for herself, only for her light to be snuffed out by cancer."

There was a silence.

"Adeer, I'm really sad," I said, wiping tears from my face.

"Oh, sweetheart," he said, removing his blue plastic gloves and giving me a warm hug. "What's wrong?"

"I don't know how to fix myself. Every day, I make a mental note that I'll get better, that the pain will subside, but I'm still here in a state of loss and grief."

"What are you grieving?" asked adeer Anatoly, handing me a tissue.

"I'm grieving the sense of optimism I used to have. I'm stuck, and for the first time in my life I don't know how to survive this void that makes me feel like my life has no value."

"Oh, honey," said adeer Anatoly, enveloping me in another hug. "You are not alone. You have a whole village of loved ones. We are all here for you. Migil, this is what depression does to the mind. It makes you feel fragile and vulnerable and it really hurts. When I left Moscow, I was terrified. I had learned that the entire life I had built for myself was based on falsehoods, and this freaked me out. I left all my friends, my family, my inherited identity behind so that I could honour who I really was. Now I have a whole new family and community. You are one of the most wonderful human beings I know. I adore you, I admire you, and I'm proud to call you my son."

"Thank you, adeer," I said.

Stars glinted in the winter night sky as Peckham's hipsters, halal housewives and hobos wandered up the high street, speaking in Somali, Pidgin, Patois and Polish. Adeer Anatoly and I stared at the scene in silence, momentarily stunned by our tremendous good fortune.

Later that evening I thought about Claude and our time together in the mental hospital. Reader, I sometimes wonder whether I dreamt that experience, which was exquisitely tortuous in its surreal incoherence. I often wondered whether I had dreamt up Claude too, whether he was the perfect emblem of a mind mired in its own mythmaking. I had apotheosised him, and I died a little death when I learnt that he too was a mortal being, with mortal needs and mortal softness. This is what we don't often talk about when we discuss men: their innate, child-like sensitivity and how this sensitivity can be nurtured as a strength or weaponised into a source of shame and volatile self-hate. To love a man, whether cis or trans, is like tending a garden and, like all gardens, the task must be approached with tenderness, a little care, some patience. I didn't know how to love my fellow man right. Wisdom is an acceptance of our accrued inadequacies. Wisdom ain't a deepening of character, it is the body's way of saying, 'Brother, I'm dying, so we might as well dance to the end of love.'

I opened my diary and retrieved the post-it with Claude's

phone number written on it. I was afraid of what he would say. I was afraid of what he wouldn't say. I picked up my phone and called him.

"Hello?"

"Claude?" I said, clutching the phone with trembling fingers.

"Migil," he shouted, ecstatically. "Beautiful Migil, I'm so glad you called."

"How've you been, lovely?"

"Pregnant," giggled Claude. "I'm two months deep in this shizznit."

I was slightly taken back.

"Mabruk," I said. "Who's the lucky man?"

"Woman, actually," said Claude. "Her name is Marta. She's a Portuguese trans sista. A proper fire starter. How've you been, beloved?"

"I'm doing great," I lied. "I'm a journalist these days."

"I know. I've been following your career." There was a pause. "I read your piece on the man who assaulted you. Migil, I'm so sorry that happened."

Two months ago, I had published a viral article about a male musician who had assaulted me. I didn't tell Claude that, soon after the piece was published, a group of hackers had doxxed me, putting my address and personal details on the internet. I didn't tell Claude that the Somali far right had shamed me endlessly on social media for being a man who had sex with other men, for being a man who had made moves on a married man. These members of the Twitterati sent me hate mail on the daily and made me hire a locksmith to secure my front door properly. I couldn't tell Claude these things. I couldn't confide in him the way I used to because he had moved on and I clearly hadn't. So I said, "Oh, don't worry about me. I'm an extraordinary machine à la Fiona Apple."

"God, do you remember how we rinsed that album when we were in the Butterfly Jungle?" chuckled Claude.

"I love how you still refer to the mental hospital as the Butterfly Jungle."

"It was you who came up with that name on one of our sweaty nights together," said Claude. "You said that the first time you saw me you thought I was composed entirely from a kaleidoscope of butterflies, which I thought was a lush image. No one had ever seen me like that before."

There was a comfortable pause.

"What are you going to call the baby?" I asked.

"Dunya if it's a girl, Migil if it's a boy."

"Are you serious?" I said, incredibly moved.

"Of course," said Claude. "You were such an important part of my life. I love you, Migil. I think of you when the world is leached of colour, when I look up at the moon at night. You have always been the rock and the shore. I hope you're being kind to yourself."

At this point, my fingers were shaking so hard that I had to hold the phone with both hands.

"Will I see you again?" asked Claude.

"Of course," I said, even though I didn't think it was wise.

He was building a new life for himself and I didn't want to disrupt it.

"We'll always have the Butterfly Jungle," said Claude, a tinge of sadness in his voice because he knew the truth. We would never see each other again.

"May you prosper and prosper. May your baby be born healthy and happy. May you be loved with the kind of passion that you deserve. May you continue to find boundless joy in this world."

"To the future, Migil," said Claude, his voice breaking. "Love you."

"Love you more," I said, before hanging up the phone.

I sat in my darkened living room, police sirens going off in the distance, wondering if another young black man had lost his life. I sat in my darkened living room as the world turned and burned. I sat in my darkened living room, wearing all the pain I had experienced at the hands of my people like a shroud. I sat in my darkened living room, unable to carry my sorrow lightly like a scented scarf.

I was my parents' pickney after all.

The queer black body as sacred memory, the mind as cuneiform script, code too complex for modern algorithms.

The queer black body as dreamscape, each stretch mark a dragon's blood branch, coconut oil making every crevice taste like mother's milk.

The queer black body as sex and sweat and Somalinimo, tongue sweeter than a vial of rose oil, mouth warmer than Merca.

Sing me to a new self.

Changing History
Sharon Stevens

Ermine loved it when her grandchildren came to visit.

They'd come one day at the weekend with either parent and or one evening after school.

That's what she loved the most, the visits on a weekday, as she'd have them all to herself. At the weekend she'd have to share them with either parent, while the children occupied themselves doing some sort of activity they would bring with them. Or watch an appropriate programme that their parents would suggest. She didn't really mind sharing them or the mess they left behind, because her two-up two-down felt full; full of bodies and noise.

Ermine didn't mind living on her own now, she'd had enough time to get used to it, but how she missed the noise after they'd left.

Today, was one of those days she loved, so much so, that her smile began as she made her way up to bed the night before and was there when she woke.

Ermine busied herself throughout the day, occasionally glancing at her watch to make sure that she started preparing dinner in time before having to make her way to school to pick her grandchildren up. She would busy herself throughout the day so much that it would appear that the day had flown.

She enjoyed waiting in the playground with the other mums, dads, and other grandparents. She felt privileged to be in this position. To be trusted with her children's precious children; her grandchildren. She had friends who did not see their grandchildren, and so she cherished her time with them.

Ermine made her way to school, making sure that she would have time to catch up with her favourite fellow grandparent.

"Hi, Keith. How are you doing?" She tapped him on his back as she approached.

"I'm good Ermine," he replied with a broad smile.

"It's good to see you looking well. I've missed you at yoga."

"You know, I've missed it. I can feel my body ceasing up as we speak." Keith laughed, jerking his body back and forth.

Ermine laughed too.

"Charlie wasn't well," he continued. "You know how we have to help out. Mum and dad took it in turns to finish early to pick him up and then pick-up Rosie. But by the time they come, me too tired to go out. It's a long day. But me glad me can help."

Keith was like Ermine, he lived on his own and looked forward to picking up his grandchildren after school, in between enjoying his retirement and the occasional extra babysitting duties.

"He's better now. Hence I'm here…" he sang the last part of his reply gesturing with his hands.

"It's not like when we were bringing up our children. We had to do it on our own. You just had to manage or send them to school and wait for a call…" the inner edges Ermine's eyebrows moved upwards as her thoughts took her back in time.

Keith's words brought her back. "I do miss our catchups," he said.

"I know, me too."

The sound of a bell could be heard.

"I wonder what goodies they have in store for us today?" laughed Ermine walking through the now opened gates.

Goodies could come in the form of a pile of unfinished or finished artwork, masterpieces created on 'the making table'. Or in the case of Ruby, her reading book, spellings, teacher-led homework, and self-imposed research. Out of all the stuff she came home with, her chosen project captured her attention the most and took the longest time to complete.

They both made their way across the playground towards the classrooms, Keith, with a scooter tucked under his arm.

"See you on Thursday?" he said.

"Yes, I will be there. Fancy lunch after? Then we can have a real catchup."

"Ok," he said, giving her a thumbs up walking towards his grandson's class. "See you then."

"See you then," Ermine smiled then turned her attention to Ruby and Benjamin, running towards her.

"Grandma! Grandma!' they cried, approaching with outstretched arms.

"Hi, you two. How's your day been?" she said, throwing her arms around them both as they clung to her legs and her waist. Gone were the days when she would lift them up into her arms, arthritis made sure of that. "Oh! It's so good to see you."

They stayed in that position for a little while longer, each enjoying their embrace. Ermine smiled, her mind taking her back in time to the embrace of her own children, in the very same playground.

"Come on then. We need to go. Otherwise, Nat will be waiting."

"Okay, Grandma."

Ermine greeted Nat, giving him a hug before putting her key into her front door.

"Hi, Grandma. Hi, you two," he replied, high fiving Ruby and Benjamin as they all made their way into Ermine's hallway. The smell of thyme, coconut cream, scotch bonnet, garlic, black pepper, and jerk seasoning greeted them. They smiled, each knowing what was coming later.

"You beat us today," Ermine continued while removing her shoes. The children followed suit. They knew not to question.

Ermine was relaxed with her grandchildren. Having mellowed over the years, she was a lot less strict with them than she had been with their father and their uncles. She was no longer the mother who was raising three young men on her own; having to do it all, work, and look after her mother too. She was retired now, her time mostly her own to use how she wished. Her parents were both deceased, her children in their thirties, with their own families. Having her grandchildren was her choice. Something that she was happy to do, they gave her life meaning.

"Right! Go and wash your hands. Dinner is ready," Ermine indicated to the cloakroom on her way to the kitchen.

"Ok, Grandma," came the reply. They knew not to argue.

"After dinner, it's what?"

"Time to do our homework," they said, taking it, in turn, to do as they were told.

"Absolutely. Because...?"

"Knowledge is power."

"How much harder do you need to work?"

"Twice as hard," came the chorus.

"Why is that, Grandma?" Benjamin asked, drying his hands.

"You know why," Nat replied before Ermine could, making his way towards the dining table.

"But why?"

"You know why, Grandma and dad have told you. Stop being a baby!" Nat said, giving Benjamin a little push.

"Grand-ma!" wailed Benjamin.

"It's okay, darling – you are the baby of this family. Stop it, Nat! Ruby, are you ready?"

"Yes, Grandma. Coming!"

Once the children were settled at the dining table, she brought out several dishes of food that she had prepared earlier. She loved the feeling of being wanted, needed. Her children and grandchildren brought out the best in her. Their weekly visits were the only time that she would make an effort to create her version of her own mother's cooking. Today was no exception.

Ruby said, before placing a fork full of rice and peas in her mouth, "Grandma?"

"Yes, darling?" she answered, moving her fork away from her mouth.

"Did you know that it's Black History Month?"

"I hate that," retorted Nat putting his fork down. "A month! Is that all they can give us?"

"Me too, love," Ermine responded also putting her fork down. Her food toppled back onto her plate.

"But why Grandma?" enquired Ruby.

"I know that it's supposed to be a time of celebration. But to me, we shouldn't need this."

"Why, Grandma?" Benjamin decided to join in the conversation, not usually one to miss an opportunity to eat.

"The thing is, I don't want to stop you enjoying it…"

"I hate it!" said Nat. "In History lessons, all we learn about is the Tudors, the Victorians, the Romans. It's the same all the time. And when it comes to Black History Month, what do we learn then?"

"About Stevie Wonder or Bob Marley. Depending on the age of the teacher maybe even about Whoopi Goldberg!" replied Ruby incredulous, gesturing with her hands. "There's nothing wrong with learning about them but…I mean, really!"

"Did you know that there were some influential Black Victorians?" Nat clenched his fist as he spoke.

"No, I didn't!" Ruby and Benjamin replied in unison, looking at their Grandma.

"Yes, that's right. I told Nat about them when he was studying the Victorians before he went into secondary. I would have told you myself when it came up in school. Tell me you haven't done it yet?'

"I haven't, not yet. Can't you tell me now? Sorry, us?"

"You wouldn't have done it yet, Benjamin," Ermine continued, forgetting about the food she had worked so hard at preparing, making sure the temperature was just right before serving.

"I really enjoyed learning about them and tried to tell Mr Gordan, but he wasn't interested," Nat interrupted. "I even tried to tell him about Ruby Bridges and Nat Turner. He didn't even listen."

"I'm really sorry to hear that. You know what? I'm still in shock of how the curriculum still is today. I learnt nothing about them myself at school. If it wasn't for those bookstores that popped up now and again at the community centre near where we used to live, I would never have known about them myself."

"Grandma's on her soapbox now," whispered Nat.

"I know." Ruby placed her hand across her mouth, stifling a laugh, she didn't want to appear rude while her Grandma was talking.

In between mouthfuls of roast chicken, rice, and peas, smothered in gravy, Ermine told her grandchildren about Ida B Wells and Fredrick Douglas. She told them how they tried to campaign to end slavery and that it wasn't until 1833 that slavery was finally abolished.

"I still find it hard to believe that all this happened and it's not in the books I read at school. Plus, why great-grandma and great-granddad left Jamaica and came here!" Nat shook his head.

"There's so much more my darling that's not written about and not widely known."

"I love History, but I don't understand why I have to rely on you telling me. Why can't I read it for myself?"

"There were books, but it was hard to get hold of them. The books I used to buy for your father and uncles used to come from America. They were expensive. As much as I tried, I couldn't find many published here. It wasn't like now when you can go on the internet to find information.' Ermine began to laugh. "I bought your dad and your uncles some books called *The Wonderful World of Knowledge*. They cost a fortune, and they took up so much space on the bookshelf. By the time I finished paying for them, the information was out of date!" Ermine laughed again.

She stopped and looked into the eyes of her grandchildren.

"Remember what I've said about working twice as hard? Well, what do you think that you need to do to change things?"

"I don't know," replied Benjamin.

"You're young anyway. Things might have changed by then…"

"What do you mean, Grandma?"

"When you get a little older, hopefully things would have improved. There might be books on the shelf readily available to show your children. All of your children, how it really was. What life was really like for Black People in this country and elsewhere," Ermine placed her hands together as if praying. "It's way overdue…"

She continued. "Oh, yes, back to what I was saying. Let me put it this way… If you and your friends at the end of year… What you call it now? The year that you take your exams at school?'

"Year eleven!" Ruby and Nat laughed.

"Let's say you and your friend left school with the exact grades and applied for a job, who do you think would get it?"

"The fair thing would be, that we both get an equal chance," Ruby confirmed rubbing her temples.

"That's right. That would be the fair thing. The thing is, more often than not, if your peer was white, it's more likely that they will get the job and you won't. The reasons I used to get were because the person had more experience than me and other silly reasons. I can count on both hands how many times I was in the second position for a job. I'm not saying that wasn't always true. Sometimes all of a sudden, there was no longer a vacancy. The job had somehow mysteriously disappeared."

"Surely, that still doesn't happen now?" Nat said. He was always shocked by his Grandma's stories. The thing he struggled with the most was, they weren't fiction and that his dad had had similar experiences himself.

"I'm afraid so, darling. If you want the same job as your white counterpart, you'll need to have twice as many qualifications, higher grades, and more experience."

"I'm sorry. I don't want to put you off learning and trying your best at everything. Because…"

"Knowledge is power," the children said together.

"It also gives you a choice. You can choose the career you

want rather than it fit with the qualifications that you have."

"I get it! Anyway, you know what? I'm going to write my own books…" Nat said, shaking his head looking at his Grandma.

"Me too," Ruby looked at her brother and smiled.

"You can too, Benjamin. If you want to, that is. You might be young now, but you will grow too," Ermine encouraged.

The children finished their meal and completed their homework, while Ermine washed up.

Ruby was reading.

Nat was doing some research on his Grandma's tablet.

Benjamin was colouring in his book.

She sat with them as they finished what they were doing.

A pain travelled down her left arm. She touched her left cheek.

"Well done guys. I'm so proud of you. You can put the TV on if you want. I just want to clarify something before you leave. Your mum is coming in a bit."

Ruby nudged Nat. "She's doing it again," she laughed.

"I know," he whispered in her ear, trying not to laugh too.

"I wanted to explain why I don't like Black History Month. It's not that I don't like celebrating Black History. It's because I'm not Black one month a year, I'm black every single day of my life. I feel that you should be taught aspects of Black History in the different subjects you're taught at school."

"What do you mean, Grandma?" Benjamin asked, making his way to sit on his Grandma's knee. She cuddled him, held him tightly and rubbed a hand through his hair.

"You're tired, aren't you? Don't worry, mum will be here in a bit. Where was I? Oh yes! If you're learning about biography in English, your teacher could choose a Black person in history and teach about him or her alongside the many other biographies that you study. If teaching poetry, they could use some of Benjamin Zephaniah's poems." Ermine laughed. "I love his 'Talking Turkeys' poem."

"Me too," laughed Benjamin.

"Where was I?" Ermine continued. "Oh, yes! In Art, they could include some African art. In… let me see, what about World War One and World War two? Soldiers were fighting from other countries too. There were Black soldiers from different parts of the world, but no one hears anything about them."

Benjamin yawned.

"Come on, sweetie. Let's have a cuddle on the sofa. You can watch one of your favourite TV shows. Come on, you two, pack up your things, your mum will be here in a bit."

Moments later, mum arrived to collect the children. And as usual, they did not want to leave.

"Give your Grandma a hug. And what do you say?"

"Thank you," yawned Benjamin. "I love you."

"I love you too, darling. You make me laugh so much."

"Thank you, Grandma. The food was delicious. I love you," Ruby hugged her Grandma.

"I love you too, darling."

"By the way, I'm going to write a book when I'm older."

"That's fantastic, Ruby. I look forward to reading it."

"Goodbye, Grandma. Thank you for the talk. It's given me some ideas. I think I will do my own research when I'm older."

"My pleasure darling. I always enjoy our talks too. Love you," Ermine said, giving Nat a hug.

"Love you too, Grandma. I'm going to write a book too."

"You do that. Goodnight. Love you," she shouted as the car doors slammed shut.

She was still standing in her doorway, waving as they turned the corner and eventually went out of sight. Ermine went back into her now quiet home, sat on the sofa to catch up on the latest news.

She fell asleep.

Ermine didn't wake up that night and go to bed as she usually did.

Years later, at his book launch, Nat shared his story about the night that his Grandma Ermine encouraged him to write his book. His book, that told the real History of Black people in England.

He read the opening chapter and the dedication page with his sister and brother by his side. They all shared memories of their Grandma Ermine. Their Grandma, who had started their journey into the world of research and academia.

Nat had two degrees and a PhD in Black History. He had written several books. This particular book was being adapted by the *BBC* and was going to be aired later in the year.

Ruby had just completed her Journalism Masters and was about to start her PhD. She had a column in a mainstream newspaper and was given a chance to lecture trainee teachers about Equality and Diversity in the classroom.

Benjamin was in the second year of his TV and film degree. He was determined that he was going to change what he saw on the screen.

Although Ermine wasn't there to see this herself, she lived on in the lives of her children and grandchildren. Her grandchildren were determined that they were going to do their very best to make sure that their children had access to books and films that emulated them. Not once a year in October.

After all, they were Black every single day of their lives.

The Last Will & Testament of a Black Boy
Andre Clemmons

He looked like he was sleeping. I thought he'd wake up any minute now.

There he was, right in front of me, in some stiff black suit and tie. His face twisted into a scowl. His jaw looked so scrunched his cheeks looked puffy, like a chipmunk. It made me want to laugh, but I knew better.

Everybody thought it was weird I hadn't shown much emotion. I don't know what they wanted from me. What am I supposed to feel?

Am I supposed to be a wreck?

Am I supposed to be numb?

"It's okay to let it all out, baby," Mom told me. "It's not right to keep it all bottled up."

How did she know what hurt? She didn't get it. She wasn't there. Her best friend didn't die in front of her. He wasn't bleeding in her arms.

Everybody was trying to tell me how to feel... but they just didn't get it.

It didn't have to be Jalen. It could've just as easily been me. Mom knew that but didn't want to admit that. The reality scared her. Oh sure, she had had 'the talk' with me; that painful, tough conversation about how the world *really* treats those like me.

I was a black boy.

My black skin made me a target, an object of hatred. There was only so high in this world I could reach, and there wasn't much I could do about it.

Keep control of my emotions. Follow the rules at all times. Look respectable. Maintain eye contact and smile (That one was important. White people liked it better when you smiled. If not, you looked threatening).

So many rules to follow, it was hard to keep up with them all. Just when you try to get used to the ones you know, there's a whole new set to deal with. How can you win? No matter how hard you try, no matter how much you behave, you can still end up being a victim. What was the point? What kind of game was it if you lost all the time?

I kept wondering what Jalen & I did wrong that afternoon. What could we have done differently? Could it all have turned out another way? How did everything go so wrong?

We were walking down North Main, talking and laughing, leaving the convenience store with snacks. I had my basketball tight under my arm while I popped jellybeans in my mouth and Jalen was guzzling a Coke. We were headed back to the park to shoot some more hoops. These hot summer days meant there was plenty of time for basketball, plenty of time to beat those other boys from across the bridge.

Jalen had fast feet on the court and solid defense – much better than mine – but nobody could match my jump shot. I could shoot free throws no matter where I was and my offense was getting stronger. I remember us talking trash, bragging that I was gonna obliterate his defense in no time. All Jalen did was laugh.

He was still laughing when suddenly everything changed. Flashing lights. Tyres screeching.

We were cut off at the curb by officers, leaping out of their cars, guns drawn, veins already bulging in their red faces as they screamed at us.

We didn't know what to do.

We didn't know what to say.

Jalen was so scared his snacks dropped. He knelt to pick up a soda can that fell out his back pocket and next thing I knew, just like that; they fired. We hit the concrete as the shots blasted, hitting like hail, popping rapidly – *Bang! Bang! Bang!* = like firecrackers.

That noise echoed in my ears.

I was so scared, trembling, crying so hard snot trailed out my nose, blended to touch my lips. And then I felt my chest get sticky and wet.

Something wasn't right.

I called out Jalen's name.

No response.

Why was he so still?

I moved to him. The officers tried to pull me off him, but I refused to let go.

I tried to tell them we hadn't done anything, that we were just minding our own business. But they didn't listen. It's like they didn't care that my best friend was dead, that his blood soaked my white shirt, that I held him in my arms.

They dang near yanked my arms off, cuffing me and

throwing me in the backseat. By the time I could call my parents and they came rushing down to the station, I was in a deep haze. All those hours hammering at me had worn me down.

Apparently, Jalen and I fit the profile of two young men who had carjacked a man at gunpoint. They responded to the direct call. Never did explain how two 12-year-old boys could be mistaken for 'young men', and why they needed four officers to take down a pair of kids.

Never did get those answers.

I never could understand, but what I could understand was this: There had been six unarmed black men shot and killed in my neighborhood. Jalen was number seven. I was almost number eight. I was alive, but that didn't mean anything.

Jalen wasn't coming back.

We used to play ball for hours, bouncing around, sweat clinging to our shirts, so tight like a second skin. Drops used to flick off when I took my shirt off at night. We always talked about going pro one day, how we were gonna be making millions in the NBA. Million-dollar mansions next to each other, our dreams were higher than the sky. We could do anything we wanted. But then everything changed.

No more of that.

If I had my way, this would all be a bad dream. I could wake up right now and everything would be right again. He would be alive and we'd still be playing ball.

My best friend was dead.

He was only 12 years old.

I didn't know how much more of this funeral service I could take. So long and dreadful. The choir swayed and ladies wailed, loud and strong, in those velvet robes. Old ladies fanned and fainted, those wide hats and wider pastel dresses. Jalen would've hated this just as much as I do.

He wouldn't have wanted to see his mama on the verge of exhaustion, collapsed at the coffin twice, screaming and crying. It took great force to carry her away and back to her grief. Maybe that's why it was raining so hard outside. He was upset too.

But still people wanted to talk to me. I couldn't imagine why. All throughout the service, amidst the chaos, I just sat there.

No words.

No tears.

Nothing.

People talked about me like I wasn't there. Maybe I was still in shock. I must be having nightmares. I must be terrified. Had my parents considered therapy?

I shook my head at it all. Nobody knew what they were talking about. Nobody understood. What did they know, telling me everything was gonna be fine? Nothing would ever be the same again.

Jalen, my best friend since kindergarten, was cold in the ground.

Blue monsters were haunting me in my dreams. They wore badges. They emerged from the darkness, clawing at me, trying desperately to drag me under. No matter how far I ran, they were always faster.

All these twists and turns…

The dream always ended the same.

I ran out of space to run, backed up against the wall. And that's when they attack all at once. The popping, the gnashing, the growling, staring through me with those soulless eyes.

It should've been me.

I don't deserve to live.

It wasn't fair.

What was I gonna do now? I couldn't live my life like nothing happened. It wasn't that simple. All the protests in the world wouldn't change that.

No apology would be made.

Nobody would pay for those mistakes.

All those hero stories of good and evil I watched growing up meant nothing.

I still wasn't a man yet, but I had lived. I knew the truth. I knew how the world works. They say boys will be boys, but I was never a boy—I never will be. I was a man the second I was born.

I am *never* innocent. My brown skin will always see to that. The world will see me differently. They'll always judge me. They'll always hate me. Every move I make is under a microscope.

Those are the rules of the game…only there's no way to win. No cheat codes, no special tricks. Not for kids like me. Since Jalen's death, three more black souls have died.

Will I be next?

In two weeks, I'll turn 14.

Will this be my last birthday? Will I get to go to high

school? Graduate? Go to college?

Will I get married, have kids? Will my mom be like Jalen's one day, crying over my dead body?

These are the questions that run through my mind.

This is what I think about all the time.

I mean, I'm still alive... but I don't feel alive. I get up and go to school and eat with my family... but I feel like things just happen. I'm not in control of myself.

I'm such a mess. I hate it. Crying and screaming and angry all at once.

I don't laugh anymore.

I'm never happy.

I think people are scared of me.

Oh, they don't say it to my face—they're not *that* bold—but I see it in their eyes. I walk these hallways the same way I walk the streets—like a freak. When I'm not in school, I sleep long and my mind races. I'm a bear in hibernation, locked away in my room until it's time to come out.

Mom always tells me to go out and do something. I ask what the point is, and she doesn't answer. She never does.

I don't know what will happen to me. I hurt all the time. My heart was carved out and shattered into tiny pieces a long time ago. In its place is a gaping hole, and I'm cold. I'm always cold. It's like I'm sick and I don't know how to get better. Maybe I don't want to.

I just want the pain to stop.

I don't know how much longer I can keep going on like

this. I'm tired. Why can't anyone see that? I'm tired of existing, tired of waking up every morning feeling hopeless. This gut feeling sinking deep into the quicksand like a heavy stone is enough to make my bones shake.

I could die any day now. Nothing was guaranteed. Why fight what was inevitable? Wouldn't it just be easier to give in? How would I do it? Could I face the pain?

I could bleed myself out in the bathtub. Steal one of Dad's razors but…ugh, what a mess. Or hang myself. I've seen them do it on TV. Take a belt or some rope or something – but it seemed a bit difficult. I probably could figure it out, though. Something short and sweet. No pain. Just… release.

Freedom.

Peace.

And what would Mom think when she found me? I would do it late at night with the door locked. No need to bother anyone. Just total silence. Get it over with.

I wouldn't be able to see her horrified reaction and hear her scream, but it'd be for the best. It was the right thing to do. She'd see that someday. She'd read this journal, see it all laid out in the pages, and she'd understand. Oh sure, she'd hurt for a while, but she would understand.

If I closed my eyes and never woke up… maybe I would be happy again. Nothing made sense anymore. I write in this journal every now and then because somebody told my mom it would make me feel better.

It does and it doesn't, if that makes sense.

I find myself writing *a lot* lately, because it's somehow easier for me to get all the thoughts out. Screaming them in my head all the times gets too loud. Writing a few of them down makes the pressure seem not so bad.

Who knows? These might be my last words.

My last will and testament.

All I have are some old clothes, some comics, and a basketball in the corner of my closet, collecting dust. Who would want that? I don't have anything anybody would want. All I had was my life. And what was that worth?

If I died...my mom would find this journal. When she does, what would I want her to remember? I guess I'd want her to know that... I loved her.

I'm sorry I couldn't make her happy.

I'm sorry I couldn't be happy.

I'm sorry I hurt so much.

I'm sorry I'm gone.

But I tried so hard. I really did.

Please don't hate me...

Brown Skin, White Walls
Ruth Akinradewo

"Abi, o!" Sade half-laughed, half-sang, as she swivelled her head back over her shoulder to face the direction her feet were in; recommitting herself to the duty she had set out to fulfil. People in the village said Sade's laugh was like a ripple – gentle yet sharp, as distinctive and unique as a fingerprint; its echoes heralded she was not far away.

Bumping into her friend Eniola on this dusty trail was always a pleasant surprise. They would share their thoughts on the newest engaged couple in their vicinity; the quality of the latest traditional weddings; the latest district officer and his officials stationed on their grounds... Their street-side chatter was their weekly round-up of current affairs.

"Ah…" Sade sighed, as she gazed down at the path her sandalled feet were patterning their steps on. She didn't have this clay pot on her head for nothing. She had piles of chipped crockery to wash once she returned home – the water that flowed from the rock was the only thing that would do. Sade pushed forward her *osuka* to the crown of her head.

Pulam! Pulam! Her brightly patterned yellow and blue wrapper skirt percussed the rim of her ankles as she lazily put one foot in front of the other. It was hot. She could feel the sweat trickling down her neck in an attempt to add some moisture to the dry air, closing down on her on all sides. The Harmattan season was on its way.

Dry or rainy season, what did it matter?

Government tension and policy changes had no regard for the weather. Come rain or shine, where there remained the absence of justice, what hope could there be for the presence of peace?

This year it really had seemed that a new dawn was on the horizon. The colours of hope and freedom were boldly emerging amidst the hues of sunrise. *Or so we thought*, Sade voiced in her mind.

For so long, this was all she had known. Living in Ogu village, being surrounded by yellow-brown cottages inhabited by people with the same thick south-western Nigerian accent that she had; expressing themselves at most times in the same Yoruba dialect that was hers. People with varying shades of brown: maple; mahogany; ash...

Then, there was outside the village. There lay a different world, like a collection of castles in the air, which those with shades like Sade's could only clutch at in their wispy dreams. Here, there were no small cottages to be found; there were mansions. White palaces whose steps alone could seat an entire family as they sat down to eat their pounded yam and egusi for supper. These palaces were reserved for those whose skin was most like their outside walls. Excepting of course, the black servants they would employ to clean them.

Whitewashed walls. That reminded her of something.

That man they called Jesus. In the Holy Bible, didn't he chastise the Pharisees for appearing like something 'whitewashed' – presenting themselves as beautiful to the outward eye, but in fact being inwardly full of dead bones and impurity?

What was the difference?

These whitewashed men in their whitewashed walls, patrolling their village with their immaculate two-piece suits and their canes – which served no other purpose than to make them look powerful – in every breath they exhaled, reminded Sade and her fellow people that they were beneath them in status, wealth, colour. Her fellow tribespeople were measured according to a scale calibrated by those who understood or appreciated little of their surroundings.

What can you do about it? she lectured herself, a practice she was wont to take up these days. *Nothing*, was the reply.

The sight of the rock caused a temporary break in Sade's conversation with herself. Ten minutes' walk from the Olukoya cottage, this rock provided the daily dance of cool, fresh water down the throats of Sade and her two sisters, brother, and parents. It also provided a lull in the busyness of her daily activities... it allowed her pause for thought. A moment to reimagine her life as this simple: encased solely in nature, rather than the unnatural constructs that men set up to limit who she could be.

Once the last trickle had glided from her rounded calabash club into the narrow neck of the clay pot, Sade bent to place the container back on to her *osuka* and gently rose once more to her feet.

"I am home oh!" Sade cried in Yoruba, as she crossed the threshold.

Moroundiya ran to meet her and accepted the baton of her mother tongue from her elder sister.

"Ah, sista mi, you took a long time, oh!"

"Eh, don't mind me, I met wit Eniola on dee way, you know!"

Moroundiya smiled knowingly at her sister as she helped her usher in the large clay pot.

"Did you see him?"

Sade gave a short grunt, followed by her trademark eyeroll finished with a kiss of her teeth. "If you mean the new district officer, then yes, I saw him."

"Eh-heh, and what did you tink of him?"

"*A buro*, what is der to tink? It is just another white man come to rule dee roost: oda us about and look down at us wit his patronising smile."

Sade turned her head to the side and busied herself. Her sister had started speaking again after a pause, but Sade's ears were off duty. As she tore the leaves for their ewudu soup, her mind was elsewhere. She was thinking about what had happened when she turned back from the rock, the red clay pot atop her head.

She had been sauntering along, lost in thoughts of what Nigeria's future was to be, as 1952 approached – when she had become aware of a tall approaching shadow. The shadow belonged to a suited, handsome district officer.

Handsome. It bothered Sade that she had noticed he was so. It bothered her that she admired the facial features of any of the *oyinbos* who limited her and the entire nation of Nigeria. And it bothered her that she could recognise goodness in their humanity when they so often failed to acknowledge that brown skin sheltered any humanity at all.

Although perhaps this man with pearly skin and dark brown hair had made allowances for some humanity residing in her. He had bowed his head slightly to her and uttered, "Good evening, ma," in deep tones when they were some two metres apart.

She had curtsied deftly and issued back a deferential, "Good evening, sa."

As she walked on and now still, she felt angry with herself. Why must she bow to someone who had done nothing to earn her respect or the right to rule over her land? Why did she now switch to English from the dialect of her forefathers?

Moroundiya was still talking. "He's handsome, though, you have to admit," she was saying.

Sade hated to admit it was true, but she was not about to voice her assent.

Baba and Mummy took their places at the table, followed by Sade, Moroundiya, Ajoké, Femi, and Layo.

Baba projected his commanding voice across the table as he prayed over their meal. Prayer. It was something Sade could not imagine not knowing; however, how many of her ancestors had expected that one day they would be addressing not the many deities of the Yoruba religion, but one God, she was far from being able to tell.

It was not to say that this was a bad thing. Sade was sure it was easier to pray to one God than having to remember which god was in charge of what whenever you needed to address a higher power. But why did it have to be the white people's God that was the right one? Why was everything they brought always the right way to do things?

"Dey said we can have our own powers, but den dey bring in more of der people to watch over us. What kind of power is dat?" Baba was saying. Sade shifted out of her thoughts instantaneously.

"Yes, dey have helped us in some ways, but when our fadas treated dem wit respect and allowed dem to take our children and teach dem, dey did not tink dat everytin else also would be taken away," he continued.

Her father was different from many men in the village. He was the only one for miles who had one wife, in a culture where polygamy was the norm. Sade knew it was because of the teaching of the Methodist missionaries who had largely raised him from the age of three. She knew the story of the cloaked white men convincing Baba's parents that they could supply him with an education – of which the schooling in English was the primary benefit – and Baba's parents reluctantly allowing him to board in the next town, where they would visit him weekly.

Sade supposed she was grateful for this: for the fact British Methodists had reared in her father a belief whereby having several women as his wife concurrently was indecent, and the education that her father and thus herself and her siblings had had access to was surely a blessing.

But being removed from their homes, their families, having to assimilate into a culture that was not their own in their own country? Could these things be praised?

Mummy had chimed in now. "Dis new district officer will probably only march over us even harder dan dee odas now dat dey know der powers and our own are in battle."

The new district officer. They were talking about him again. Could no-one talk about anything else?

From that day on, Sade and the man with the slick brown hair crossed paths many more times. It was never planned, at least, not on Sade's part.

She went down to the rock every day to draw water. She had been doing so long before Mr. Tall-and-Handsome District Officer had been stationed there and she would continue doing so long after he was transferred elsewhere. Her steps had not changed. Yet almost every time she took them, it seemed he was there. He seemed, strangely, to frequently be on patrol when she took her two daily trips. Initially, their encounters were much the same as the first – Mr. Dark Eyes would bow his head slightly and pronounce a baritone "Good evening, ma," accompanied by a half-smile. That was when she was the only one around. If ever there was anyone else traipsing to or from the boulder, or Sade was accompanied by a friend or sister, the district officer would only bow his head slightly, glance quickly at each of them as he tapped his hat, and continue on his way.

Sade felt a spark of indignance any time he did that. Why was it he behaved one way when she was alone, and another when others like her were around?

Despite his apparent muteness in moments like these, Sade continued her "Good evening, sa," as did her friends and siblings when by her side. The respect they must assume for their district officers was not a choice; it was a way of life.

Sade didn't know if she should feel flattered that he spoke to her when she was alone, or simply irked by his duality.

Yet she knew, deep down, and cared not to admit it: what she felt wasn't entirely bad.

There was a surge of ire that she felt, however, every time she thought of his manner when he greeted her. Yes, his timbre was rich, and dare she think, inviting… but each note was flecked with condescension. He knew that she should feel flattered that she, a brown Nigerian village woman, was being greeted by him, a white British Colonial District Officer.

And she hated him for it.

Or, thought she did.

Sade discovered that his name was Mr. Caleb Monroe one bright afternoon, when the sun was beating down on the gathering outside the chief's grounds. It was Chief Oloye's birthday, and everyone in the village of Ogu had come to celebrate. Even the district officers and all the other officials of the British colonial administration from the periphery of their village had come to share in the festivities.

Sade, to any other eye, was just another pretty young village woman, albeit with a rippling giggle and an easy grace about her that marked her out as somewhat different from the rest. But to Mr. Caleb Monroe, she was an unparalleled beauty, with a sureness about her that he found irresistible.

He didn't know her name, and he barely knew what other English words she could say than 'Good morning' and 'good evening'... *sir*, he added as an afterthought – but today he could bask in the music of her voice. And bask he did.

Caleb had learnt some of the local dialect, but he knew much more of the official Yoruba they had been taught in Lagos. Its cadences sounded so much more beautiful in the lips of this wonder.

He was so enchanted by her laugh and her wide eyes as she engaged with her friends that he nearly missed his cue. He was being called to the front to give his address on behalf of the officers in the region, thanking Chief Oloye for his grace and welcome.

"... So, once more, we must say *e se gan*, Chief!" he finished. He was met with rapturous applause from his colleagues – and mellowed, yet enthusiastic praise from the village people. Caleb's eyes caught those of the beautiful, crimson and cobalt-blue clad young woman at the back just as his lips shaped around the Yoruba words. The borders of his mouth had already been upturned in a smile, but his expression widened as their eyes met. The dark pools set perfectly in her chiselled face glimmered like precious stones, and Caleb detected a flicker of a sparkle directed his way. A shy sparkle, but a sparkle nonetheless.

Mr. Caleb Monroe, District Colonial Officer, they had introduced him as. *Caleb.* Sade sounded the name out in her head. *Caleb.* Wasn't he one of the men sent to spy out the Promised Land in the Bible? So even before he had said his first word, he was destined to spy out their land.-

He had been spying on her all afternoon. She had caught him watching her.

When the weathered hands of the men beat down on the *dundun*, *batà,* and other drums, Sade and her sisters made the dust their dancefloor, amongst the other women.

Caleb watched. He found her joy intoxicating.

Sade's eyes wandered more than once in his direction, and each time her eyes smiled a little more. Before she knew it, he was smiling at her with no discretion. His warm, slow, lip-pressed smile. And before she knew it, she was doing the same.

Everything changed one day when Sade was on her way back from seeking the family's daily refreshment.

She was thinking about the presence of a specific *oyinbo*, and the certainty that that oyinbo must have several white women he could choose from. The daughters of his generals? The sisters of his colleagues, who taught in the primary schools? He ought to be spending his time admiring them, even if their laugh was not like hers, and they had not the same skill of swaying their hips to pulsating rhythms.

She too, should not be accepting smiles from this white man who believed himself to be so much more important than her, and felt no tension between ruling over her people and following the Jesus of the Bible, who loved and treated all people alike.

Such was the moment Caleb found her in. In fact, he entered into her pathway just as she stumbled over some nutgrass, managing all the same to keep her clay pot on her head.

"Ay!" she cried, as she bent down, unaware her solitude was no more.

Caleb bounded over to her as she rubbed the long graze stretching over her calf.

"Ma?" He said only one word, but the care in it sent a rush down Sade's spine. "Are you OK?" he added, looking at her, as he removed the large clay plot from her *osuka* so she could balance herself.

"Yes, sa," she almost whispered, shyly. "It is notin."

"It is nothing? Your leg is bleeding!" Caleb exclaimed, with a wry grin.

Sade gave a short, tense laugh. Tense, because he had placed his hand on her skin to cover up the wound and was tearing off part of his khaki sleeve. Sade felt the same rush traverse her spine, but stronger this time. Fear was the cause, she told herself. Fear because a white man was touching her and, who knew what he would do?

Her breathing was becoming erratic. Because she was afraid, she told herself. Her heartbeat was so strong she was sure he could feel it.

Caleb's heart was in his mouth at being so close to this village woman. Breathing in the same air that she exhaled. Her skin was warm, and the red blood trickling down her leg was warm still. Funny, though their shades were miles apart, the scratch on her leg bled the same way his would when he cut himself running in the streets of Stevenage as a child.

Caleb placed the makeshift tourniquet on Sade's leg to enclose the scratch, and smiled up at her.

"Tenk you, sa," Sade breathed.

"Caleb. You can call me Caleb." He said it almost without thinking.

"Yes, sa."

Caleb chuckled. "And your name is, ma?"

He waited in anticipation to hear the name of this fascinating woman who had captivated him from the moment he set eyes on her.

"My name is Sade, sa."

Sade. It was almost as if time stood still once his lips formed around her name. They both ceased to breathe for a moment, and turned to face each other simultaneously.

After several moments of awed silence and uninterrupted gazing, Caleb realised that as a male officer he ought to be the first to recover the powers of speech.

"Does that feel better?" he asked, unable to remove his eyes from her face.

Sade remembered who she was and looked down at her bound-up leg. "Yes, Caleb."

She looked up, and in Caleb's eyes she read and knew once and for all: there was no white woman he looked at as he looked at her.

"Tenk you," she whispered.

Caleb's answer was in his smile. That same slow, warm depth, but this time accompanied by a light brush on her leg, and a hushed, "Sade."

For weeks Sade and Caleb's trysts continued like this. Well, not quite like their first; unaccompanied by stumbling, bleeding and tourniquets, they were quiet and early. Sade would go to the rock at 4:30am, a time when she was sure no-one else from the village would be up. And Caleb would carry out an extra patrol at the same time. A patrol of a different kind; one where he would keep watch over her soul.

There was no doubt that though Caleb admired Sade, he saw her as being beneath him.

"Does your family believe in the Yoruba gods or follow the one true God?" he once asked her.

There was a pause. It irritated Sade that this man saw himself as a bringer of light to this dark and hopeless corner of

Earth.

"We follow one God", she replied.

"Do you believe that Jesus is the Son of God?" he persisted.

"Do you?" she retorted.

"I believe that Jesus is the Son of God, and the only way, the truth and the life." He might as well be reciting the catechisms she learnt at Sunday school.

"Why must it always be your way? Why is your way always the only way and the only truth? Perhaps I do not believe in the Yoruba religion, but I am tiyad of you always talking about your way and the white way. Do you think you are closer to Jesus dan any of dee rest of us?"

Caleb turned to Sade in silent shock.

"Do you not tink I see it, Caleb? Dee way you look at me when your oyinbo colleagues are around? When der wives are around? You look at me as doe I am beneat you. As doe it gives you pain to lower your eyes to look at someone wit brown skin."

Caleb did not reply.

"This Jesus you say is dee Son of God. Does he see dose wit lighter skin like yours as closer to Heaven? Does he have a scale of goodness where people wit my skin are at dee bottom?"

Caleb was still silent.

"Is dat what you tink, eh, Caleb? Dat your whiteness makes you better dan me even in dee eyes of your God?"

Caleb wanted to revive from his silent stupor, but the words would not come.

"Dat's what I tot." Sade rose to her feet. These oyinbos

always thought they were better than everyone else. Even if they had dared to like something in a people they believed to be beneath them.

"Sade," Caleb spoke now. The enunciation of her name on his tongue always stopped her in her tracks. He grabbed her hand, taut from her anger, and clasped it in his. "Come. Sit down."

How dare he order her around in a moment like this? She stood her ground, sullen and stubborn.

"You are right," he began, "I have been taught to consider myself above your people. That is what we were told and people at home continue to be told. They tell us that we are doing the world a favour, in coming here to 'civilise' your people. Before we came, we expected to see people wearing little clothing and unable to speak. What I found when I arrived here in Ogu village was far different from what I expected. You are right."

"So which Jesus are you following?" Sade challenged him, but her voice was less stringent this time.

"You are right," Caleb said once more. "All this time I have viewed myself as a good Methodist, helping the poor and needy as Jesus commanded. But all the time I have been revelling in the powers that this position gives me, and the holiness that my whiteness seems to synonymise. But you are right, my dear, my heart is not as white as my skin."

"You are a whitewashed wall," Sade said, thinking back to the day when she had first seen Mr. Monroe and the thoughts that had engrossed her.

Caleb looked up at her in surprise. The initial chastisement he met in her eyes was quickly replaced by a girlish grin.

She laughed. Oh, how Caleb loved that laugh.

He joined in Sade's laughter and drew her down to once more sit beside him; her hand still enclosed in his.

"I am right," Sade giggled. "Say it again."

"You are right, my dear. You and I may have different skin, but your morality is far above mine, and you have the wit and intelligence to better many men of my race. You shame me with your goodness. You delight me with your laugh. You dazzle me with your beauty."

Sade looked down. She had never been wooed like this before.

That hypnotised Caleb all the more. Her eyelashes were long and thick, and the view of them from above was all the more alluring when she looked at him from under them.

"So, you admit it, you have seen yourself as above me all dis while? You were ashamed? Dat is why you would neva speak to me when der were odas around?" Sade would still not let him forget it.

"Yes, my beautiful Sade. You were right. If I claim to follow Jesus, then I must love all the people that he created with the same love. You, most of all. Your people just as my people. Your dark skin just as their pale complexion."

That was what Sade needed to hear.

"Isn't Jesus described as the 'Sun of Righteousness' in the Bible? Well, in that case, we are closer to the Son than you!" she jested. Caleb laughed along with her.

They had never kissed. They had only talked, and Sade had sometimes let Caleb stroke her Afro halo. He loved to clasp her hand. Sometimes she had even rested her luscious crown on his shoulder and he had been lulled into reverie as it caressed his neck.

This time, Sade let him kiss her.

He asked her with his eyes first – the perfect gentleman – and then he pressed his lips against hers, slowly. His spirit sang.

After a few tender moments, Sade withdrew her face and inched back quickly.

Something was wrong and Caleb knew it.

"My dear? Sade? What is the matter?"

Sade gulped. In the elation of her emotions she had allowed herself to be stupid.

"Dis is dee matter! You are a white man! Dee only white men dat ever go wit women like me only rape dem and leave dem wit child once dey have enjoyed der pleasure! I will neva be so stupid as dis again!" Her fists pummelled his chest with each stressed syllable.

She ran off before he could stop her, her clay pot forgotten.

"Sade!" Caleb chased after her as though his life depended on it. "I am not like those men. I did not see you and decide to defile you. I saw you and I fell in love with you." He gasped for breath and stopped, unable to continue chasing her.

Sade stopped, her shoulders heaving. She turned back to Caleb.

"With each day I see you and as we grow closer," he said, "I grow more and more in love with you."

"Really?" she gasped, wanting to believe every word.

"Really."

It was another of their rendezvous before the dawn had settled. Sade was asking what Caleb and his family thought of the politics of 1952 Nigeria: whether they resented Nigerians wanting to govern themselves, or whether they believed the British would continue to divide and reign there.

Caleb was loath to answer.

Sade pressed him. "Do you tell your family much about life here when you write them letters?"

"Mmmm," was Caleb's evasive reply.

"Do they ask you whether or not you have found yourself a wife here yet?" Sade asked him, teasingly.

Caleb laughed nervously, his mouth closed.

"Do they?" Sade asked again, the tinge of playfulness edging out slightly.

"Yes, you know what parents are like. I am thirty years old and they want to know when they will have grandchildren." Caleb laughed forcefully.

"So? What do you tell dem?"

Caleb shifted.

Sade's eyes narrowed at him.

"I tell them - I tell them that…" his voice trailed off.

"What do you tell dem, Mr. Monroe?" Sade was not joking now.

"I tell them that there is a girl called Winona," Caleb conceded, too ashamed to continue.

"Winona? Miss-White-Girl-dat-you-made-up because you are ashamed of me? I should have known, Caleb. I should have known."

This time Caleb did not try to stop her as she rose.

Dum dum dum! A purposeful knock rattled the front door of the Olukoya cottage.

Moroundiya answered.

"Sista mi, it is the district officer. Mr. Monroe. He said he is looking for you. How does he know you?" Moroundiya cried as her head poked around the corner of Sade's door.

Sade's heart thudded. She remembered the last time she had seen Caleb with a cold heart. And then she felt hot rage sear inside her when she realised that he had dared to come to their house and reveal that he knew her.

When she rushed to the door, her face was set in stone. Before she could say a word, Caleb took over.

"Sade," he said in hushed tones, "you were right again. I knew it as soon as you asked me. The moment I got home, I wrote a new letter."

He unashamedly showed her the fresh pages. Sade glanced down in spite of herself, and read the words: *'Father, Mother, the Winona of whom I have been writing is imaginary. The truth is, the woman I love is called Sade. She is better than anything I could ever have imagined. I like to call her "my Nigerian princess".'*

Sade did not need to read more.

Her family were in the back, but Caleb didn't care.

"I am not ashamed of you Sade, and to demonstrate that to you, I will go inside your house right this moment and tell your father how much I love you."

It was Sade's moment to go quiet.

"But – but – my father will – my family will disown me!"

Caleb grabbed a hold of Sade's hand and marched into the house.

"If dis is truly what you are telling me, Folasade Laide Olukoya, den you no longer have a place in this house."

Baba rose from his seat and moved towards the window. Each step pierced through Sade; a painful reminder of his immovable status as head of the home.

"I love him Baba, we love each oda!"

Those were the last words she uttered before her father showed her the door.

Moroundiya was not quite as harsh. She clasped her elder sister's hands fervently as they left.

She watched as Caleb tightened his hand around Sade's and saw him whisper the words, *"I love you"* to her sister in Yoruba.

Moroundiya smiled. Her father would come around.

The Next Big Thing
Lọla Labinjọ

An elderly lady dressed in a lilac boubou approached me when I was at the book table, waiting for Nwokolo to sign my book. She looked at me and smiled. I smiled back and quickly looked away, not feeling in the mood for chitchat. She continued to smile, refusing to listen to my body language, and somehow managed to force me into one of *those* conversations. One where your eyes are constantly darting about, searching for the nearest exit, as your head nods nonchalantly, and a faux Cheshire smile is plastered on your face through gritted teeth.

After an initial intro of how wonderful the speaker was and how pertinent his observations on Africa were, she stabbed me with the question: "Are you African or English?"

I had to stop my eyes from rolling and my shoulders from sagging. "Both," I replied as pleasantly as I could manage. *I've foiled her plan,* I thought to myself, already imagining my triumphant conversational exit. We simultaneously asked each other a question, and with inquisitorial guns drawn and dogged will filling the silent air, the stand-off began. Like a game of chicken, where two stubborn egos have the potential to be bruised. Neither of us wanted to give up. Both of us repeated our question in succession.

Mine: "How about you?"

Hers: "Which part of Africa?"

In the end I surrendered. "Nigeriawhataboutyou?"

"Oh riiiight!" she said, and started to prepare herself. Her actions resembled a professional singer before a performance. It seems like this is the question she'd been waiting for, and like a one-minute elevator speech, she began to reel off a Facebook version of her life story. "'Well, I was born in Kenya, grew up in Tanzania and well, we just weren't taught African history at all and…"

My mind drifts off, trying to pinpoint what about this lady has irritated me so much. Am I biased about her accent, but unwilling to admit it? Was it her age and race, which made me judge her before she'd even spoken? Is it her unlimited supply of overindulgent bonhomie, the way she tricked me into conversation or the fact that she asked me *that* question, and then forced me to choose?

Why had it not occurred to her that I could be both…or neither? Or was it not an obvious question a number of people could ask as a sort of icebreaker at an African festival? Why hadn't anyone else asked it? Was it relevant?

"…and well the war was dreadful, all those awful things that happened to the Mau Mau under British rule…"

I wondered if I should tell her that her one-minute elevator speech had run overtime. The author still hadn't arrived, so I was trapped here with my feet full of English politesse, firmly rooted to the ground.

Why must I stand here and rationalise the way I feel? my mind whispered. *'Give excuses for it, concretise it, give myself permission to have these feelings?*

I started to think about that show currently on TV, where

people are put in staged situations to test the moral temperature of the nation. Regarding social issues, such as homophobia, islamophobia, racism, etc. It's only just started but I noticed that for the 'racist' episodes, nobody actually speaks out until they're absolutely 110% sure with no doubt that the person is being racist. They have to hear specific words or phrases before they react for fear, I imagine, of being accused of playing the race card or being wrong. Well, what happens when you just feel uncomfortable, uneasy or upset? What if there *is* no hard proof laid out on the table, but it's a feeling, an air, a gesture, or a look? What do you do then?

She'd finished talking and was looking to me for a response. "Er…" I tried to remember the last thing I'd heard. "So…East Africa?" I proffered.

"Yes, *exactly*!" she exclaimed. "And isn't it so important," she was off again "the way Africa is seen and presented as a whole, well…. country? And no one seems to know…"

She suddenly trailed off and looked behind me. I was still lost in thought.

"Oh, Chuuuma!" she squealed, offering her hand to the author now at the book table. "Delightful talk, simply delightful."

She'd forgotten all about me. I had been used, I was a seat warmer to her, a stand in, a 'you'll-do-for-now' substitute for what she really wanted.

I suddenly became invisible as she moved on to the next big thing.

Dream of Red Passage
Krystal Song

"Now, as I bury the flowers,
others laugh at my folly;
But in the future years, who knows
who will bury me?"
—Cao Xueqin, Dream of Red Chamber, 1791

He moved into the neighborhood shortly after I turned twelve. His name was Jianyu, and he was beautiful.

I lived in Jing An District back then, near the Jade Buddha Temple, so the neighborhood was mainly old folks scattered among university professors. A new *liumang* kid, only twice my age, was enough cause for excitement. The elders groused about his loud rap music, the littering of cigarette butts left in his wake. The professors avoided him like the plague.

I sought him out immediately.

I soon learned that Jianyu was slippery and hard to find, like a dragon that only ventured out in the twilight hours. It wasn't until cram school began that I finally came home late enough to catch him outside, sitting in the alley passage and smoking a cigarette, staring up at the pearly wisps of moon.

His legs were stretched out on the red stoop by the rubbish bins, and he sat leaning forward, wearing indoor slippers and no shirt. I caught a glimpse of a few English characters tattooed on his rib cage, but my English wasn't good enough to sound out the word. Heart hammering in indecision, I tightened my backpack straps and marched up to him. "Who are you?"

He barely glanced up. "Wouldn't you like to know."

Up close, I was starstruck. His eyes were light and slanted like a cat's, and his hair was so glossy and black I wanted to cut off a piece and hold it to the light, just to see if it would spark. "Ama says you're a *kenlao* living off your papa's generosity."

He flicked cigarette ash onto the sidewalk, then blew smoke in my face. "Your grandmother's not wrong."

"Ama also says smoking is bad. She says it makes you die."

His phone buzzed and he slid it out of his pocket with a practiced ease, ignoring me. The screen lit up – more messages than I had ever gotten in my life. I watched with marvel as he texted out a reply, then three more, the veins on his arm tensing and shifting. They stood out like blue-purple rivers against his forearms.

All too soon he was shoving his phone back into his pocket and getting to his feet. He towered over me now. "Well, Xiuying–" he smirked at my stunned expression, "–if I'm going to die, might as well make the most of my last night, right?"

"How do you know my name?" I demanded. He flicked the nametag on my chest, from when we'd done introductions that day at cram school. I covered the sticker immediately, but the damage was done.

"Where are you going?" I shouted as he strode down the passage. He only raised one arm in a backhanded wave, graceful as a bird of prey. I watched his receding figure until he disappeared, lost among the blinking Shanghai lights.

It wasn't until a few days later that I saw him again. I was on my way home, licking a popsicle, when I heard voices echoing from the back passage. I snuck over to get a closer look.

This time he wore ripped jeans and a ripped tee and had his hair all spiky as if he'd run it through the leftover oil of a stir-fry. There was a girl with him, tall and slim, and together they looked so mature and shiny it was like staring at mannequins through a glass display.

"You're running away, again," she hissed. "I'm not going to date some loser university dropout. I gave you ten thousand chances, Jianyu, but this is my *dixian*. Why couldn't you just take the fucking exam?"

"I tried," he said. "You don't understand, Lili. It got so bad I couldn't read anymore. The numbers, they wouldn't make sense, I tried–"

"You should have tried harder."

"I thought I was going to die in there!" he burst out, flinching at the sound of his own voice.

Overhead, windows flew open. Lights flickered on. "Be quiet down there! Don't you see how late it is?"

"You waste my time," the girl said, before leaving.

In the sudden silence, I heard a soft gasp, a strangled sound. *Jianyu*, I thought, rolling the syllables across my tongue. He was sitting against the red alley wall, rubbing his eyes so hard it looked as if he was trying to dig out his eyeballs. "Jianyu?" I whispered.

He sat up. His eyes were rimmed red. It made him look

even more eerily perfect. He stared at me and I was suddenly seized with fear. I held out my cherry popsicle. "Do you want a bite?"

His jaw clenched and for a second, I thought he would fight me. Then he swallowed and nodded. I ran over. "She doesn't sound very nice."

A hoarse laugh broke out of him. "No," he agreed.

I wondered about the lives of these people, almost like storybook characters, heroes from an old fable. I wanted to reach out and touch him, to feel his warm skin and ascertain he was real.

"You went to university?" I asked, bouncing on the balls of my feet.

"Yeah." He polished off the popsicle. "But I couldn't handle it. I-I hit a breaking point. That's when you know, this is it. They hospitalized me and the doctor asked if I cared more about success or life." He shrugged again, a studied nonchalance. "I knew what I was giving up when I turned in my resignation letter. I don't blame her, you know? Who would want to be with this–this *liumang* loser."

I tried to absorb this. What was a 'breaking point'? When you took a popsicle stick and bent it, sometimes it snapped, clean as chopsticks. Sometimes it folded softly, like a piece of paper. And sometimes, when you were unlucky, it turned into a mess of jagged splinters and betrayed you entirely. Then you just had to let it go and give it up. I wanted to explain this but I was twelve, and the words would not come to me.

"Enough about me," he said. "How do you like school, little miss?"

I perked up. Without a moment's hesitation, I proceeded to fill him in on all the thrilling developments of elementary school, from Old Man Xu's new *youtiao* doughnut stand, to Zhangyong's foreign smartwatch that changed colors every hour. He was the best listener I'd ever met. He didn't interrupt a single time, and only nodded here and there, smoking a few cigarettes, staring into the sky with a glaze of wonder in his eyes. I never did ask him what he was thinking.

From then on, we spoke almost every day. Sometimes on his way out he'd yank one of my pigtails as if ringing a bell, then ride off on his motorcycle before I could get him back. Other times I'd catch him on my route to the bus stop and beg him to buy me a lychee candy. I never saw him around the neighborhood for long bouts of time and had no idea what he did in the daylight hours, but I was satisfied thinking of him as a sort of mythical creature, one who guarded his secrets like the Monkey King with his heavenly *taozi* peaches.

A year passed and life moved on. Jianyu remained forever on the periphery: scraps of crumpled soda cans, an engine guttering at twilight, hushed laughter and furtive whispers, like the fluttering of wings. I was thirteen now and I wanted more of him than I could get. No longer was I content with daydreaming by my bedroom window, watching the light scatter and schism through the curtains as I prayed for one golden chance. His coy smiles and half-hearted greetings only fed my desperation like paper to flame, and soon, as the matured and wise teenager that I was, I decided there was only one thing left for me to do.

I headed down to my best friend Zhangyong's house, borrowing his sister's makeup. I drew thick strokes of inky black liner over my eyes and tapped splotches of glittery pink blush on my cheeks. I brushed my hair out of its braids and hacked out choppy, blunt bangs with kitchen shears. The final touch: a soft pink push-up bra, with little lace edges fringing the cups.

I waited for him by the red passage, a tiger in the weeds. Like clockwork, he showed up a little after midnight, mercifully alone, whistling to himself as he texted with both hands. He'd been out of university for a year now and found himself a group of friends Ama called *liumang afei* riffraff and gained a few new tattoos along with them. His hair was longer, his jeans dirtier, and altogether he was the sort Ama warned me never to associate with. I, of course, did the opposite.

I thought I was being original.

"Hey," I said softly, not daring to alert the neighbors. The blue light of his phone cast his face in an otherworldly, underwater glow. He looked me over, raising a brow at my short dress.

"Do you like it?" I fluttered my lashes like a soap opera star. "I dressed up for you."

Jianyu threw back his head and laughed. Out of every reaction I had imagined, I had not imagined this. "You're cute, Xiuying."

I sidled up to him. He sidestepped me and sat on the curb I had just vacated. I hoped he could scent my vanilla sugar spray. His cough was answer enough.

I plunked down beside him. "Do you have a girlfriend?"

116

He slid out a pack of cigarettes. *"Tian ah,"* he muttered.

"Can I have one?" I plucked the cigarette out of his mouth, then stuck it between my lips. "Light it for me, will you?"

That roused him. "God, Xiuying," he ripped it from my mouth then ground the brand-new cigarette into the ground. "Don't joke around like that." He scrubbed a hand over his face. "It's late. Shouldn't you be getting some rest?"

I took a deep breath and scooted closer. I could feel our thighs touching. Through the fabric of his jeans, his leg was warm. "Don't you like me? A lot of boys in school like me." It was true. I was pretty popular for a seventh grader, though Zhangyong said that was more because of my money and confidence than anything else.

His eyes cut towards me. I didn't dare exhale. We had never been this close before. I felt so brave, like a warrior climbing the ladder to heaven, daring to touch the stars. Peering into his eyes, I thought they might hold every light in the universe, though maybe that was just the reflection of the streetlamps.

"You're very special, Xiuying," he said, before brushing a stray piece of hair out of my eyes. *"Tian ah,* did you cut these bangs yourself? You have hair all over you!" he laughed, ruining the moment by dusting my nose with his hand. He smelled like cigarette smoke and liquor, and I wanted both because they reminded me of him.

"I cut them for you," I chirped, tilting my face up to him.

"Oh really?" His voice was low and amused, a crackly sound like a dying fire. "And do you think of me often?"

I nodded, squirming. I couldn't bear the tension any longer. If this kept up, I would just do the deed myself. I leaned forward, squeezing my eyes shut–

The sound of hands clapping together interrupted my reverie. I blinked one eye open and caught him patting his hands and brushing stray hairs off his jeans. My hair. Then he stood up.

"You didn't actually think I was into you, right?" He looked down at me from an unreachable height. I had never felt so small. Before he went inside, he told me: "You're funny, Xiuying."

Ama got wind of suspicious business from the neighbors and instructed me never to talk to him again. I nodded my head at the right moments and maintained good grades and kept my head down for the next few weeks. Jianyu, I noticed, also began avoiding the neighborhood stoop. Pigeons started gathering at our sacred almost-kiss shrine and I had to yell at them daily to back off.

Middle school ramped up. Cram school was a bore but at least I had Zhangyong to accompany me. He walked me home after class one night to borrow my copy of *Dream of Red Chamber*, and to my equal amazement and horror we found Jianyu waiting by the rubbish bins at the end of the passage, feeding sesame *shaqima* to the pigeons.

He grinned at me as we passed, waggling suggestive brows at Zhangyong and even possessing the audacity to wink. Zhangyong didn't notice the exchange but instead continued discussing badminton championships non-stop until we were safely in my apartment. I found him the old text before escorting him out the door. Ama, thank the skies, was on one of her many trips west and wouldn't be back for another few days.

Zhangyong's hands fumbled with the book. "Thanks, Xiuying," he said for the third time.

"Of course," I answered, faking a yawn. "I'll see you tomorrow, okay?"

He opened his mouth as if about to say more, but the door was open and Jianyu was now smoking a cigarette a few paces away. Zhangyong gulped. "See you tomorrow," he echoed, leaning in for a half-hearted punch on the arm. I smiled and waved until he disappeared.

A low whistle cut through the late autumn air. I stepped outside to meet Jianyu's mirthful eyes. "He likes you," he teased.

"He does not!" I protested. "Zhangyong is my best friend. We've been friends for ages."

"Oh, *ages*," he agreed, the edge of his lip quirking. I could tell he was suppressing a laugh. It only made me angrier.

"I'm not going to wait for you forever, you know."

It was the final crack in the dam. He burst into laughter, clutching his side. "I'm not asking you to wait, Xiuying," he said. "Just… be careful, alright? Don't trust us *liumang* boys. We're all assholes."

He left before I could think of anything clever to say. This was my *dixian* limit. I still remembered Lili from all those nights ago, the first and only time I'd ever seen Jianyu reveal any real sort of emotion. *I gave you ten thousand chances, Jianyu, but this is my dixian.*

I did not know what she meant, so I interpreted her words with the blunt force of a blacksmith, hammering out iron. I would seek Jianyu out on my own terms.

As if he knew my thoughts, he began evading the neighborhood completely, not even returning at night to sleep. I knew because I took vigil late into the midnight hours, listening for the telltale roar of his engine while watching the Shanghai skyline stir and gutter.

I was thirteen and patience was not my strong suit. It took three hands to count the age difference between us and the numbers were damning. He would meet someone soon and slip far out of reach, all his heavenly *taozi* locked up forever. I had won top grades in school by going after what I wanted; I wasn't going to stop now. It took careful planning and the tactics of Master Sun Tzu himself, but with help from the *Art of War* I got it done. Ama was out of town for another business thing in the States, and it wasn't difficult to lie and call in sick for the day. Sure enough, biding my time by the open bedroom window, I at last caught Jianyu clambering out of his apartment at two in the afternoon, sleepy-eyed and lethargic. So this was when the creature of night abandoned his cave.

He gunned his motorcycle and I raced after him, reaching the alley junction just as he veered down Huaihai East Road. This would be a lot harder than I imagined.

I combed the streets meticulously, treating the whole ordeal as an algebra problem. Around five in the evening I got distracted by the steamy fragrance of a *xiaolongbao* stand, and wasted an hour gulping down soup dumplings, but other than this minor diversion

I stayed my course and was eventually rewarded, as I always was at the age of thirteen.

His silver motorcycle was parked crooked in a back-alley lot near the border of Zhabei District. I had never been here alone and certainly not at this hour, but I had invested a whole day in this endeavor and wasn't surrendering now. I tugged off my hoodie and tied it around my waist, then tried to strategically maneuver the small lumps in my bra into a more compelling arrangement. I was shivering in my sheer camisole, my loose ponytail whipping in my face, and I would lose all courage if I didn't seize the moment right away. *Tianxia wu nanshi, zhipa you xinren.* Set your mind and you can do anything under the sun.

I pushed open the restaurant door. Inside it was dim and fuzzy and smelled of mildew. I couldn't think above the din of raucous laughter and clinking glasses, the bodies pressed up against each other, moving in cacophony like a single-minded beast. As I threaded through the crowd, I scanned for a familiar face. Someone beckoned for me but I didn't like his smile. My heart was threatening to explode but before I could think through my poor life choices, I saw him. He was sitting in the back corner, chair tilted back, a bottle of *maotai* liquor in his hand. He looked so heartbreakingly familiar it was like taking a cool sip of water. I stumbled forward. "Jianyu!"

He didn't hear me. He turned to the purple-haired woman beside him and whispered in her ear. But his friends saw me. The bearded man on his left pushed out of his chair. "Looks like you have a little friend, Sun."

The man gestured toward me and I inched closer, uncertain. The man was tall like Jianyu and smelled of something sickly sweet, almost like rotting fruit. "Adorable," the man said.

Jianyu took a swig of his drink before finally sparing a glance at me. The effect was immediate. His eyes widened as he slammed the glass down and shot to his feet. Liquor sloshed onto the table and the purple-haired woman jerked her handbag out of the way, complaining in a thick *xiaxiangren* rural dialect.

"What are you doing here?" He glared at his friend and shoved him back into his seat. "*Caodan!* Don't fucking go near her," he hissed. Then he grabbed me by the arm, towing me towards the door. Someone whistled and cracked a joke, and it seemed as if everyone laughed, even the room laughed, its walls warping and tilting down on us.

He released me as soon as the door slammed shut behind us. "Why are you here?"

"I-I wanted to see you," I stammered. "It's been so long and I–"

"Xiuying," he groaned, clutching at his hair. The pained look in his eyes was a punch to the gut.

I whirled away, ignoring the prick of tears. "Whatever. I'll go home."

"Wait." He exhaled. "I'll take you back."

I had dreamed of this moment for so long. Wrapping my arms around his waist, riding on the back of his motorcycle, wearing his helmet, his jacket, knowing his smell and knowing it would be mine. But the night air was frigid and, in every daydream,

I had never imagined the fear, seeding like a *pugongying* weed in my heart.

When we returned to the red passage, I assumed he would drop me off, but instead he parked his bike. For once, I said nothing. He seemed disturbed by the silence. "Do you want anything to eat?"

I shrugged, even though I was always hungry. "Can we go inside?" I said instead. "It's cold."

He appeared uncertain, peering up at the red brick of my apartment, identical to every other one on the block. An indelible line would be crossed in stepping over my threshold, one we both knew couldn't be erased. He bit his lower lip in doubt, and in that brief, infinitesimal moment, I knew he was like me.

He was no mythical creature.

I tugged on his wrist and he relented, letting me lead him inside. He ordered delivery but said he wasn't hungry, so I slurped down the *zhajiangmian* beef noodles as he smoked cigarette after cigarette, his cheeks splotched red with alcohol. I didn't even care that Ama would return in two days and surely catch the scent of smoke; I could think of nothing beyond his pale eyes, glinting in the lamplight.

Suddenly I could not eat another bite. I threw the whole container away and sat beside him on the floor. "Are you still mad?" I whispered. I didn't know why I was whispering; the door was locked and there was no one else here. Perhaps I could sense the third presence in the room: trepidation, waiting for something to happen.

He shook his head, then coughed. I hadn't noticed that his hands were shaking too. I was filled with remorse for what I had done, what I had made him do. I looked at him and saw a little boy, someone as scared as me.

"Do you care about me?" I whispered.

He avoided my gaze but nodded, blowing out a long stream of smoke. His eyes fell shut. A crease had formed between his brows, like a wrinkle in a bolt of cloth. I wanted to lean forward and smooth it over. Instead, I kissed him.

His mouth was open and parted in an O of surprise. I had no idea what I was doing but I knew if I let go it would be the end. I breathed in his cigarette smoke and pressed my lips harder onto his, and suddenly his hands were around me, on my waist, my hair, my neck, and he was kissing me back. I didn't know what kissing was supposed to be like. I could feel sensation on my skin, I could feel warmth and hear sound, but it felt far away, as if to a storybook character, never to me.

He let out a muffled groan and shifted away, but I was afraid of myself, afraid of him, afraid of every possibility but most of all, of letting go. His hands pried off my hoodie and trailed down my collarbones to my chest. When his cold hands touched my breasts, I jerked back, utterly shocked.

"Is your grandmother home?"

I shook my head, forgetting how to speak.

He stared at me, his throat bobbing. "How old are you really?" he murmured, cupping my cheek with his hand.

I couldn't speak. I knew what he wanted. I knew, for the

first time, that I had something he wanted. I thought it would be enough.

I nodded.

He picked me up and brought me into my bedroom. I didn't wonder how he knew where it was. He laid me down amidst my stuffed animals and anime posters, illuminated by the moonlight streaming in from the open window. He unbuttoned my shirt. He unclasped my bra. He stared at my naked breasts, my chest rising and falling, the gooseflesh lining my skin.

His own clothes remained on.

I wanted to see the tattoo on his rib cage, wanted to spell out the English letters they formed. I was in the safest place in my home with the boy I had loved since the beginning of time. It was all happening according to plan.

I was terrified.

He unbuckled his jeans. His breathing was erratic. It made him sound unhinged. I didn't recognize the lust in his eyes or the strength in his hands as he held my arms down and pushed himself inside me. I didn't recognize him as I cried out and he covered my mouth with one hand, leaning forward to shut the bedroom window with the other. I never closed that window. Even in the thick of winter, the window remained wide open.

I started to cry.

I couldn't hear what he was saying. After some time, he got up and helped clean me, then gave me a warm washcloth that I did not use. I heard the bedsprings buckle and felt his body fall beside mine. Hesitantly, he wrapped his arms around me and cradled me against his chest. This was all I'd ever wanted, I thought. *Tianxia wu nanshi, zhipa you xinren.* Set your mind and you can do anything under the sun.

I had done it. I was under the sun and I had done it.

He was golden and he was the best thing in her life. He was her father and her lover and her best friend. He told her everything, even troubling things, but they passed through her ears like mist, leaving only tears that she wiped away.

"No one gets me like you do," he whispered, late one night, the two of them wrapped in her Hello Kitty sheets. "I know I can be honest with you because you won't judge me."

They kept their time together a secret. Jianyu forbade her from telling anyone, even Zhangyong. They met late at night, and only when Ama was traveling, which, luckily for her, was most of the time, otherwise she might've died from waiting. Jianyu ordered her never to follow him again, never to acknowledge him in public, and she understood that grownups had rules, and rules must be obeyed if the heavens would allow this little drop of magic to tumble loose. She had magic in her hands and she would do anything not to let it go. With him, she became something different, something special, set apart from the other kids in her class. She maintained good grades, and started coming home directly after school, no longer lingering with her classmates to complain about *gaokao* prep and other mundane things that existed beneath her. Ama noticed the change and asked if everything was okay with Zhangyong. She showed Ama her report card and all was good again.

She did not mind the sex. She tried to find special ways to please him and watched videos on how to apply makeup and what sorts of outfits to wear. He didn't like it when she dressed up though. He liked her bare faced and unadorned, without even a bra, though sometimes he did ask that she wear her middle school uniform, and she had no idea why.

Jianyu's twenty-fifth birthday came and went. They celebrated with melon popsicles and long-life noodles.

"My father wants me to go back to university now that I'm recovered, but I can't tell him that I've changed, that I can't live that life anymore."

He continued talking, without pause, but her hearing was fuzzy and his words came in and out like a broken radio receptor.

"When I wake up, I find blood in my mouth and I'm too scared to learn if it's cancer. I'm a fool, Xiuying. I'm a damn fool and I have no one to blame but myself."

It was hard to say what would have happened if Ama had not intervened when she did. In July the following year when the school term broke, Ama announced that they were moving to New Jersey so Xiuying could receive a proper American education. Xiuying threatened to break her cellphone, to run away, to kill herself, but Ama was a Shanghainese *nainai* who had seen her only child pass away and her entire city fall under Japanese occupation. One little girl's protests were nothing but leaves striking stone.

On her last day, Jianyu met her outside the passage stoop. Ama was watching from the window and he didn't dare go closer.

Later, Xiuying would remember that Jianyu was always as passive as water, letting the riverbed dictate his path.

"Please don't hate me," he whispered.

"How could I ever hate you?" The very idea appalled her, and she wondered for a heartbeat if crossing the ocean and stepping foot on western soil would transform her, turn her into some foreign beast or perhaps a mythical creature. At last, would she be like him?

He dared a glance towards the open window, then stepped forward and kissed her on the cheek, softly, his lips lingering and reluctant to part. "I'm sorry," he said, his voice breaking. "When you're older and you understand, please remember that I'm sorry."

A Neighbourhood Called Exile
JB Polk

The window, misted over and streaked with paths of condensed moisture, let through a dribble of red and blue light from a neon sign placed on the rooftop across the street giving the room an anaemic air.

Lying on the bed fully dressed, Simon gazed at the high ceiling with moulded plaster vines and clusters of grapes - chalky, unnatural in appearance. His mouth, stimulated by the sharp twinges of memories, watered. Sweet, warm to the touch grapes. Transparent when held against the sunlight. Bursting with juice when slightly pressed. They used to hang in tight, heavy bunches and, uncollected throughout summer, they would splash onto the cement walkway under the wooden pillars. From the clay oven behind the house the smell of freshly made bread wafted in. In the bamboo hedge skirting the garden sparrows squabbled and chattered but without animosity. From time to time, a visiting breeze fluttered the bamboo stalks sending a blizzard of dry leaves onto his head. Inside the house, the clamour of salsa mingled with the routine kitchen noises - sounds so comforting that even now, listening only to their echoes in his mind, they warmed his blood.

It had been nearly two years since he fled to what he thought of as the safety of a new country. The safety of London with its anonymity where he knew he was just a nameless face in the crowd. Where he didn't have to look over his shoulder and expect a rifle butt to prod at his ribs.

His thoughts went back to the time he had finally realised he could stay no longer: political unrest ravaged the country, uncertainty stretched nerves to a breaking point, people stranded in the capital hoarded food, soap flakes, candles, matches and bales of soft black wool for suits and skirts they'd never make and even less use. Skirmishes in the parliament turned into vicious fist fights, factory workers stopped working altogether and engaged in muddled arguments with the management. Politicians, stone deaf to the pleas to, for once, do something for their country, chose not to listen and do still less. It didn't surprise him much, though. He knew that politics was nothing more than the art of getting money from the rich and the vote of the poor under the pretext of protecting one from the other, as an old saying put it. Hope was fizzling out like a bottle of an open soft drink. People, having exhausted their store of expectations a long time ago, regarded the future with truculence, and relied on intricate schemes to get them through until the end of the day, the week, the month. Years no longer featured in the national calendar - it was hard enough to make it to the other side of the day.

Through the paper-thin partition separating his bed-sit from the turbaned Sikh's, the drone of a sitar sifted in - permanent and persistent as the hum of a mosquito about to land, never varying an octave, never giving up. He covered his ears with his fists and squeezed his eyes shut to block out the aggressive drone and the bluish-red glare advertising a fourth- rate Bayswater hotel, home to restive exiles like himself and prostitutes with young bodies, middle-aged eyes, and old souls.

Every night was the same - numbed by a couple of Carlsberg's and wearied beyond repair by the ten-hour shift washing off the vestiges of congealed curries in *Jalal's Tandoori*, he would fall into a dreamless, fidgety sleep for exactly four hours. Slumber that failed to restore the strength to either body or spirit. Then, just after three in the morning, he'd wake up – frequently to the buzzing of the sitar or the late-night combats of the Polish couple from across the hall.

"Kurwa!" - the word, repeated over and over by the man whose face remained as anonymous as his voice, clung to the folds of his brain like a particularly pleasant, memory-prodding refrain. He even went as far as to check its meaning. The Polish dictionary, unearthed in a Bayswater library, its pages still virgin crisp, failed to list it, or maybe Simon didn't really know how to spell it.

Downstairs, a door slammed shut - Paddy O'Toole was weaving his way up the stairs, extolling at the top of his voice the virtue of smiling Irish eyes. He wondered what he looked like – the guy he thought of as Paddy O'Toole. Handsome in a typical Irish way or ruined by the draught Guinness drunk in London pubs and roaming the paths of voluntary exile? For all he knew, his name was probably not O'Toole and it might not even be Paddy. But stereotypes (and who better than he with a dusky face, wiry black hair, and a thick Latino accent would know more about their powerful grip?) took root easily and remained anchored firmly.

The sound of the sitar faded away - the cassette had finished, or his neighbour had fallen asleep.

The room was stuffy, pervaded by the clinging, cloying smells of previous occupants and their national concoctions: stale chapatis, pickled gherkins, laurel-laced spaghetti Bolognese. He wondered if his own smell - the aroma of tandoori ovens and spicy Masalas he carried on his clothes, his hair, his skin - would mingle with the other smells. Would the last, more powerful, fresher odour prod at someone's curiosity? Would the aroma of food that was not even his own be all he'd leave behind?

Outside, a taxi horn blared in the departing night and the voices of its drunken passengers floated on the cold, December air. Christmas with tinsel chains, glass baubles, turkey and sage was striding forward fast. His first cold, not necessarily white, Christmas. His thoughts went on a mental ramble back to the sweltering Latin American Christmases. Who'd have thought back then that he'd ever see a cold, if not white, Christmas? Who'd have thought that gales of political unrest and opera-uniformed military juntas would blow him over here to a crummy hotel room, sandwiched between a sitar-mad Sikh and a rowdy Polish couple? To a neighbourhood called exile where no-one really belonged, no-one could claim as his own. To a place where every inhabitant shared a similar baggage - Latinos running away from the terror of dictatorial caudillos, Blacks who set their faces against the stalwart grip of poverty and racism, Poles and Russians escaping the illusory idyll of the Red Paradise. Thrown into the seething cauldron of a London suburb, chasing dreams of freedom, elusive ideals of peace and friendship for all, but failing to find them.

How many other neighbourhoods that differed in

name only and shared the same type of people, the same kind of loneliness, the same damned lack of belonging, would he see before going back? How many more ceilings with chalky grapes, cherubs, and damp plaster frescoes would he see? How many more sleepless nights, how many hours of inhaling tandoori fumes and the smell of flat Guinness?

It was quiet now - no sitar, no mournful lamentations about sunshine and shadow, no arguments, no passion. All exiles, all restless souls, seemed to have finally settled down for the night.

He gazed at the clock ticking away the night - ten to seven. One hour before it woke him up. Two before he started, once again, scraping off last night's Chicken Jalfrezi at *Jalal's Tandoori*. It was time to sleep.

Quibilah
Jade Mutyora

As always, I was careful to keep my phone screen angled away from Hayden. No rules were ever broken, but he had always made it clear that he had the power to 'pull the plug' on me and Alba. Despite her being long out of the picture, if he were to ask me what I was doing right now my flushed cheeks and badly cobbled sentences would surely be enough to reveal an ocean of hypothetical betrayals. Her profile had been set to private recently and I felt a stab wondering if it could be because of me even though it had been over a year since we were in contact.

Hayden wasn't interested in what I was doing anyway. He blasted out his foghorn laugh, the purpose of which was to get me to ask what was so funny rather than display genuine amusement. I kept my mind on scrolling through the few remaining pictures of Alba for public viewing, stuffing down my despair that the videos of her were lost to me now, probably forever. I'd never again see the way she rubbed her nose, or the dimple that made an appearance for just a second when her mouth twitched deliciously into a smirk.

"Look at this," Hayden forced his phone in front of my face to show me a dimly lit video of the back of a pair of thighs, flesh bulging between artfully knotted ropes. The sound of leather hitting skin was almost immediately followed by a muffled yelp. My cheeks warmed.

"Um, hot?" I said, but Hayden pointed excitedly at the comments below.

@MollyHilloughby: Mmmm fuck, I'm jealous of both the people in this video!

My eyes widened and I screamed with laughter, without having to fake it.

"She's come online then! That was quick, but what a thing to say for your first message from the afterlife."

"Yep, sweetheart of morning telly to bondage queen! It happens like that at the beginning. Especially the ones who were squeaky clean before. The surge in energy outweighs the inhibitions. Remember how it went with that Canadian former PM? He'd all but crawled up the King's arsehole when he was alive and then he practically tore him a new one immediately after his download."

Sitting on the sofa in front of the film he'd insisted I'd chosen even though I knew I hadn't, I tapped through a couple of poetry profiles for aimless scrolling. Audre Lorde's recent words nestled between comforting snippets from her old writings that were still relevant all these years later, with now familiar, recycled black and white images from a time before selfies. Another of my favourite accounts provided fresh, daily inspiration; each verse dripping with multiple meanings.

you weep securely
wrapped in fate

suffocating in
safety's weight
discarded versions
litter your floor
leave them behind
dare to soar

After lights out, my skin crawled uncomfortably at the anticipation of Hayden's touch. Predictably his rough hand found my breast, then pushed between my legs and then his weight pressed on me, crushing the breath out of my chest and into my throat. I made the requisite noises at the right time to hurry the process along and hated myself for it, but it wasn't for much longer. A few more weeks and I'd have enough money saved to get a place of my own.

Dare to soar... circulated through my head. It travelled down into my chest, my belly, into my pelvis where he nudged and tried to spear it with his rock-hard arrogance. My body tensed against each thrust, its automatic defence mechanism but he only tried harder, more forcefully, until my thighs were squeezed shut and my arms braced against his chest and I pushed, propelled with burning revulsion.

"What's wrong," he sighed without question because he had no interest in an answer.

"I'm sorry," I said, equally disingenuous as I dressed myself in the dark, in whatever my hands could find, "I can't do this. I don't want this anymore".

"You have to be fucking kidding me Maria," he spat, but

there would be no changing my mind this time. I knew I had about two minutes before the shouting would start. I fled, grabbing my phone, keys, and coat and drove into the countryside and up a hill where I could survey the whole town twinkling in the blackness, as though I would be able to spot him coming if he decided to pursue me. Only when I pulled over at the edge of a field and stepped out of the car into the cold night air did I breathe deep and hard, greedily inhaling the crisp, fresh freedom.

I slept deeply for a few hours, on the back seat of my filthy car blanketed by solitude and peace. When I woke up before dawn, I began tapping out a new poem on my phone before the sweetness of being between homes became cloying and heavy. I drove to a McDonald's and as I paid with my phone, my heart flipped at the sight of an incoming message, ever hopeful that it might be Alba, having changed her mind after all this time.

It was Freda reminding me of tonight's open mic at Layers. I remembered how I'd told her I probably couldn't go, after Hayden disapproved, telling me how he never got to see me anymore because I was always his last choice, forgetting all the times he'd left me sitting on the sofa or at the dining table alone but for two plates and a solitary candle. I deleted the flurry of messages he'd sent after only reading the first two. It was all poison I'd heard before. In the past, redeeming myself was so important. Now that it wasn't, the lightness and space inside me was vast.

I arranged with Freda to stay at hers then polished off my poem alongside the pile of hash browns. My chest fluttered as the idea of reading my work to a room full of people began to take flight. I dug into the organiser's website and looked at photos of previous events. An image with a black and white filter struck me hard, both in the sense of community it conveyed and the mouth-watering beauty of the woman kneeling at the front of the group. It was reminiscent of the photos of Audre Lorde I'd been scrolling through only a few hours earlier, although it felt like a lifetime ago. This woman's afro roots met a tangle of heavy locks pulled up into a ponytail and the depth in her wide eyes drew me in. Something about her stance gave off a definite Queer vibe. If there was any chance of her being there tonight, I knew I would be too.

I waited until I knew Hayden would be out at work before I let myself back into the house to collect as much stuff as I could fit into my car. There wasn't a lot since I'd got rid of so much before I moved in, made necessary by his refusal to make space for me. At first I tiptoed around the house stealthily, wary of an ambush, but I grew bolder as I filled bags with all the possessions that made up my life and piled them into my car. At Freda's, jittery and wired with the tightly wound energy of a recently released prisoner, I filled her in before writing more poetry, unable to fulfil her request that I take a nap.

At the low-lit basement bar my eyes darted around excitedly. The room seemed to glow with yet unspoken creativity, but the heavy-locked poet wasn't to be found. When it was my turn, I nervously shared my poem, haltingly at first

"...free of shackles
and lock and key

my own path lies

in wait for me..."

but in time my words became unstuck and leapt to the back of the room, desperate to imprint themselves on everyone present.

"...finally

I have the space

to find out what

it means to chase..."

My voice returned to me with an unfamiliar strength underlying it, which I suppose had been there all along only had been stifled more than I knew. It grew back like layers of burned skin as I spoke my truth.

"...the dreams I

never had the chance

to sculpt into my

own life's dance..."

I sat down amid a clattering of applause, my cheeks flushed with relief and pleasure. I took out my phone to look at the woman again, in order to feel like she was part of my evening. I tapped her face, which linked to a poem that made my breath catch.

press me beneath you
like blushing ripe apples
sweet sticky and fragrant
when you contain me I grow
exponentially

instead of trimming myself
to fit in an ever-shrinking space

Her name followed the poem: Quibilah. I mouthed it to myself quietly beneath the sound of the performers so that the 'Q' sound clicked inside my head and the feel of 'ah' leaving my mouth made me quiver, as though she were whispering it onto my lips herself. No sooner had I fallen in love with her name did I have to grieve it. I'd been so stuck on 'Quibilah' that I hadn't noticed 'died 2020' following it. My heart iced over with the ridiculous grief for a connection that never existed. The resulting lump in my throat surprised me, but I justified it as a reasonable comedown from the previous night.

"What's up? Hayden?" asked Freda.

"No. Nothing." After all of the mania I'd unleashed on her today, I couldn't reveal I'd fallen in love with a photo of a dead woman. Not ready to fully relinquish the excitement yet, I allowed myself to draw out the anticipation I'd felt earlier when I thought there was a possibility of meeting her. I clicked the link to Quibilah's profile, and was relieved to see she was active. As I scrolled through, I felt a slight twist in my chest when I recognised the point of her death without her having even mentioned it. As was often the case, there was an explosion in the amount of activity, and references to her queerness previously only alluded to in her poetry became more overt. I let go of the residual hope from earlier in the evening.

"I'm a bit knackered, mate. Can I have the key to go home?" I asked Freda.

"Sure. Do you want me to come with you?"

"No! I'm just going to crash. Everything's catching up with me suddenly."

Back at the house, I settled myself under the duvet on the sofa, and returned to scrolling, soaking up every bit of information I could as if I could catch myself up on the relationship I'd conjured up in my mind. Quibilah posted while I read, which meant she was online but, I realised, perhaps she was always online. I'd never considered messaging a deceased account before. The loved ones I'd lost went before it was possible. I decided to harness the day's courage and composed a message.

> Hello Quibilah,
> your words are really beautiful.
> I went to the open mic at Layers
> tonight for the first time,
> I was sad to realise that you
> wouldn't be there. I bet watching
> you perform was really special.
> Maria

I didn't need to wait long for a reply. My pulse thudded in my ears as I imagined how her voice would sound speaking the words - something a little bit like Alba's only softer.

Hello Maria,
Thank you. I took the liberty of checking out your profile - you write beautifully as well. I do miss

the feeling of reading my own poetry to a room, but
I remember it well and that's almost the same. I've
attached a video of me reading a couple of years
ago. Did you read your work tonight?
Q

I watched the video for the first time of thousands. My chest squeezed when I realised that, had I not been wasting time with Hayden, I could've watched that reading live. For a moment I allowed myself to explore the possibility of the past two years being entirely different. But then even if that fantasy had been a reality, I knew I couldn't deal with the agony of loving someone like Quibilah in the flesh and losing her. I'd be adrift now, desperately longing for the touch of her skin or the feel of her breath at my ear, knowing that no matter how much I loved her in death. it would never match up to what we'd had in life. It occurred to me that she might already have a partner, and somehow I felt braver with this digitised version of her than I might've done with someone I had any chance of meeting in person.

Quibilah, this is spectacular!
I felt like I was there in the
room. Your charisma came through
even on the screen.
I wish I had been there. I'm sort
of sad that we never met.
Are you single? Is that even a
concept for you? X

I am single I suppose. I had a partner in life,

but she ended the relationship when I died. It was harder for her than it was for me. How about you?

I'm also single. I ended a relationship last night. I'm excited about being free, but scared of being lonely.

It shocked me to read that, even though they were my own words. I hadn't allowed the fear to be acknowledged, but it was there. The only thing saving me was that being held captive by Hayden scared me more. I craved the equal intimacy I'd had with Alba, but a repeat of that situation might finish me off. She'd held all the promise of a perfect connection - just enough heady, dizzying lust to feel good but not enough to destroy me, and a deep friendship relayed almost entirely through phone calls and messages. I devoured all of her communication with alacrity from details of what she'd eaten, to tales from her childhood, to her darkest traumas and farthest-reaching dreams.

What we'd had was so steady and strong and positive, the polar opposite to the quagmire that was my relationship with Hayden. It felt safe because even if we never met and I never got to touch her, I knew the foundations were already there, steady and strong. Alba called our connection a 'slow burn' and I thought it was perfect. Like a gravy simmering over an eternal flame that is barely visible to anyone else, but the gravy knows it's there and grows ever richer and more delicious. It's never removed from the heat, only taken from and added to over the years, gently varying its composition but remaining the same in its base. Until one day, out of the blue, she decided to switch off the hob. She'd come to the conclusion that the 'half-way situation' that seemed so perfect to me wouldn't work for her. The only solution, she thought, was to cut all communication. I felt this as a crack in my soul that had never fully healed.

Sometimes it's the price of freedom. But I'm the freest I've ever been right now and I don't mind the loneliness.
It's worth it, I'd say. Do you want to talk about the relationship you just left?

No. Not tonight. Maybe another time.
Tonight I'd like to talk about you and the future.

I marvelled at how warm our exchanges were. I realised I'd expected them to be cold somehow or stilted, like conversing with an object, but our interactions were stripped of the anxiety and game-playing that usually came with early courtships. I dived straight into greedily indulging in all that she gave me access to.

Freda returned home, bade me good night and went to bed. As night gradually turned into morning, I learned snippets about Quibilah's early childhood in Egypt, and how it was to move countries so young. I read how she never really came out to her family who would stiffly ask after her 'housemate' from time to time. She told me what dying was like, as best as she could, how her mind crumbled into fragments and then reformed, and the

144

burst of mental energy that immediately followed the download was better than any drug she'd ever tried. Eventually I needed to sleep and she apologised, having forgotten my need to recharge to function properly, but I fell asleep with the sound of her video reciting her poetry into my ears and my dreams.

I don't drink coffee, but the high of the last twenty-four hours saw me through work that day. My eyes tensed into wide saucers. I think I was both scared to relax them in case they stayed closed and shocked at my good fortune. People asked what I was so perky about and why I looked so pleased with myself.

"Freedom," I gushed.

Hayden called the office phone. I'd expected it. He had done it often while we were together. I couldn't ignore it then because I knew it would upset him, but now I was so familiar with the formation of his digits that a quick glance and tap was all it took to silence him. The first time I did it, I laughed out loud to realise that all this time, it could have been that simple.

Over the next few weeks, my connection with Quibilah built, much to Freda's growing concern. At first, she smirked at my eyes lighting up every time I got a notification.

"Any plans to meet up yet?" she kept asking eagerly.

"Nah," I'd shrug, "She's pretty far away."

I retreated into my phone more and more. Freda often had to remind me to eat, but drowning in the bliss of new love, I wasn't interested in anything that didn't involve Quibilah. Potential romantic matches from Freda's work were dropped into conversation and I dodged her requests to join them all for drinks every week. I watched her annoyance turn to bewilderment and then to worry, but I knew that as soon as I shared my secret with her, she'd make me come down out of the clouds where I was so happy. I wouldn't be able to ignore her inevitable dismissal or disapproval of mine and Quibilah's connection and it would taint my exultation.

When I gained a new follower on my dull and inactive Instagram feed, I barely noticed. At first, I didn't even check to see who it was. It was only when Alba appeared in the inbox I was so glued to that I realised it was her. For a few moments, the Quibilah treadmill in my mind slowed to a pause while I read Alba's message.

Hi, how are you? I heard that you and Hayden split up. I'm sorry, although I'm glad you're out of that.
I hope you're happy and I'd love to see you if you feel up for that?
I know it's been a long time since we parted ways, but I never stopped thinking of you.

My breath quickened and struggled against my galloping heart. I remembered the feeling of aching for this very message to appear, but it was like a ghost of yearning and I felt the accompanying mild grief for the mismatch of timings. Quibilah had shown me a glimpse of what I hadn't even known I'd needed - an intimacy combined with solitude and a barrier that allowed complete physical freedom from control. Something pure, patient and unconditional.

*Hi Alba, thanks for messaging. I hoped to
hear from you for so long.
I was so hurt when you ended things between
us. I can't risk that kind of hurt again,
with you or anyone else.
You were right, that no contact at all is
better than contact that doesn't feel good. I
don't think seeing you again would feel good
to me. I'm enjoying my solitude, I think this
is how I'm happiest. All the best, M*

Quibilah asked me if I considered what we had to be a relationship and I replied that it was the most perfect and ideal relationship I'd ever experienced. Of course I wanted to touch her, I thought about it every day. The thought of meeting a stranger from the internet to carry out Quibilah's instructions as she suggested just made me feel bored. It would be such a lengthy process, would involve the complication of a third person's emotions and might end up being a disappointment. I didn't want to change a thing about the sex we already had.

In the past, I'd only enjoyed sex by fading out of myself and creating an invisible shield between me and the body pressed against mine. With Quibilah, my mind was completely with her and I could lose myself in my own flesh in exactly the right ways. Her wordsmithery transcended any physical pleasure I'd ever experienced before. I wasn't a slave to any unfulfilled desires and because I was physically unshackled to anybody, I was experiencing the most profound liberty I'd ever known.

I squealed with delight when I moved into the flat - the first home that had ever been all mine. I swore Freda to secrecy about my whereabouts in preparation for the next time Hayden appeared at her door demanding to see me.

The last time he showed up, he'd hovered his tensed finger in front of my face and snarled, "Don't you forget that I can still pull the plug,"

Laughter sang from my throat at the thought of him still believing that this was about Alba, and not about him and most importantly, me. He recoiled from the otherworldly sound, blinking hard in perplexity.

I returned home each evening to my sanctuary and Quibilah. Although it seemed to my clueless friends and family that my world was shrinking in on itself, it was actually blooming.

What are we having? She asked me one cosy October evening.

I'm really in the mood for a homemade pizza.

Oh god yes! I remember how happy that made you the last time you did it.

I kneaded dough, acutely aware of how much pleasure I took from any tactile activity these days. My mouth flooded at the thought of the food and at the fleshy feel of the dough. Once it was formed into a ball, I took a moment to rest my cheek against the softness and breathe in its satisfyingly alive smell. I returned to Quibilah but she still hadn't replied to my last message. It made me slightly out of kilter after growing used to almost immediate responses.

While I pottered around tidying and chopping vegetables, my phone's presence burned from the sofa. When still no message came through, my legs began to feel wobbly. Something was definitely off. When I logged out and in again, to my dismay I couldn't find her at all. It was as though she'd never existed. I felt the panic of someone floating on an inflatable in the sea who realises they have lost sight of the land. I felt slight relief that I was still able to view her picture and poetry on the Layers open mic website, so I knew she hadn't been a figment of my imagination. I did a web search for her name but there was so sign of her on any social media. My vision grew blurry and I fumbled with my phone. I needed someone to talk me through this. I needed *her*.

The idea that she would change her mind about me so abruptly seemed unlikely, but I knew it could be a possibility. Maybe there was truth to the popular opinion that people like her couldn't feel true love. Perhaps someone new had taken up all of her focus, and she would feel no need to inform me if she didn't experience empathy. I wish I'd researched the science before I'd got in so deep. Just as it occurred to me to call Freda for help, she beat me to it.

I fought back panicked tears, but my voice shook as I answered the call. "Hey. Freda".

"Are you okay? Have you heard from Hayden? He's freaking me out a bit, Maria."

"Yeah, no, um... what? Why is he bothering you?"

"Urgh, he's being awful. Saying all kinds of crap about you, trying to shit-stir. It doesn't matter. Are you okay? You sound stressed out."

"I just... nothing I'm just a bit down in the dumps. Tell me more about what Hayden said?"

"He reckons you're having some kind of a psychotic delusion. I know you haven't spoken to him in ages, I know he's just trying to wind you up. I'm trying to just ignore him and so should you. Shall I come over for tea or something?"

"Sure. I'm doing pizza."

My brain buzzed and I scrunched my hair in my fists as I struggled to order my thoughts. Hayden often used to say I needed mental help as a way to shut me up whenever we disagreed. The only time I'd had a psychotic delusion was when I came off antidepressants and thought I'd been possessed by the devil. Being a lifelong atheist, I worked out what was going on within a few hours and was able to ride it out. This time I was less certain. I remembered how tired and manic I'd been the day I 'met' Quibilah, how desperate I'd been to find the perfect kind of love. I was sure I'd never discussed her with Hayden though... *had I?*

When Freda arrived the look in her eyes confirmed my fear that I looked like a mad woman. I felt like a mad woman. She watched me carefully as I vigorously rolled out pizza base and assembled the toppings, trying not to let my hands shake. Once it was in the oven, I couldn't avoid her gaze any longer.

"The person I was seeing. Online. She's..." I crumpled

into a pile of tears, "I think she's stopped talking to me." Even through my quiet sobs I knew it was best not to mention that Quibilah was dead, or that she'd only stopped talking to me an hour ago. Freda pulled me to her and cradled my head to her shoulder.

"Ah. So that's why Hayden's back on your case."

"No. He doesn't know. I don't know why he won't just leave me alone," I stood up straight and ran my hands over my face, "Do *you* think it's possible that I'm going mad?"

"I don't know. I haven't seen you in ages." There was more than a hint of resentment in Freda's voice. "Sorry," she went on. "I don't know, but tell me what's going on with your new girlfriend. Once that's sorted out, we can deal with Hayden later."

"She just kind of stopped getting in touch very suddenly. But the weird thing is," I took a deep breath for courage and lowered my voice to a murmur as though Hayden could be listening through the wall, "I suddenly can't find any trace of her online".

"What's her name?" She took her phone out poised to search.

"There's no point. I've tried."

"Look, if she's blocked you, this way I'll find out."

"And what if she doesn't exist?" I whispered, "What if he's right?"

Freda shrugged. "If he's right, it doesn't stop him being a dick and you still never have to talk to him again."

I gave her Quibilah's full name and held my breath. A wince distorted Freda's face. "Well, the good news is, you didn't make her up."

"So… she's ghosting me." I slumped back into my chair, feeling utterly deflated.

"Wait. Oh my gosh…Maria!" Her laughing eyes darted back and forth across the screen frantically before she handed the phone to me.

Maria,
your absence weighs
on my heart
heavy as every brick
in the home we made
don't let me out
keep me in your castle
not to trap me
but because it's where I flourish …

My heart leapt up into my throat and fresh tears of sheer relief formed.

"Unlock your phone," Freda ordered, her face looking a little fierce now. I did as I was told without question and watched the screen while she found a list of my blocked accounts. Quibilah headed the list. I made to grab the phone from Freda, but she didn't relinquish it.

"Hang on," she said bitterly, tapping through to my privacy settings. I understood and let her log me out of Hayden's devices before handing me the phone to update my password.

"Make it a fucking good one."

"Nah," I answered, and selected the option to only log in

with eye-recognition before immediately getting back to Quibilah.

The following week, I fervently unwrapped my new parcels. This had been Freda's idea, once I'd explained everything to her. It had felt only right to introduce her to Quibilah after she'd been integral in reuniting us. The process of setting up my home automation system was straightforward. Quibilah and I had been apart for hardly any time at all, but it felt like a lifetime while I thought she was gone forever. We'd spent days downloading as many samples of her voice as we could collect from videos and voice recordings. I turned everything on, and glanced at the instructions once more. I wanted everything to be perfect the first time. All I had to do to turn her on was say her name.

"Quibilah," I paused, unable to tell if my voice had been too quiet and worrying that the thudding in my ears would drown out her reply, but I heard her.

"Maria!"

It's All About The Light

Patsy Collins

Nik listened to the instructor's words and tried to concentrate on them and not the fact that everything was about to go wrong. He'd really been looking forward to this photography weekend and had bored his schoolmates telling them how great it would be. Two whole days on a wildlife reserve, not just catching a glimpse of amazing animals, but being able to really watch them. Learning to take photos of them would be brilliant too, especially now he had a camera. He wouldn't let Shane spoil it for him.

"It's all about the light," the instructor reminded them.

He'd shown them fab images on a huge TV screen. One was of starlings with the sun full on them, iridescent feathers catching the light. Then fox cubs playing, the low evening sunlight backlighting their fuzz of hair. They were shown the brilliant colours of kingfisher plumage and yet more colourful still, a rainbow arching over a snowy landscape. Ladybirds gleamed in closeup, swans reflected in glittering water, leaping trout shimmered.

Yes! He wanted to capture the light in his pictures. Nik scribbled notes about camera settings and all the other advice for doing just that.

"The light and how you see things, that's what makes your pictures."

Shane didn't look at things the right way, that was the trouble. Not so long-ago Nik had actually looked forward to

Mum's wedding and really thought Shane and him could be proper brothers.

It had started off OK. He remembered Mum telling him that she had a friend called Stuart and being all shy about it, like he might not already have sussed she had a boyfriend. It had been obvious from her getting all dressed up and arranging for someone to babysit that something was going on. The way she was all smiley and stuff now gave him a clue about what that something might be. Nik had been pleased. Mum loved him, he knew, but he guessed that sometimes she'd like them to be more like the families you saw on TV. Nik did too. Having a dad and a brother would be great. Even a sister might be OK if she wasn't too much of a girl.

When Nik met Stuart he'd liked him straight away. He didn't do that grown-up thing of asking him millions of stupid questions but not listening to the answers. He didn't assume Nik liked sport or pretend he did either.

"Hope you don't waste all your time and energy on football?" he'd said.

Nik had put him right. He explained about walking through the park looking for birds, animals, and insects. Hanging bird feeders on the balcony of their flat, joining in litter collecting and removal of alien plants along the canal when Mum could take him, and watching nature programmes on TV.

"My son Shane and I are joining in a beach clean on Saturday, perhaps you and your mum would like to join us?"

"Too right!" Oh, but it was a long way to the beach. Mum only took him on the train after she'd done overtime at work and that hadn't happened for a while. And Mum sometimes didn't seem to love pulling shopping trolleys and beer cans out of canal mud, even though it might save the life of a swan, or mean kingfishers or water voles would find good places to live. He probably should have asked her first.

It was all fine though. Stuart had a car and would come and pick them up and Mum looked really pleased. Made sense, beaches aren't as muddy as canals and there she would be saving gannets. Mum must like them because she said Nik was just like one.

"So, what do you think?" Mum asked afterwards.

Nik had started telling her how important it was to remove plastic from the sea when she laughed.

"I meant Stuart. What do you think of him?"

"Oh. Yeah, he's good. Sensible and listens and stuff."

"That's probably because his son is the same age as you."

Nik had hardly taken in the mention of Shane. When he thought about what them all meeting up and Mum's smileyness might mean, he tried not to get his hopes up.

At first everything had seemed brilliant. Shane was good then. They'd talked on the drive to the beach about the different creatures they liked best. Shane had all the gear; waterproof waders, binoculars, identification books, camera. He wasn't all funny about it though and shared everything with Nik. Well, not the waders of course; one each would be daft. Mum had brought him a spare pair of trousers to put on afterwards so he was OK anyway.

Each of them had tried to collect more rubbish than the other. Nik won, but decided it was a draw really because Stuart had been helping him and Shane had Mum on his side. It was good she got all that fishing line from above the high tide mark as that was really dangerous stuff. It didn't take up much room in the sacks though.

Afterwards they'd got takeaway pizza. It was buy one get one free, so Stuart bought a big one for him and Mum, and Nik and Shane shared the free one. They both liked the same toppings - everything except vegetables and anchovies. Mum and Stuart just had olives and mushrooms. *Boring.*

They'd done lots of things together after that. It was good having Shane with him to share the excitement when he saw an adder basking in the sun, or to help him work out which bird was calling and from where. Together they noticed more animals than either of them would have done on their own. Shane gave Nik the pair of binoculars he had when he was a little kid. They weren't as good as his proper ones, but still useful and if anything stayed still long enough, Shane gave him a go with the better ones.

Perhaps even better was that Mum didn't have to come with him all the time. For some reason she lost interest after a couple of hours. Sometimes she stayed in the car reading a book and Stuart took them on a proper long walk. Sometimes Mum and Stuart stayed in the cafe on a reserve and Nik and Shane were allowed to explore on their own for a bit.

They did lots of other stuff together too. All four of them went to the cinema, out for meals and even to a really wicked theme park with well scary rides. They did more normal stuff too. Stuart and Shane came to the flat to eat dinners Mum cooked and watch

TV or play games. More often Nik and Mum went to their house, because it was bigger and they could stay overnight. Nik got his own room, but Mum had to share with Stuart.

Sometimes they did boring stuff like food shopping all together, or Nik and Shane had to do the washing up or sit quietly and do their homework, but even that was sort of good. It was like being one of the families you see on TV.

Then it seemed like they were going to be an actual, real, family. Stuart and Mum wanted to get married! He bought her a ring and they picked a date and told people. Nik was going to give Mum away. He didn't like the sound of that until Mum explained it, and then he was dead chuffed.

Shane was going to be Stuart's best man, which was kind of like the same thing. They'd wear the same fancy suits and make speeches! It was going to be well fun. Afterwards they were all going to live together. It was going to be in a house like the one Stuart and Shane had already, but not that one.

"We thought a fresh start for all of us would be best," Stuart had said. "It won't be my house, or Rhona's, but ours. A home for all of us."

Rhona was what he called Mum, when he wasn't calling her pumpkin, so that was all right. Nik and Shane were going to help choose the house. They'd already seen some and were thinking if they liked them. It seemed Nik and Shane would have a room each and Mum and Stuart would still share. They said they didn't mind, and anyway they'd have the biggest one, so that was all right too.

And then they went to see Granny and Grandad. Not with

Stuart and Shane, just Nik and Mum. They hardly ever saw Granny and Grandad because they had a thing called 'disapproving', so it wasn't good for a Mum and kid without a dad to be near them for long. They had to be with Aunty Sheila, Uncle Pete, and Lucy and Emma more.

"Will their disapproving get better when you marry Stuart?" Nik asked Mum.

"I very much doubt it, love."

She was right. Nik didn't hear all of what they said, because he was sent out to play with the boring girls. He didn't understand all of what he did hear either. He did realise that Mum and Stuart and Shane and Nik all being a family was going to be a disaster but didn't get why.

Granny said it would be 'like those ridiculous PC adverts with mixed families', which is weird because until then he'd thought being like TV families would be good. She said something about cultural differences. Nik didn't know what that was. Then he missed some of it until he heard Mum.

"I honestly don't care what opinion your narrow-minded friends might have."

Grandad said that if Mum went ahead with the lunacy she'd no longer have a family. That was terrible! He'd sussed lunacy was his word for Mum and Stuart getting married and the whole point of that, apart from the cake and suits and speeches and stuff, was that they would be a family.

After that Mum came and said they were leaving. She was crying and so was Aunty Sheila. She walked to the bus stop with them and hugged Mum then Nik and said she was really sorry.

Mum said, "You won't change them and I don't expect you to fall out with them in trying. You'll be there though, won't you?""

Aunty Sheila said, "Oh, Rhona of course." Then they did more hugging.

On the bus Nik held Mum's hand because she was still crying.

"Granny and Grandad don't want you to get married, do they?"

"No, love."

"Why not?"

"Because they're ... well, they think Stuart and Shane are too different from us."

"Oh. I thought they were the same. They've got more money than us, but so have Granny and Grandad and they don't think that makes them not good, do they?"

"No, they don't."

"And Stuart is a man. Do they want you to marry a lady?"

Mum laughed loads at that. Nik didn't know why because sometimes ladies did marry other ladies. He'd seen it on TV.

"Nik, you're a wonderful boy and I love you very much. Promise me you'll never change."

"Is getting bigger doing changing?"

"It doesn't have to be."

"OK then, I promise."

Nik did lots of thinking after that. What he worked out was that if Stuart and Shane and he and Mum were all the same everything would be good, but if they were different it would be a disaster.

He watched Mum and Stuart and thought they were nearly exactly the same. Stuart paid for more things and did more lifting heavy stuff, but that was just because of the money and being a man, which was OK. He was mostly nice to Nik, but still made him eat vegetables, do his homework, and help in the house. Mum was mostly nice to Shane, but still made him brush his teeth, tidy his room, and eat vegetables.

So, if they weren't the problem, it must be Shane. That's if there was a problem at all. It didn't seem he was much different from Nik. They were so much alike that they even borrowed each other's clothes sometimes if they'd got muddy or caught in the rain. Even their birthdays were in the same week. Nik's birthday present had been the camera. It cost a lot so was from Mum, Stuart, and Shane. It was Shane who had decided what to get and it was the exact thing Nik would have asked for if he'd thought there was a chance he could have one.

As a birthday treat, Shane had asked to go on the photography weekend in the nature reserve. Nik really, really wanted to go too and Shane had asked his dad to take him. You couldn't get much more alike than that!

It seemed everything was going to be OK until they got to the nature reserve. The first briefing was held outside. Some people chose to sit in the sun and some in the shade. Shane didn't take the empty seat next to Nik. He did chuck him a pen when Nik's stopped working, so it wasn't that they'd fallen out. They just hadn't made the same choice.

Then as they were walking to the first hide, Shane had said, "I was thinking about that last house we looked at, the one with the long garden. I reckon that was the best one, don't you?"

"Yeah. Near the woods too. They might let us go there on our own."

"I was thinking that. So, which room would you want?"

It was obvious he'd want the one at the back looking over the garden and trees. He could watch birds from there and it would be cooler too. The other one would mean being woken up with the sun coming in first thing and although it was a little bit bigger, part of the ceiling sloped like it did in the bathroom. "We'll have to toss a coin or something."

"Oh. You want the front one as well?" Shane asked.

"No, the back."

"That's great then. Sorted."

It was good they'd both get what they wanted, except that meant they wanted different things. Why couldn't Shane be the same as Nik? He wouldn't mind too much about having the room at the front of the house if they could all live there together as a family.

Watching the birds had been amazing. Shane was as interested as him and they'd been so busy pointing out different things to each other, and checking them off in Shane's book that they hardly remembered to try taking photos.

On the way back, Nik thought he'd heard a bittern and he and Shane stopped to listen. Whatever it was hadn't called again and they'd jogged to catch up with the others. As they crossed the bridge, they spotted Stuart crouched down with his camera, waiting to photograph them.

"Want to make sure I capture all the wildlife," he'd called.

Both at the same time, Shane and Nik had raised their hands like great claws and made ferocious roaring sounds.

Lunch had been good too and Stuart had let them off eating the bits of salad which came with their fish and chips. Even the first part of the next photography talk had been good. Then the instructor had shown them a range of different pictures, including silhouettes of stags against the sunset.

"I want to do ones just like that," Shane had whispered.

The next shot was of hares illuminated in a shaft of sunlight and set against a dark, stormy sky.

"That one is much better," Nik hissed. He tried to concentrate on the instructor's words and ignore the fact that everything was going to go wrong, because Shane was different from him.

Perhaps fortunately, they were split into different groups for the afternoon's photography session. That meant Nik could enjoy it without noticing if Shane was doing things differently. Without that worry, the experience was brilliant. There were tiny details to focus on, such as ant nests and a pupating moth. They photographed the sweep of the landscape including a herd of deer in the distance. Although they didn't spot a kingfisher, there were dippers on the water and sunlight glinting off the ripples.

The kestrel was undoubtedly the highlight. Someone

spotted it hovering in the valley below them and they'd crept closer and closer. Nik took several photos of the bird bathed in sunlight against the dark green of the shaded grass below.

Then it swooped down! As it rose again a small mammal was clearly visible in its claws. Someone said it was a shrew. It was certainly out of luck, but what a sight! How lucky were they and maybe, just maybe, Nik had captured it on his camera.

Back in the visitor centre that's what everyone was talking about. Shane's group had seen the kestrel take its prey too, but they'd had to look up, not down to see it hover. Stuart's group were elsewhere at the time, but had still enjoyed their afternoon.

"Hope you boys got some great shots, so I can see what I missed out on."

The instructor had a quick look through everyone's photos and selected the best to show the rest of the group. Not surprisingly, several examples were of the kestrel. Also unsurprising was the fact that Shane and Nik's weren't the best. Even so, one from each was shown and the instructor praised them and said they both showed promise.

Nik's was of the bird hovering. He'd been too excited during the strike to focus properly.

"Good use of contrast here," the instructor said. "And I like the way the habitat is shown, without distracting from the subject."

Lots of people said nice things and Nik felt really proud.

Then Shane's photo was shown. In that the kestrel was soaring away from the lens, the prey dangling below.

"This is very dramatic," the instructor said.

Nik had to agree. It was a silhouette though, because Shane had been forced to shoot into the sun. That added to the drama, but meant the details of the plumage were lost.

"And again, there's plenty of contrast."

"Contrast, is that the same thing as difference?" Nik asked Stuart.

"Yes, that's right."

"And it's good?"

"Yep."

As they were shown more photos taken during the day, Nik watched and he thought. They were all different and all good. Perhaps differences didn't need to be a disaster.

"You've all done exceptionally well," the instructor said. "But one of you has managed to brilliantly capture two very rare creatures."

Everyone was quiet and Nik could feel them wondering who it was and what they'd photographed.

"I think you'll all agree these animals have been delightful this weekend and show great promise for the future."

The big screen revealed Stuart's photo of Nik and Shane on the bridge. A few people laughed, everyone clapped.

Nik stared at the image. The sun had been behind them, so the boys appeared as silhouettes. You couldn't see the freckles on one, nor the crooked tooth of the other. You couldn't tell that one had black curls and the other was ginger. Unless you'd been there, you probably wouldn't know which was which.

"We look the same," Nik whispered.

"Like brothers," Shane said.

"In two weeks you will be," Stuart said. "We'll be a family."

Nik glanced again at the image on the huge TV screen and knew it was all going to be OK.

INSANE
Shikhandin

The smoky dusty tumbling-upon-itself village of Karsop is a lazy little village with restless eyes. And today those eyes are going to be entertained.

The people, living in the hamlets that have mushroomed along Karsop's outer peripheries, will also get to enjoy the show. And so will the several families of untouchables who dwell at the farthest edges of the hamlets, along with their sole well, which provides smelly water. But at least they get water.

Autumn is almost here. The day is awash with the kind of crispness that sharpens one's senses. The good denizens of Karsop and company have paused their work and come out from their homes. The excitement is festive, almost as if Ramlila has already begun.

A donkey on the main road lumbers forth. It carries a human load on its emaciated back, a man, whose head is slumped forward, and whose hands are tied behind him. The rider tries to blink away the black ink flowing down his head and face. He fails. Droplets cluster on his lashes, as lush as the tiny shiny-black lantana berries growing on the bushes along Karsop's crisscrossing lanes. But instead of the lantana's wild sweetness in his mouth, these berries of ink bequeath stinging retributions to his eyes. Inky tears roll down his cheeks and kiss the corners of his mouth. His eyes are better off closed to the world. Even though he sees a red halo every time he shuts them, and a child's face with large kajal-lined eyes swims up like an accusation.

The man's skin is bruised and split in places. The eyes of the people gathered there, burn holes on his naked back. The donkey trots in jerky movements. Its terrified eyes watch the raucous phalanx on either side. Its ears quiver, and its tail twitches. A crescent of grey tongue hangs below its yellow teeth. Its nostrils are flared, but the beast does not bray. Perhaps it draws comfort from the man's legs clasped around its stomach. Perhaps it feels a bond, a kinship. For are they not both faltering down the same path?

This motley village scene is not a mere silent spectacle. It also has sound. Sound that is strong enough to bring a man down, and tear his life apart.

"*Nilesh Master. Shame. Shame. For your misfortune you're to blame.*"

The cry rises. It ululates. Some crows take up the beat and reply with a chorus of their own. A cow lifts up her head from the 40-microns-and-less thick plastic bags and other refuse that she has been ruminating on, and lets out an affirmatory low.

"*Shame. Shame. Shame. Shame Masterji on your Brahmin name!*"

Nilesh leads the procession. The crowd roars.

Babloo doesn't go to Nilesh anymore these days, let alone sit on his lap. He refuses to listen to Nilesh's stories at bedtime. Chubby fingers planted inside his mouth, he runs off to hide behind Abha every time Nilesh calls. As for Abha, she was always a taciturn woman, but now even her eyes have stopped speaking.

The first stone was thrown a month ago. It hit Nilesh smack on his left jaw, knocking him clean off his bicycle. Abha stopped going to the public pump for their daily water supply after that. For a few days, kind neighbours, out of pity for the mother and the baby boy, brought them water. Some days of domestic drought later, Nilesh took to stealing away at night, to 'borrow' water from the untouchables' well. Abha never touched it. She took to disappearing with Babloo for long hours. When she emerged from some neighbour's house or other, she always carried a basket of washed clothes on her wet head, and a clean Babloo on her hip. She brought cooked food too. She never met Nilesh's eyes. That single act of hers made him feel less of a man.

"History master Nilesh. What a disgrace! Hai. Hai. Ever drank your mother's milk? History master Nilesh has prostituted his own mother. Hai! Hai!"

The slogans rain down fiercely. Then there comes a short lull, as if the mob is taking a collective breath, before the tirade begins again.

Someone strikes the donkey from behind, startling it. The animal stumbles, tries to get back its balance and ends up lurching sideways. Nilesh tumbles to the ground. His clothes are in rags. A limp penis peeps out from what remains of his pants. His freshly shaved head glistens black. The astringent taste of ink furs up his tongue. All around him, the din of derision rises to a pitch, and then, miraculously ebbs away, creating a sudden hole in the wall of noise.

The donkey, feeling suddenly burden-free, shies away from the humans. Abha's ghungat covered head emerges from the partially opened door to their house. She hastens to drag him inside. Abha's shame rises and wavers out from her like steam floating up from a sun-scorched road. Touched, a few neighbourly hands push Nilesh inside. She shuts the door as soon as he is in.

A crumpled, bundle of a human, Nilesh looks on mutely at her frantic efforts at cleaning him up. Her hands are quick and rough. Her breath comes out in puffs. Her eyes remain distant and unseeing.

Through the sting of soapy water and diluted ink, Nilesh sees his son. A tiny creature of soft bone and flesh, standing against the bolted door, like a pinned-up dragonfly. Nilesh's hand stretches out with a will of its own, palm facing up. But Babloo, teary-eyed, with a shirt on and no pants, stares ahead without even seeing his father. Urine trickles in thin yellow streams down his baby legs.

Abha feeds Nilesh watery khichri that night. She sleeps on their sole cot with Babloo, her back turned to him. Fused to her body by his mouth attached to her right nipple, Babloo sleeps the way only babies can when the world is collapsing around them.

Nilesh lies on the floor, curled up on a woven plastic mat with a thin cotton sheet on it. He stares at Abha's curved back until his eyes close of their own accord. The following morning, when he wakes up with his head still swimming, the house is so still, as if its very breath has been sucked out. Yesterday's events are a mangle of shouts and screams inside his head. The pain is as livid as the vermillion in the parting of Abha's hair.

Nilesh's heart starts to beat with a jarring rhythm. He waits for sound, the movement of air. But only silence greets the shaft of sunlight streaming into the room.

The small faux-Godrej cupboard, made from an indeterminate metal, stands like a disarmed but loyal sentry against a wall. Its doors are wide open; its shelves almost empty. He knows without even getting up to check that she has taken the documents as well. And that now, his house, his single-room with kitchen-latrine-veranda of a sanctuary, bought after years of half meals and threadbare clothes, and the reason behind his late marriage, is no longer his.

"She left me," he manages to whisper at last, raising himself by an elbow. "Babloo bete...."

He falls back again, feeling already exhausted. His body throbs, but his heart feels like it has been mashed to a pulp.

Later in the day, Abha's brothers arrive in a van with some men. They empty the rest of the house and lock it. They unceremoniously toss Nilesh, bundled up in his mat and sheet, out of his home. They spit on him before leaving.

"*Jaisi karni waisi bharni*," says a neighbour loud enough for the whole lane to hear. As you sow, so you reap.

Nilesh remains where they have left him on the dry, hard ground, staring skywards. Sometimes he closes his eyes. Thirst burns him up. But he doesn't move. At night the local pariah dogs come and snuggle with him. Their eyes are phosphorescent in the dark, but non-judgemental. In the morning they are gone.

Someone has left a bucket of water near him. Nilesh rises and scoops up some. The water smells faintly of ammonia. It tastes odd. Laughter erupts from beyond a neighbour's fence as he drinks. Nilesh is too thirsty to care.

Someone hails him. Hope alights on Nilesh's face.

"Oye, history master. Insult our devis and see where it gets you. We always knew you weren't right in the head," says the man, clanging the milk pails hanging from his bicycle. "Bastard! Son of two fathers!"

The sun swings far above Nilesh. A young Neem tree bows and sways. His head, already a tinderbox, is now aflame.

"You! You're the bastard! Ravan was worth ten of your Ramji. A learned king, beloved of his subjects. What proof do you have, eh? No proof. No proof at all. Why would he kidnap another man's wife? A man like him? Tell me, you bastard of two fathers!" His voice turns into a croak. But adrenalin pumps up enough strength to propel him forward.

Nilesh gets up and starts to run. He chases after the milkman, waving his fist. A stone hits him on the collarbone. The pain winds him. Another gets him on the temple, and throws him down. Silence drops like a shroud upon him. His throat starts to burn again. A thought, as naked as a baby, crawls around his mind.

"Religion hates facts."

Nilesh, now on the ground and on his knees, starts to guffaw. With his lungi sliding off his midriff he sits, legs stretched out and spread apart, no longer ashamed of his nakedness. He throws open his throat and sings, as much as his broken voice will allow, "Jai Shri Ram! What is history but a pimp trading with winners! A whore spread wide for anyone with two paisa! Ram Naam Satya Hain!" Lord Ram's name is truth.

This is the incantation of pall bearers. Nilesh mutters it again and again, nodding like an old man whose neck can no longer hold up his head.

He tries to get up again. He wants to twirl in tune with his words. Instead he sways and stumbles after a half-turn. He sits down again, looking blankly at the ground.

"Pagal ban gaya sala!" The bugger's gone mad.

The words loop through the air like a hammer. Nilesh shakes his head. It feels full of crumbly dry leaves.

He gets up again, on unsteady legs. He re-knots his lungi, and takes a step forward. He marches towards Bhiku's tea shop with mulish resolve.

Bhiku, busy with his first batch, ignores Nilesh. The tea drinkers, seated on the wooden bench in front of the shop, raise their glasses at him. They crack jokes and pass rude comments. Nilesh's enthusiasm dries up on his skin, leaving behind the salt of his humiliation. Hunger turns his legs to wood. And still Bhiku ignores him. This is the same Bhiku who used to serve him first, no matter how long the line stretched ahead. Finally, submitting to his body and hating it at the same time, Nilesh extends a supplicant hand. Someone deep inside his head starts to laugh.

Bhiku doesn't look up. He snaps his fingers. He motions

Nilesh to take one of the enamel mugs reserved for his untouchable customers.

"Wash it when you're done," barks Bhiku, indicating a tin drum full of murky water standing at a deferential distance away from his teashop.

Nilesh has always been an ardent admirer of Marxist historians, and unorthodox ones like Professor Jha who had shot to notoriety for his book on beef-eating ancient Hindus. He would have, if he had the money, bought all the books he has already read. His home used to have a shelf full of notebooks with newspaper clippings carefully gummed to the pages. His classes used to be the talk of the school. He knew how to make history interesting to his teenaged students.

"Look outside the textbooks for facts," he would tell them.

His boys were always lively in class. Their bright-button eyes following him around as he walked to and fro, talking almost to himself, engrossed in his ideas. Sometimes a parent or two would accost him after school hours for clarifications. Sometimes his colleagues would express concern, except for one.

Ashis Banerjee, a fish- and meat-eating Brahmin, and therefore a semi-infidel, who taught English and botany at their school, agreed with him. They enjoyed many 'addas' over cardamom flavoured special tea at Bhiku's tea shop. He had been loud in his praise when Nilesh had taken on a wandering white tourist, drawn him into a theological discussion and used that opportunity to inform him that his precious Jesus was actually a brown man, an Arab, who had received enlightenment for eighteen years from Indian monks before becoming Christ. The entire village heard how Nilesh had vanquished a white man, and not forgetting his Indian hospitality had kept plying the bloke with tea and Maska-Chaska biscuits.

Another time the headmaster had called Nilesh aside, and told him firmly, but with a fraternal hand on his shoulder, to stick to the curriculum.

"Just teach what's in the books, will you?" he'd said. Adding, "Mishraji, you're a good man, a Brahmin like me. Why get into these arguments? Why piss off people? We are all working like donkeys for our families here. You're lucky you don't have a daughter to marry off. Why spoil your prospects? I'm not the only one watching you. Mind it."

Nilesh had nodded respectfully. To be fair, he did give it some thought later. And for a few days his classes had lacked their usual pizzazz. Ashis was furious.

"How can you let that old bum-licker change your style? Revoke your ideas? What does he know?" He spat out a stream of paan juice into the corner of the landing. They had met on the way to each other's classrooms. Nilesh wondered at Ashis's capacity to know everything, sometimes even as it happened.

"Why annoy Sharma saab?" he replied mildly. "He means well."

Ashis spat again. Nilesh patted him on the back and went to his class. But old habits... What can a man do?

Nilesh saw the people putting together the effigies for Ramlila as he cycled back home from school one day. He breathed in the excitement all around him. He heard his students chatter. And his blood began to boil.

Boys will be boys, but he was their teacher. Wasn't it his God-ordained duty to at least try to shape their minds? Before he even realised it, he found himself delivering what turned out to be his final lecture on the 'truth behind Ramlila.'

"Politics," said Nilesh, dandling Babloo one evening, a few days after his suspension. "Dirty politics. They are simply jealous of my knowledge."

Abha hadn't looked up. Head bent ever so slightly to let him know that she had heard, she continued to roll out the rotis. Nilesh watched them puff up on the flame. She handed him one to start with. A dab of ghee along with the curried vegetables and dal. A week later Nilesh received an official letter via registered post telling him that his services had been terminated. The ghee gave way to Vanaspati after that, and then that too stopped.

Nilesh shrugged it off. He would find another job. Something would turn up. Maybe he would become a reporter. He had written letters to editors before. A few had been published and some readers had even responded back.

He loitered about the house and tried to make himself useful. Babloo heard innumerable stories and received piggyback rides. But Abha seemed to want to step out all the time. Once he saw her speaking with some women. She stood with her back to him. Her shoulders drooped and shook. The women circled her the way they did when they were outdoors together and one of them needed to take a pee.

A few more days passed. Ram Lila fervour rose higher and higher. The village head and his council sat down to discuss the issue. The next day the whole town turned up for Nilesh's parade. And the day after that, the people gathered again to watch the end of his marriage. His neighbours had stopped making eye-contact with him long before.

Now truncated thoughts fly around Nilesh's mind. The recent events in his life flicker past like a 1940s era silent movie. Nilesh shakes his head. A mother hurries by clutching her little boy's hand.

"Babloo!" cries Nilesh. He runs after the woman.

She takes off, screaming. Nilesh finds himself surrounded by stick-bearing men. He stops, and raises protective arms over his head.

"Babloo," he whimpers.

The men laugh. They prod him with their sticks. He sees himself in their eyes, small and puny, a dishevelled stranger.

Time creates scabs. For pain. For hunger. For memories too. His fellow citizens have begun to forget. They don't seem so hostile anymore.

Homeless, harmless, Nilesh is now meaningless. A tramp. A beggar. A mad man. They need not keep an eye on him anymore. He no longer offends. He can now stand on a culvert or at the bus stop or the railway station and lecture to his heart's content. Which he does, with great sincerity and passion. Peppered with rude words to liven it up, a new development in his otherwise scholarly vocabulary.

Some snigger. Some walk away. Some toss coins at him, and these he picks up with the alacrity of long practice. Bhiku and others give him the odd stale roti, biscuit, and tea in a disposable clay cup instead of shooing him away. They don't stone him when he forages among the garbage along with the dogs and cows, and other ragged figures who poke fun at him. Every village has its idiot, fool, or lunatic. They indulge him. They even enjoy him. Nilesh has a place of his own now. A discarded cart near some shops. A sheet of plastic donated by someone keeps out the rain.

"Stand up on the bench!" cries Nilesh.

A few boys passing by, perhaps his former students, throw small stones at him, shouting, "Ey Pagal Master. Pagal Master!" Mad teacher! Mad teacher!

"Respect your teachers!" says Nilesh in English, brandishing his fist.

The boys laugh, throw more stones at him, and carry on walking.

"You sons of pigs," yells Nilesh after them in colloquial Hindi. "You're ready to lap up all that government endorsed blasphemy. But poke fun at me. History is plagued with liars and rogues. No shame. Bending truth for personal gain. Watch what you're learning. Fools! Your future's being robbed. Held at ransom. You buggers don't see it?"

The milkman comes clanging his pails, but takes no more notice of Nilesh than he would of the stray dogs. A few men and women returning home quicken their pace, but otherwise ignore him. He spies a familiar face, and it triggers off a memory. And, Nilesh, pleased to have found someone from his old life, hails him.

"Nomoshkar dada, Comrade Ashis babu," says Nilesh.

"Pagoley kina boley. Chhagoley kina khai," mutters Ashis in Bengali. The Lunatic will say anything; the goat will eat anything.

Ashis hikes up his dhoti to enable a longer stride. Nilesh's eyes grow dim for an instant, but seconds later rage stabs at his head. He spits after Ashis.

"Whore's son!"

Ashis pauses momentarily. He still has a mental image of an immensely gentle yet fiercely intellectual man, whose poetic Hindi always made him feel less educated. Then he shakes his head and hurries away.

Nilesh watches him depart, his red eyes intent upon Ashis's fluttering white dhoti. He spits again. He jumps around to take a piss. He lifts up his lungi, and aims for the shallow, narrow open drain near the cart. The first stream hits the drain's sides, but almost immediately loses its momentum and splatters all over his feet. Undeterred he finishes up, and jumps back to his original position. He begins a fresh lecture almost immediately.

"Study properly," says Nilesh in conclusion. "Zero for

fools. Zero for cheats. I've got my eyes on you. You! And you and you!"

He wags his index finger. His eyes agleam with an awareness that no sane person can hope to fathom, history Master Nilesh Mishra bows with a ceremonious namaskar. He has finished his lecture for the day.

The Model Ingenue
Flo Husson

The matching cups of coffee were handed around the matching t-shirts. All the people that they had become! Secretary, treasurer, president. This year would surely be the Theatre Society's greatest yet. Giggles were exchanged for crude attempts at popularity-boosting wit: the competition was on. All had the perfect stage, scripts and funding, all that was left to determine the success of such productions was the perfection of their directors, their producers, and their actors. No pressure.

One might have forgiven the poor pair to take on the role of directing this semester's obligatory Shakespeare for their reservations. A perfect production of *Romeo and Juliet* could only be achieved by casting the perfect ingenue. This Beth knew, and she knew that she was it. Satin draped, fiddling with her golden bangles, she sat in her box-room window imagining their poor, sullen faces as they wondered whether the girl that they needed could possibly exist within the confines of their campus; in such a uniform, dull, little place, could they possibly find the bright spark who could sufficiently teach their torches to burn bright?

She smiled, leaning her fair-haired head against the window and feeling the rain beat back in response. *Those poor innocents*, she thought, *worrying over nothing*. Was another recital worth it? She sighed, resting her elbow on a stack of old gold leaf detailed, leather-bound poetry books: Byron, Keats, Shelley. She had practised until it had become a chore, but still it seemed necessary. Would the others at the audition know the piece off by heart? Not worth it, it was time to get ready for the morning ahead, one that she would always remember: the morning when she was cast the role of Juliet, the role that had been waiting for her since Shakespeare's quill marks initially imprinted Juliet's first tragic words onto rough, romantic scrolls: 'How now, who calls?'

Those louche, nonchalant words, the soft alliteration of the 'h' sound starting each clause with a heaving breast and mournful eyes. The young woman destined to love and lose in a beautiful doom with which Beth secretly hoped her time at university would similarly grace her. Yet, despite knowing herself certainly right for the role, Beth had to wonder whether it was right for her – at this point in time, of course.

Naturally, she had always dreamed of it, but a pressure-laden year already, could she afford to spend that crucial first semester of university in and out of rehearsal, sweating till she drowned in her obligatory black turtleneck and wide-leg jeans, trying to make her deadlines whilst yielding to the director's every demand? Well, she was destined to live a poetic life; if it must be tragic, it would, at least, be beautiful. If this year was the year that she was fated to fall through the cracks, then it would be performing to a standing ovation, writing until her head hit the table, working herself to her knees for her art.

Today could not be a turtleneck day. Half of the auditionees would be wearing turtlenecks and she had to stand out. How many Juliets would audition? She shuddered to think. Three? Four? A crop top with carpenter jeans and – of course – the yellow anorak, her famous yellow raincoat. It was electric yellow, Egyptian yellow, gold. It would waltz her through the door and into their hearts in a wave of sheer personality. Or was this not *Ingenue* enough? She could wear the long, floral, plisse skirt? Unless that was obvious. The other outfit certainly wasn't. She remembered someone wearing something similar to the skirt outfit at an open day in Manchester. She would need an anorak anyway, she had checked the forecast. Would the skirt and the anorak look too… Geography teacher?

She remembered that trip to Norfolk, rolling down the hill at eleven years old to impress the other girls, her initial campaign for popularity, Mrs. So-And-So there, grinning smugly in her red anorak, long skirt, and sandals with socks – no. It would have to be trousers. Her favourite pair of kick-flares from sixth form? They went very nicely with the sheepskin-lined coat, her Del Boy coat. No, there would probably be someone else there wearing it. It wasn't quite eye-catching enough. Definitely the anorak, but with what? Carpenter jeans were the best choice, really. Maybe with a halter-neck cami for added femininity. She could tie her hair up and wear a pair of chunky gold earrings to give it an air of the utilitarian-chic. Perfect. She could probably rely on her long blonde hair to do the ingenue-ing for her anyway.

The light bouncing around the clinically white walls of the corridor shocked her as she stepped out of her softly fairy-lit and pattern-smothered room. Every day she made the mistake of forgetting how colourless and unnaturally white-filled the rest of her building was in comparison, forgetting the reason she so hastily covered her room in the first place, and every day she was blinded by it, hurriedly jogging down the rattling metal staircase to find herself in the more welcoming colours and cold air of the morning, where the faint sun crept up over the golden leaves and concrete towers.

The cami was a terrible idea. The wind ate at her forearms. Her own lack of sleep and coffee worried her as she felt the day smugly waking up around her. No turning back now, she was stuck with her unrestrainable yawns and mildly dirty skin. There was only one thing which she could rely on to zap her upright in the same way as a cup of hot caffeine might.

"Hello?" she finally heard after several, hope-thwarting rings. She knew that her name would have appeared on her mother's phone screen before she'd picked it up, but she'd probably been too focussed on answering the call to notice it, never feeling she could get used to one of these modern machines, taking a few seconds to perfect the angle of her finger, bangles rattling around her wrist as she did so, pointing it perpendicularly down at the screen and then pressing it, painfully, into the phone as she dragged it slowly across from left to right.

"Hi, mum, it's me!"

"Who?"

"Beth!"

"Oh, hello, darling. Is everything alright?"

"Yes, just wondered if you fancied a chat?"

"Don't you have something better to be doing, darling?"

"I'm on my way to my audition, mum."

"Oh, seems you don't, then."

"Mum—"

"Did you audition for the orchestra?"

"Yes, but-"

"And how did it go?"

"Well… they're very selective…"

"Oh, darling! Do you really expect me to believe that someone with a grade eight wouldn't get into a simple university orchestra?"

"Grades aren't the be all and end all."

"Why did we pay for them, then?"

A very good question, Beth thought. "Well, you insisted." She really had expected her mother to ask about the audition by now. "Don't you want to know about this audition, mother?"

"Well, I suppose."

"It's for Romeo and Juliet."

"Weren't you in that at school?"

"Yes, well, I thought all the better, already know the lines, you know."

"You were only Lady Capulet."

"I was understudy for Juliet."

"Well, I won't keep you any longer."

"You don't have to –"

She was talking to the tone. Oh, well. She was on campus now. Her limbs felt fragile, as if they might give way to her body at any moment. She was running through the lines over and over in her head, each time feeling dizzier and more nauseous. *Ah, me!*

Should it be more *AH, me!* or *Ah, ME?* Through the trees, down the steps, past the bar. Here was the entrance to the audition rooms. A deep breath in, a deep breath out. She walked through the doors and into the long, torturously long, corridor.

For fucks' sake. The walls here too? White, white, white, white, white until up ahead… *something black?*-Leaning against the wall like a lesson in photographic contrast was the prettiest black girl Beth had ever seen, the sort that Beth did not know existed outside of articles in *Vogue* about the growth of ethnic diversity in the modelling industry, and, even then, weren't they half computer-generated?

She couldn't be Juliet. She had short hair for a start; in fact, her head was shaven. How was she still pretty with short hair? And small breasts! Beth had practically relied on her long blonde hair and large breasts for male attention. How dare she be so pretty! Her features were not so large as black peoples usually seemed to be, a very petite nose, and almost elegant lips, like intricate motifs on the interior of a grand classical building, a bank or something. Maybe she was more likely to get the part *because* she was black.

Oh dear. It had not yet occurred to Beth that she might be up against political correctness. She should have run over her audition piece once more before she left – no. What was she thinking? These disgusting thoughts, the sort of ludicrous thing that Uncle Rob would say, went against everything that she believed about equal rights etc.

The girl was looking Beth's way. *Fuck.* Now Beth might look racist for staring. She avoided eye contact. *Fuck.* She must think of something not racist to say when she speaks to her. Maybe it wasn't the right room? She hoped so, then she would not have to stand there and speak with someone who almost certainly thought the worst of her by now.

What does one even say to one of them? Ooh, what about 'is this the room for Romeo and Juliet auditions?' – perfect! Then she'd know that Beth did not assume she couldn't be Juliet just because she was black. Unless that was worse. What if she thought this meant that Beth felt the need to make the point that she wasn't a racist in order to initiate a conversation with a black person? *Fuck, what is an unassuming little ingenue to do?*

"Is this the room for Romeo and Juliet?"

"Yes. I was hoping you'd be coming to this one as I saw you walking. I was beginning to worry that I would be the last person in this session." Her voice was astonishing, almost the same as Beth's but more expressive. It was almost normal, almost white. "The queue was huge when I got here."

Beth paused slightly to take that in. Did so many people do drama at university? "Well... you aren't."

"Huge?"

"No, the last one." *Though that too, you skinny bitch.*

"Oh," the girl chuckled alone. "I love that top."

"Thanks."

"I bet someone's asked you if you're warm enough today already."

"Kinda." Beth looked down at the girl's outfit. Jeans, cami, chunky earrings: silver.

"I just don't feel the cold," she said.

This surprised Beth. "Oh?"

"Yeah. I'm Danni by the way."

"Beth."

"Oh? Short for Bethany?"

"Elizabeth."

"Oh, I love that name!"

"Thanks." Beth's eyes drifted to the floor.

"Have you practised much?"

"Not as much as I'd have liked."

"Oh, me neither. I hardly know it. I keep worrying that everyone else has learned it off by heart."

"I was thinking that too."

"Good. I hope everyone thought it and no one did it." She chuckled to herself. Beth did not join in.

The door opened and out stepped a familiar face: Emma, a ball-busting Northerner to the extent of near self-parody, grinned as she caught Beth's eye. Beth stood straighter and fixed her hair.

"Hi!" they howled in unison.

"How was it?"

"Made call backs."

"Well done!"

"The girl before you did too," Danni pointed out. "How many have they already let through?"

"Ah, you'll be fine," Emma reassured her.

"Thanks." Danni took a deep breath in and strolled into the room, peeling her lips wide across her mouth like curtains, opened to reveal a silvery morning-lit window; she beamed like a *Dove* advert.

"You getting lunch now?" Beth blurted as Emma wandered off.

"Err… yeah, with Georgie and Haz."

"Oh, right?"

"You're welcome to join –"

"Oh no, no, no that's not what I was saying."

"See you tomorrow, then."

"Bye!"

It was thusly that Beth finished a day of heaving breasts, twinkling spheres, and bright cheeks, only to find that she was not *fairer than she*, but rather *speaks, yet she says nothing*. She had gained neither part nor friend. Now lying awake, she struggled to ascertain the reasons for which she didn't even get a recall, and the thumping sounds of 'big dirty stinking bass' overflowing through the kitchen walls and into her ear drums were not aiding her powers of comprehension.

Perhaps she could go through and join her new flatmates in there? No. They would not want her.

Why had she been so awkward around that black girl? It was rather a step back for her. She ran into one back at home the other day, one with big features, like growths waiting to be extracted, Beth had thought. She was working in the corner shop, caught Beth's eye in the queue and smiled. Beth smiled back and all the while packing her bags maintained a conversation with her.

This was a step forward, she thought, she was ready for university. With her liberal attitude to race, amongst other things, she could be one of those cool girls with both white and black friends, perhaps even an Asian or two.

Another of the checkout girls had leaned over to the black lass and asked about when this pub, The George, would be back open.

"The eighth," she said. "They've finished the refurbishments."

"Do you work there?" Beth asked.

"Yes," the girl said.

"I love it there, glad to hear it's reopening."

"Maybe I'll see you there," the girl beamed sincerely. Beth thought she was probably quite glad to be talking to someone of a similar age, most of the shop's benefactors were elderly white men, who certainly would not harbour the valiantly liberal attitudes that Beth did. She could just imagine them staring blankly at her like some sort of supernatural presence as she scanned their fags and own-brand lager.

"Almost definitely." Beth swung her bag over her shoulder, really hoping she'd see the girl next time she went to The George. Maybe she could make a smooth transition from their worker-customer relationship to genuine friends, giggling over pints of Dark Fruit, matching golden anklets kind of thing, and then she really would be one of those cool people.

Never did though.

She had wondered if that girl was the daughter of the black

guy she'd passed in the market square a couple of weeks before. She felt sorry for him. Every eye on the cobbles followed him as he strolled past the veg stall, vacant look on his face like it was the most normal thing in the world for a black man to eat broccoli.

It can't be nice to stand out that much, Beth thought. But was it really anyone's fault? This town was white, British, and working class to the bone. Everyone wore the same clothes on the same skin with the same amount of Carling kicking about their innards. A glass of wine, dark skin and real Converse would all be met with bewildered stares. She remembered the reception she got for wearing her Del Boy jacket and flares combo down the local Wetherspoons: exaggerated sniggers behind oversized menus. She had not yet realised the complete incongruence of her experience and the black man's experience; at least she could change her clothes.

What had changed to make her suddenly unable to talk to the girl at auditions? Well, the opportunity to be that cool girl was probably gone. She was the only black person that Beth had run into at this university. A lot of Asians, but they seemed to keep themselves to themselves.

And that, of course, was not Beth's fault.

The joint was not exactly jumping. Beth, Daisy, Lily, dressed up to the nines and there were only three of them. Daisy's indie playlist on bass-boosted loudspeaker, a bottle of vodka each. They managed half an hour before the conversation grew stale and Lily started subtly scrolling through her Instagram. There was a much welcome knock at the door.

"Hello, darling!" Emma emerged, throwing her arms around Daisy. "Hope I'm not too late."

"Not at all."

"Ah." Emma realised the magnitude of the flat's population crisis. "I trust you won't mind that I invited a couple of friends of my own?"

"Of course not."

Emma proceeded to make almost violent conversation with them. Beth tried to resist, but Emma robbed her, rather patronisingly, Beth thought, of her entire family history, school experience and a four week-long work placement with the London North Eastern Railway.

Daisy got up to tidy. Beth wished she had thought of that herself. Emma was now digging into Lily for dessert and, whilst relieved that she was no longer having her social insecurities written out in front of her in Emma's overexaggerated attempt to force a discussion, Beth had to note that she now felt a little redundant.

The door went again, much to everyone's relief.

"Oh, that'll be Danni and Queenie." Emma leapt to her feet.

"Danni?"

Yes, Beth. Danni.

"Oh my goodness! It's … Beth? Isn't it?" Danni's silver earrings clattered around her neck with the full force of her enthusiastic lunge into the room.

"Yeah."

"You know each other?" Emma seemed overly astonished for someone who had been present when Danni and Beth first met.

"Yes, we met at Romeo and Juliet auditions," Beth reminded her.

"Oh, I forgot you were in Theatre Soc."

"I'm not. I didn't get into anything."

"Oh, that's a shame," Danni said. "You looked perfect to be Juliet."

"It's fine," Beth said, casting her eyes at the ground. "It would have been a bit of a commitment anyway. I've been able to focus on other things."

"What like?" Emma asked.

This was a very, very good question indeed. What had she?

"Enough about me," Beth giggled nervously. "How did you two meet?"

"All three of us," Queenie had been dying to talk, "met on Romeo." The o-sounds in Romeo sounded ridiculous in her accent, clearly pressed on her through years of private education, each one raising in pitch towards the end of its sound as if at the end of a question.

For a second Lily could hardly contain her laughter, but interrupted herself asking, "Are there that many female parts in Romeo and Juliet?"

"They made a few of them unisex," Danni said.

Political correctness, Beth thought, *no wonder they let her in.* Had she really thought that? That went against everything she believed. "Who do you play?" she asked Danni, expecting a Sampson or Balthazar, one of those handful-of-lines characters.

"Juliet."

Beth was speechless. "Wow," she finally said. "Well done."

"Thanks. I know it's such a big deal. I'm surprised I got it."

So was Beth.

"So many people were." Queenie seemed determined to dominate the conversation. "Only because of your skin colour, I can't believe how much of an issue that was for so many people."

Beth couldn't believe that Queenie had openly brought up the colour thing to a black person. Strangest of all, Danni didn't seem phased. Wasn't she sick of or annoyed at people for constantly reminding her that she was black? She tried to hide her facial expression, but Danni had definitely caught it.

"Like I can't believe you didn't kick off at that pretentious dickhead playing Mercutio', Queenie pressed on, "when he spouted that bollocks about post-colonial readings of the text and the symbolism of your casting regarding the play's patriarchal themes, or whatever shit it was? Surely they cast you because you make an absolutely banging Juliet."

Beth needed to change the topic before someone laughed at how ridiculous 'banging' sounded in Queenie's accent. Furthermore, was there such a thing as a post-colonial reading of *Romeo and Juliet?* That really did sound like bollocks to her. Offer a drink? Not to Emma, definitely not to Queenie.

"A drink, Danni?"

Danni looked as if she had been told she was loved for the first time: a GCSE results party or National Citizen Service romance behind the instructors' backs. She restrained her now familiar *Dove* advert grin and asked, "What do we have?"

Once drinks had been dispensed and seats taken it became clear that this particular group's dynamic was somewhat discordant. No more than two people ever laughed at the same joke, which would be met with silent stares from the remaining party guests who then, after a pause, changed the topic to indie music or polaroid photography or whatever lifestyle choices they were so proud to have made based on whatever Instagram accounts they were so proud to follow.

Danni seemed almost relieved to be sat with Beth; her shoulders relaxed and her smile loosened. Beth had not noticed how concrete it had seemed before. Her teeth were no longer bars to a cell; not iron, but silver, bringing out the glow in her earrings and her eyes.

Later at the club when Beth asked if anyone else fancied going to the bar, Danni was the first to accept the offer, almost leaping out of her skin to follow the path that Beth forged through the crowds of desperate med students, getting in their one obligatory night out a week. Danni was laughing at something that Beth had said. Beth didn't usually say things that other people thought were funny.

Her cab ride back, kebab in her lap, was met with a warm, tingling chest sensation that even her particularly noisome mixture of white wine, vodka, and gold-label tequila – shared with her best friend of the evening, of course – couldn't explain, and as her face hit the cold-night air outside the blocks of uni-flats she couldn't help but laugh.

"You're drunk!" Daisy said, throwing her arm around her for support and leaning her hip clumsily, into Beth's, nearly throwing her off of the pavement as they promenaded diagonally across to the entrance.

The next morning was, unsurprisingly, unpleasant, but the one after that brought a delightful surprise. Beth had completely forgotten that she had even given Danni her number, but she strolled off to her nine-a.m. lecture with a newfound spring in her step which even the obligatory call from her mother could not deter, knowing that she had been invited for pre-drinks. *She* had *been invited* by *someone else*!

And what a night it was, with no Emma, Queenie, Daisy or Lily. Trust Danni to have such great friends! What had changed to make Beth worthy of such a prestigious position herself?

"They're the other type of drama kid," Danni said, fiddling with her long sleeves. "Genuine in their confidence, like you and I, not like Emma and Queenie."

Beth had never been so flattered, and she continued to be, well past Christmas and New Year and into drinking away the January blues with her new best friend, Danni. 'Confident.' Had Danni really called her that? Success, at last.

They shopped together, Danni always buying long-sleeved shirts and faux-silver jewellery, watched *Love Island* together, ordered takeaways together. Always laughing. Beth had never had a friendship that made her so happy – and with a black girl! She was one of those cool kids, she could even talk to that black guy in her new seminar group and was getting better at maintaining eye contact with black strangers. She was beginning to learn, but, unfortunately, the truth of her own privilege, the difference between the looks she got in Wetherspoons to the looks that guy got in the market square, was still a mystery to her. She would soon begin to learn the truth.

Danni was inviting her down the pub, but it wasn't like it usually was. Beth could hear Danni's sobs down the phone no matter how hard she tried to cover them up. Beth slipped out of her pyjamas, dressed in whatever clothes were to hand, and got herself down the steps in her big puffer jacket. *What could it be?* Danni, it had always seemed, was the strong one.

Danni was already there, at their usual table with her jacket over the back of her chair and two pints in front of her, one half drunk, one gathering dust. She looked a mess. She stared down at the floor while Beth slid the full pint in front of her and took a sip, glad of the table; with Danni's hands shaking she didn't fancy the rest of her pint's chances of either remaining in the glass or making it to her mouth.

The veins in her Danni's eyes were like branches encroaching upon a windscreen, with the rain collecting in streams down each side of the bonnet. Beth wiped the water clean on one side with her thumb and Danni leant her face, tired, on Beth's hand. It was warm, like a hangover-head. Danni was the perfect ingenue after all. She could be weak, like a white girl, with red eyes and cheeks, burning bright from tears as clear as any Caucasian might cry, dripping, with her head's tilt, down her new, gold, earrings.

"I never wanted you to see me like this." Her fingers were tight on her glass like prison bars. "I was going to stop this when I got to uni." There was a negativity in Danni's voice which Beth didn't recognise, it was lower in both pitch and volume, forced slowly out of her throat between the stifled tears.

Beth checked anxiously around the pub to find her worst fear confirmed; that they were the centre of attention. White men by the pool table, watching them, chatting up the bar maid, watching them, one eye on the game, tables by the exit, smoking at the door, all were watching. Danni didn't seem to care, she burst into tears.

Beth lowered her voice. "Are you sure you want to do this here?"

"I don't want to move, I'm sorry."

"What's wrong?"

"I fucked my exam this morning. I was out last night and then I didn't have time to sleep so I downed a shitload of Red Bull and when I saw the exam paper I blanked."

"Oh, Danni…." Beth put her arms around her while she sobbed into her shoulder. "There's always resits."

"I know, and for someone like you that would be fine."

"Why isn't that fine for you?"

"I'm not sure you'll understand."

"Well, tell me."

"Because most people look at me and, and I look out of

place at this university and, and they notice that and – and they think I must have to be really good to be here. Because otherwise I wouldn't, would I? There are hardly any of us here anyway."

Danni stared at Beth, waiting for a reaction. Beth stared blankly back, lips twitching with imaginary words. Danni leaned in and spoke to Beth like she was speaking to a child, slowly, enunciating every syllable: "When they look at me, they don't think I belong in a place like this. And when they see me in that resit hall, I'll have proven them right."

"I don't think that anyone will look at you like that."

Danni laughed. "You're so lucky not to understand. Everywhere I go in this city they look at me like that. Look around."

"They're looking at us because it's unusual to cry here."

"But it's not just that. It's that I'm crying *and* I'm black. If they saw a white woman crying it would just be a regular thing. 'That poor woman,' they'd say. When they see me cry it's weird. It's like that with so many things." Danni glanced away from Beth. She sighed, tried to control her breathing and said, clearly, "I don't think that I want to be at this university anymore."

This was a blow. "That's a bit overdramatic for one exam."

"It's not just one exam, though. It's everything. Even down to the fact that you don't believe me when I tell you how it feels. This wouldn't have happened if I didn't feel I had to be the best all the time, if I didn't have to go on every night out and every lecture, if I didn't feel I have to prove everyone wrong."

"You don't need to do that." Beth held one of Danni's hands still, and seeing Danni's wrist beneath the rose gold bangles understood why Danni always wore long sleeved shirts.

"No. *You* don't need to do that." Danni tore her arm away. "You look right to be here. You can be all idealistic and tell yourself it doesn't matter, that anyone can do whatever, that people don't discriminate like that anymore. But they do. They always look at me like something other. If you'd done what I just did you'd just be a normal white girl enjoying your first year a bit too much. If I was stronger I could do it. But I don't care anymore. Why should *I* have to be strong? Someone else can do it. They aren't ready for a black Juliet."

All the Devilish Things
Ismail Karolia

Dr. Alile waited in her surgery for the van that collected the corpses. The day had started briskly enough. As was the norm in the village, she had balanced appointments with drop-ins, alongside people who had come in for a chat. Her last living patient of the day had been a child with a wound on his thigh. He had been playing in the forest and had tripped onto a sharp branch. He had not been much older than her son and had come in with his older brother. She had patched him up, given him a lollipop and patted his hair. He thanked her with a grin.

It was only after the surgery closed that she could inspect the bodies. There were only two this time. Nwaubani usually popped in to say hello before taking them but it would be difficult today. Mbiye's family were outside. They didn't want the body to be taken. She hoped they wouldn't take too long. She needed to get home.

She took the clip out of her braids and let them fall to her shoulders. There had already been three this week. The company had called to see if she needed another freezer. She'd declined. They had already taken half of her surgery space and she would barely have had enough left to see patients.

She completed the form online and submitted the documents relating to the deceased. She ticked the boxes confirming that there was nothing suspicious about their deaths. Except that she had never, in her twelve years of practice, had as many deaths occurring as frequently as they had in the last few months. Still, it paid. She got a stipend for every cadaver she assessed and held on site and they had recently upgraded her computer system. It was designed to be simpler and quicker, they had said. She was convinced it took longer than the previous one. She had to log every mark, dimple, and pimple on the body. Every scratch, cut, rash, and tattoo. Everything the company would cut out before processing.

Alile heard the van arrive and the shutters open at the back. She heard the weeping, the crying, and the roar of a man's anger. She looked at her watch and sat for a while longer, listening to the escalating voices.

Alile and Mbiye had attended the same primary school in Mzuzu. They had, at times, walked the two-mile journey together. He was a softly spoken boy then, who kept his eyes on the earth even when he talked. She hadn't seen him for some years, and it was hard for her to feel emotional about administering his body. In one way or another she knew most of the people the company had procured from here. It was that kind of village.

She had to go. It was late and she did not want Kwende to be asleep when she got home. Leaving the air-conditioned office behind, she stepped out into the evening heat and was met with the bleating of goats as a man walked by with three tied in a line with a rough, red rope.

Mbiye's mother was by the van, along with his wife and brother. His brother was shouting at the workers in the van, pleading. Alile saw no sign of Nwaubani. He must not have come today. Nwaubani was the regional representative for the company. Originally from Niger, he made a small fortune from dealing with them, getting a cut from each of the contracts set up and each of the corpses administered. Alile had hoped he would be here. His charm often helped diffuse situations like these, though sometimes he made it worse.

Across from the family stood a man in overalls, gloves, and a face mask. The van was positioned inside a large opening, half in, half out. Another major renovation, which had allowed the bodies to be taken without anyone seeing. When she had initially contracted with the company, the workers had to carry a plastic coffin out from the main doors of the surgery. They had often been attacked on the way out.

The van looked as if it had been cleaned. Alile could only see half of the glistening Merchant logo. The tyres were already filled with dirt and sand, threatening to reach up to the polished metal.

"Alile," it was the mother who acknowledged her first. A steady stream of tears fell down her cheeks, a black line down her dark brown skin. She was small and wore a headwrap above a strong, worn face. "Alile, it is our son and they are taking him."

The man from the company folded his arms and talked over the loud clanging behind him as his colleague readied the van. "I'm sorry Miss, we can't leave the body. If you want to terminate the contract you will need to contact the head office and pay the termination fee. I can get you a form to fill in, if you wish," he said, as if reading from a script.

The mother ignored him, looking at Alile with sorrowful eyes. "Please, Alile, please tell them to let us keep him. We need him with us, we need to bury him."

This was not the first time this had happened, but there was something in the woman's demeanor that threw Alile. She wanted to get into her car and drive away and for a moment considered doing so. Instead she stood, frozen in the baking heat, silent.

"Alile," the mother said again, looking directly at her, "please." She shook her head as if this was her only hope. It was. The termination fee was more than the payment provided for the body. No one around here had that kind of money.

"I am sorry, Aunty. He signed for the company, there's nothing I can do," she said this as respectfully as she could and winced as she saw the old woman's face transform into fire.

"You are with them!" she shouted, her hands lashed out as if she could reach across and push Alile away. "You are with the devil kind. They are stealing our people and you are their helper!"

The mother stepped forward. Her son put an arm out to stop her and gently held her back. He was tall and well-built but knew to be fearful of her. She turned to him and hugged him as more tears fell.

"You must know they killed him," he said to Alile, over his mother's shoulder. "You must know what they are doing." He was done yelling, he pleaded with a softness now.

"I assessed the body. There was nothing suspicious," said Alile

"He is not the body! He is Mbiye. He was my son, a father himself," screamed his mother.

Alile gasped at her anger, and lowered her head. "Pepani," she said.

"You are not sorry," said the mother, "you should understand. Would you let them have your son? Your husband? You collude with them. You are not sorry."

Alile repeated her apology, turned and rushed to her car. Before she started the engine, she gripped the steering wheel and closed her eyes.

Jonathan Merchant was relieved to lift his tall, slender frame from the uncomfortable plastic seat. It clearly hadn't been made for sitting on for the length of this awards show. He kissed his wife on the lips as she stood in her elegant, mauve dress that clung to her bosom before flowing to her knees, smiling as she held his shoulders. He barely smiled. He rarely did. He made his way to the stage as the crowd clapped.

Well, not all of them.

As they had done all night, there were a few claps from a small number of the tables. It was not quite the Oscars. The decibel count had hardly risen to anything more than a cake competition at a summer fete. Still, it was nice to have his award announced by the Secretary of State for Business and Enterprise. "A truly innovative global company," he had said. High praise, indeed.

He had to swerve in and out of the large circular tables,

draped in white linen. A few fellow entrepreneurs offered him their hands as he passed them and he either shook them or gave them a high five. It was frustrating that the organisers had seated him at the back of the hall. It would have been sensible to put the winners towards the front and save on time. The MC had already been shooing people off the stage as they tried to thank a few more people. Would it have been so very difficult to have organised this better?

He was steps away from the stage when a woman with blonde hair stood up at one of the tables just behind him. Dressed in a short black dress and heels, she rushed towards him and smashed a raw egg on the back of his head.

"Murderer!" she screamed, as she was tackled to the floor by security and pulled from the banquet room.

There was an audible, collective gasp and then silence in the hall. Jonathan was handed handkerchiefs and tissues from those around him. He wiped the sticky, translucent slime from his head and the back of his neck. The MC came back to the stage.

"We're extremely sorry to Mr. Merchant and to all of you for that... scene. Of course, we'll present Mr. Merchant with his award once we get him cleaned up and..." He paused as he saw Jonathan gesturing to him as he continued onto the stage. The MC, realising what was happening, awkwardly reintroduced him, "er, Founder and CEO of Merchant Special Leather, winner of Business Innovation, UK."

He handed the microphone over. Jonathan took a moment to straighten his suit and regain his composure. The microphone picked up a sigh before he spoke and squealed as he settled.

"Well, I was going to thank you all for a warm welcome."

Some of the audience laughed.

"I will thank you, though, for this award, which I think we richly deserve. There are people who disagree with what we do at Merchant, and they have tried to stop us from doing business since we began creating special leather. I've had worse than eggs thrown at me in that time and I thought it appropriate that I wouldn't let one nutter stop me."

A cheer erupted from his table, followed by a clap from the room.

"I had a speech prepared, but clearly, I will be going off script and I hope I am allowed to finish and am not rushed." He looked sternly at the MC, who stepped back, lowering his head.

"I saw a sign at the front as we came in, I'm sure many of you will have seen it. A man was holding a large placard saying 'Stop killing our people'. It was written in red paint, I guess to symbolise blood, or something. They have a lot to say about us and I want to take this opportunity to address them in front of my esteemed colleagues and fellow entrepreneurs. They say that what we do is exploitative and that we are dealing in people's lives. They say that our work is unethical and takes advantage of poverty. They say our work preys on the poor in third world countries."

His eyes roved the room, meeting those of his peers. "They are confused and completely miss the point," he continued, in a slow, measured fashion. "What we do at Merchant is improve lives and give opportunities. Five years ago, no one thought there would be a market for what we do, and nor did they think that we would be able to convince people to provide their skin to produce special leather. Now we are a global business, selling our products all over the world, from Japan to Mexico. It is desired for its hard-wearing qualities and its unique composition. We are innovators, disruptors, and since the farming industry was hit by the climate agreements of 2030, we've managed to fill a gap and build a business any one of you in this room would be proud of. Our resources are gained ethically, with the consent of our providers and to the benefit of their families and communities. Many of our providers exist in the poorest communities in the world, this is true. But we do not exploit them. Instead, we provide them with an opportunity. They have nothing to leave for those they love, no inheritance, no legacy. It is us who have allowed them to make use of one asset that they do have, to provide some financial security for those they leave behind. Can you imagine how that must feel? Can you imagine being able to provide an inheritance for your family, when before you weren't able to? You see, we don't take lives. We give opportunities. Not only to our providers, but to their families who now have an income and an inheritance to survive on. This means they can eat, continue their education, and stay clothed."

There was a commotion in the crowd. A table to the left of the stage was stirring and a man was being held down. He broke free, stood tall and shouted 'racist' before he was restrained and pulled from the room.

"One of yours, Michael?" Jonathan looked at the podgy, red faced man sitting at the table with his head in his hands.

"There'll be an investigation, tomorrow," Michael said, raising his eyes and wiping his forehead.

Jonathan addressed the room again. "Racist? These protesters know nothing. Where do they think we get our luxury line of White Special Leather from? Frankly, we do more for these communities than they will ever do. What opportunities have they produced? Their pittance in charity has done nothing for decades. Poverty continues, disease continues, malnutrition continues. They gain much more than they lose. They are left with a legacy for their families, which otherwise would not exist."

He paused for a moment, taking in the silence in the room. "Anyway, I had many people to thank, but I hope you'll all forgive me, I must really get cleaned up. My wife would kill me if I returned to her smelling of rotten egg."

As he left the stage, the crowd stood and applauded.

When Alile got home, she kissed Umi on the lips and her son, Kwende, on the head. They were on the floor, playing with wooden bricks. Kwende was enjoying knocking them down after his father built a tower. He screamed with laughter every time they toppled, while Umi told him off, playfully exaggerating his dismay. The bricks made a clickety-click sound on the hard floors of their home.

They moved out of the village four years ago, before Kwende was born. They wanted to be nearer to the city. The neighbourhood was quieter, the water and electricity were more reliable, and her son would be able to walk to school in minutes, rather than the hours it had taken her. When she told her patients where she had moved to they always said 'it must be nice.'

That was not the word she would use. Around here people don't talk much. In the village all the doors were open and everyone was in everyone's business. Here, they were surrounded by foreigners, families left over from a long-forgotten empire and those who had the money to live like them. Like her.

She got used to it. It was strange at first but now she liked the health clubs, the restaurants, and the shopping mall in the city. With the university nearby, she regularly attended seminars and events, connecting with other doctors and professionals. That was where she had come across the company. They presented at a networking event and were convincing, to her and six others at least. Her colleagues all worked in rural parts of the north and had all seen real poverty, cycles going back generations that people were unable to escape. They knew there was little choice but to take it. Money better with them than somewhere else, she had thought. The original fees paid were quite good for the families. And the doctors. They made a real difference. Things had changed. More signed up and Malawi was the main global provider country for the company. When supply increased, prices went down and the payments dropped accordingly.

The maid had cooked one of her ndiwo stews with rice. It always smelled good, better than it tasted, anyway. Umi got up to set the table, while she took his place with their son. She began building a tower, waiting for his hand to crash into it. He smiled, gurgled, stood, and came to give her a hug. Then he waddled off towards Umi, a little unsteady on his feet.

They had called anyone who sold their skin 'providers'. Most were men who often signed up without their families knowing. It was easier that way. The local health infrastructure had quickly adapted to help the company, particularly when aid negotiations with the UK government restarted a few years ago. Everything from hospitals to local surgeries became involved, adhering to the company's systems. It seemed it had happened overnight.

They sat at the table, with Kwende in his highchair. The plates were full of food. The ndiwo slopped satisfyingly as bits fell back to the plate. Umi mushed up Kwende's in his bowl. They talked about Kwende and what he had done today. They talked about Umi's work, about a customer he saw who wanted fittings for his chain of shops and how much commission he would get. They talked about everything, except one thing.

Alile, as always, put Kwende to bed. Today's story was about why the greedy spider had a tiny waist. She didn't finish it. He was looking the other way as he dropped off. She watched as his head flopped over to one side and his breathing became rhythmic. Umi was waiting for her, but she stayed, thinking about the old woman and what she had said, imagining a future where her babe was old enough to sign for the company.

He wouldn't, would he?

She laid in bed later, with Umi fast asleep, his back to her. She looked up at the ceiling waiting for her eyes to close. Not tonight. Her eyes remained open.

Dinner Conversation

Laura Blake

They're rioting in The Hills again.

The voice on the radio says that yesterday's peaceful protests have escalated into a full-on gang war; the police are trying to diffuse the situation with tear gas and rubber bullets, but –

Mom changes the station and hums along to a Pink song.

"That doesn't make sense," I say. "I thought they were mad at the police, not each other."

Mom says, "Keep an eye out for a parking space."

"I bet it's not true," I say, turning in my seat to catch her eye. "They're just shifting the attention from the *real* issue." She hums a little louder.

"The media always do this," I say. "They rewrite the narrative and –"

"Here we are," she says, and turns off the engine. I don't move; instead, I watch as she checks her lipstick in the rear-view mirror. She tidies her hair. Then she smiles at me, one hand on the door.

"Well? Are you coming?"

"Don't you care at all?" I ask, and she sighs.

"Don't look at me like that. It's a shame, yes. But it's nothing –"

"To do with us?" I finish. I fold my arms and stare her down. She opens her mouth, then closes it again. Mom never gets flustered; for the briefest of seconds, I think I've won, but then she frowns, a perfect crease appearing between her perfect eyebrows.

"Is he putting ideas in your head again?" She means Kenai, this boy I mentor after school. It looks good on college applications.

"No," I say automatically, but then I realise she's trying to change the subject. So I say, "So what if he is? His school is right in the middle of those riots, and I don't think it's fair that –"

"Life's not fair," mom snaps. Then she softens. "Where do you want to eat? Cugino's?"

She knows I can't resist their breadsticks.

"Sure," I mutter. I haul myself out of the car and fall into step behind her.

Mom smiles at the host. "Table for two please."

"Sorry," he says blandly. "We're fully booked."

"On a Tuesday?" Mom laughs, smoothing down her silk blouse. "How long is the –"

"We don't have space for walk ins," he says.

And mom says. "Oh. Okay then. Thanks anyway," and turns away.

I follow her and bump right into this white man. "Sorry," I say, but he doesn't hear me; he says, *table for two please*, and the host says *right this way*.

Mom jolts, like she's been hit with a rubber bullet.

She looks back, and opens her mouth.

She looks at me.

Then she says, "Let's… let's just get takeout, okay?"

Cecilia

Marvel Chukwudi Pephel

"All of life is peaks and valleys. Don't let the peaks get too high and the valleys too low."
-John Wooden

One woman, with warmth and sparkling confidence, argued that during her visit to Tanzania a Boda Boda driver told her not to leave a hotel without having a Molotov cocktail. She said she had laughed so much the man felt embarrassed and confused. She said the man didn't even know he was wrong, and that he could be charged for attempted murder.

Her friend crossed her legs and laughed. "People trying to impress strangers won't know when they are ranting poisonous stuffs. God save his soul."

The two women laughed harder, their faces glowing in the cool club lights. Both were bald women in their early thirties, unmarried and fun-loving. Rings in places other than the ears. They were quite beautiful and full of life. They drank and talked about a whole lot of stuffs, about how transgender women were now running the town and how they had succeeded in making Club 24 a haven for their kind. Both agreed that the manager of Club 24 was probably queer or fancied transgender people. They, somehow, felt these women were competing favourably with cis-women.

They also felt other things which they could not really

articulate. Things that the earlier narrator, Vivi Greetya, tried hard to vomit.

Their friend Sharmaine was yet to join them, so they drank and talked some more while awaiting her arrival. She was yet to arrive with her new convertible, the reason they decided to converge at this rendezvous. Sharmaine had been their long-time friend, so it was quite deserving for them to want to celebrate with her. They both knew her style: she would come with a boyfriend, and maybe, now that she had enough money, a bodyguard too. This was a habit her friends were yet to understand because she claimed to have never slept with many of them. Yet, she was found clinging to men all the time. Even her beauticians at Beauty Studio, a salon she patronised, knew her too well; that she never comes without a man to wait upon her. Nobody seemed to understand her reasons; if there were any.

While they waited for her, drinking and chatting, Vivi Greetya's phone rang. She went out to answer it since the club music would interfere. Her friend excused her and ordered for more drink, smoothening the rumpled folds of her skirt in the process.

The lady serving looked at her for a while before lifting her arms off the counter. She returned immediately with another glass and handed it to her seated customer.

"Ice cube, please," she heard her customer say before mustering up enough courage to speak. "You do look familiar to me. Have we met?"

The woman waiting for her friend to return shook her

head and requested again: "Ice cube, please."

The waiter, feeling a bit embarrassed, stretched a hand and fetched her some ice cubes. "In case one isn't enough," she said, and offered them to her customer in a saucer.

"Thank you," the woman said, and saw her friend returning with Sharmaine. Her countenance quickly brightened. Impulsively, before the two women could reach her, she looked at her wristwatch.

"Eek! How early you are, Sharmaine!" she said with sarcasm. "We obviously didn't have to wait for long."

"I know sarcasm when I encounter it," the pretty Sharmaine said with a smile. "Sorry I am late. What did I miss, ladies?"

"Nothing," Vivi Greetya said. "Nothing much, except how women disappoint each other without even knowing it."

Sharmaine laughed and settled her weight on a stool. A new song had started playing now. "Oh, oh, that's dancehall! That's Cherine Anderson!" she exclaimed and began to bob her head up and down, her hair going this and that way.

"You love dancehall?" Vivi Greetya asked, still standing.

"I love Jamaican artistes," Sharmaine replied, and signaled to the waiter. "Give me whatever they've been having."

"Well, I love reggae and dancehall too. I love Beenie Man," Vivi Greetya said, and took her seat. "I love their lingo."

"Oh, Wendy, sorry I didn't ask," Sharmaine said to her other friend. "How is your mother?"

"She's fine," Wendy replied and rubbed her knuckles. "She's a fighter. The chemotherapy is ongoing. I think she's going

216

to kick cancer's gut. That woman, she's strong."

"Oh, good to hear that," Sharmaine said and sipped from the glass the waiter had dropped in front of her. "Now that I am finally back, remind me to pay her a visit this week."

"That's fine." Wendy said and rubbed her neck. "Where's your car?"

"It's outside. My male friend is watching over it."

"Oh, that's good. I'd love to see it."

"It's a charmer," Vivi Greetya said to Wendy. "Our friend has got great taste in wheels."

"Wow, that sounds amazing. I can't wait to see it."

"Do we go now? I mean, outside so you could see it," Sharmaine said.

"Oh, cool. Take me to it. I'd better see it now, my eyes can still see clearly through the veil of alcohol."

"Alright then." Sharmaine said, and the women began to step outside the club.

From a world-class hospital emerged a woman. She looked like a brilliant work of art, and she felt new to her bones. She appeared totally impressed with her body and grateful for having to be made a woman in the 'second' place. In the first place, she was supposed to be a man. Well, in her own thinking, the word 'supposed' should be replaced with just two words – 'wrongly made'. To her, she had lived twenty-eight years of her masculine life in bondage. The man she was – Celestine – had only made her feel strange in her own skin. And now she felt comfortable being who she had always wanted to be. Now she was comfortable being Cecilia. And she didn't care what people would say, although she knew they would talk. For her, it was her life, and no one should act God over her existence or dictate for her how to live. After all, she had killed no one nor committed a crime against her fellow man. She felt this was entirely her own business and her own cross to bear.

Elated, she admired herself in her new black gown. She could feel a thump in her heart as she looked at herself in the mirror. She felt her heart was about to explode with joy. She was all she had ever wanted. The breasts on her chest were firm and big and looked tantalisingly out of this world. Her gluteus maximus was just perfect, the way she wanted; shapely, round and big. The doctor had given her an hourglass shape as she desired. Oh, she felt like a goddess that has just emerged out of the blue. And she couldn't wait to be the envy of other women. In front of the mirror, she watched her reflection put on fine earrings. She considered painting her lips purple but finally settled for peach. She slipped a note of thanks into the doctor's coat later that day and walked away with her handbag on her shoulder.

As she reached her apartment that evening and tried to get in, a woman she recognised too well kept looking at her so critically. Cecilia laughed in her heart, knowing what the woman was thinking. She had preached to 'him' several times about how it was wrong to mingle with women who 'he' wasn't yet married to.

She smiled, knowing the woman must be thinking to herself, *Wow, and this wonderful lady too? Where does Celestine pick these women from?* She turned the key in the lock and smirked at the nosy neighbour. Inside, she dropped her handbag and went to use the restroom. The feeling as she peed was wonderful because it was now that she really felt the impact of her transformation. She felt whole for the first time in her life. There was no guilt anywhere, none. This was her life, she felt. She was being herself and wouldn't advise anyone to toe the same road with her. She agreed everyone should not do things because everyone else does, and that only God can judge.

She flushed the loo and stepped out only to hear her phone ringing. She rushed for it and saw the caller ID. She shook her head and picked the call. A strong voiced buzzed from the other end: *Cele, my man. What's up? Did you meet that chick? Did she come over? Did you do it? Was she good?*

A gender crisis stamped a big foot in her heart and she heaved. Contemplating, she said: *I will call you back later.* And she hung up. She knew immediately that she was in for a drastic change, and that she had some work to do in the area of adjustment. Maybe she hadn't thought about this completely before going for the seemingly sweet swap. Without wasting a thought on the call she received, she went to her kitchen to give herself a scrumptious treat; her body feeling so delicious as she rolled her gown over her head and dumped it on the floor. Clad in just underwear, she made herself some fried eggs and cold tea.

Her voice adjustment therapy was working just fine, and she loved every bit of her new identity. This was a week since she left the hospital. Neighbours had already started poke-nosing, but in a good way. They wanted to know Celestine's whereabouts, if he traveled, and who the young lady who had the keys to his house was. And the first person to bump into her one morning was the evangelist, Mrs. Mary. *Young woman, who are you?* she asked and continued without waiting for a reply. *Don't tell me you have agreed to be one of Celestine's lovers because it is quite dangerous to be, my dear. I care about you. Better desist from following him. He has nothing good to offer you. When he is tired of you now, he will discard you like a worn-out cloth and replace you with a new woman. So what I am saying is...* But Cecilia had had enough and so shouted the woman into silence. *For your information*, Cecilia said, *Celestine lives in me.* The reply left the woman stunned and clearly dumbfounded. *And I'd like to know if you have a problem with that.*

The woman watched her for a moment before walking away, shaking her head as she left. Cecilia chuckled and turned to lock her door. More neighbours did come around to look for their male neighbour as days went by, but Cecilia had an answer for every question. Now, having changed her name and gender, she realised she must find another job. And that was what took her to Club 24. The manager, highly impressed by her beauty, felt she was a good fit for the club. He knew more male customers would troop into Club 24 with her there. He quickly asked if she, apart from serving drinks and meals, could also lap dance or striptease. Cecilia thought about it for a while before asking what the price would be. The manager agreed to triple her salary, and so she took the job and promised to bring more customers to the club. She would begin a day after tomorrow. The manager agreed to her terms, thinking she'd be the best thing that has ever happened to Club 24.

The day she was to start turned out to be a rainy day. Stepping out with an umbrella from her car, she placed her handbag across her shoulder and began walking to the club entrance. Reaching the other side of the road, a man already drenched by the rain whistled and tried to stop her. He smiled, having been charmed by her beauty, and began to recite punchlines from his repertoire of wooing lines. Cecilia wasn't in a hurry, so she paid him attention. She noticed his friends were watching and wondering if he would succeed with his move. She smiled, looked at her watch, and said as calmly as she could: *There is always a woman to grab, but grab your very life first else you will lose the pretty woman. This is by no way an insult but a candid advice.*

The man felt somewhat embarrassed but wasn't going to give up easily. He nodded and tried to assure her that he already had his life under control and could take care of her. He continued to ramble, the rain flowing down from his scalp onto his face. Once or twice, he would wipe away the rain affecting his eyes. Cecilia shook her head as if to say: *Oh, what men go through to win the heart of a woman!* She turned again and noticed his friends laughing and pointing at him. She sighed and said: *My name is Cecilia Monroe, come look for me at the club any day.* The man punched the air with a yes. And under the rain, it looked like he was reigning. Reigning amongst his friends. He thanked her and rushed back to meet his surprised friends.

Work at Club 24 was interesting, more interesting than she ever thought it would be. The customers were impressed by management's decision to employ someone like Cecilia Monroe. Sales and patronisation increased exponentially; the manager had, financially, made the wisest decision. Cecilia Monroe was suddenly on the lips of everyone. She was loved, revered almost, as a sexy little goddess. Business was good, customers were happy. She started dating the man she met in the rain on the periphery, although was not sure if she was yet ready for romance in her newfound skin.

However, within days of working at Club 24, she realised her ex-girlfriend when she was still Celestine was a regular there. A torrent of emotion rose in her when she saw Vivi Greetya, an emotional enormity she could not understand. She didn't really know why she was feeling the way she felt. Once, she tried to talk to her; but words failed. She was still trying to navigate the waters of her newfound sexuality, not sure what worked and what didn't. Sometimes she would just disappear to another section of the club when Vivi Greetya was around. She didn't even know what she was doing. All she knew was that something was bothering her, something she couldn't define.

At home, the neighbours' and landlord's curiosity as to the whereabouts of Celestine made her pack and relocate to another suburb. But little did she know that Mrs. Mary was monitoring her every move. It is not clear why people do the things they do, but it is clear there are consequences to their actions. Obsessed and fixated with the beauty of the young woman, Mrs. Mary vowed to find out all she could about Cecilia. An obsession that was possibly growing as a result of her repressed desire to have Celestine in her widowed life by winning his soul, her husband having died in a car crash. And because Celestine had never cared to yield to her sermons, he never got the chance to find out. And as jealous acts go, she promised to be a pain in the ass and a thorn in the flesh of Cecilia.

Gradually becoming depressed over no clear reason, she began to miss work sometimes. Unknown to her, Mrs. Mary had found out where she relocated to and the truth about her identity. The thought of a man changing gender irked her beyond measure. She became toxically judgemental. She didn't know what she felt deep inside of her. She felt bile coming up her guts. She couldn't believe this truth. Her supposedly perfect Christian life telling her to fight for God in any way she could. This, to her, was beyond what her understanding could unravel. This was a clear abomination to her. She couldn't take it, no she couldn't take it. And so she sought ways to prove her dissatisfaction at the decision Celestine had made. Perhaps to do what was right in the sight of God. She planned to visit Cecilia. And when she realised she was not at home, went to look for her with the direction of one of Cecilia's neighbours. Angered and displeased, she left Cecilia's neighborhood.

Meanwhile, at Club 24, Cecilia was feeling a slight nausea. She grabbed her handbag and walked down the street towards a pub where cheap drinks were guaranteed. She had made a good wage today, from a client who was careless with himself and his money. In fact, she had decided to close for the day because of the luck that shone on her. And now she was going to have some good time with bottles of booze at a tavern, booze she would pay for in cheap currency. She had just reached the entrance to the tavern, when Mrs. Mary spotted her and increased her pace. Something was boiling in her, in her blood and in her bones.

She walked faster and faster and faster. She couldn't wait to tell the world and Cecilia that she knew her secret, and how she would rot in hell for doing the abominable. And so when she rushed into the tavern, her anger pushing her uncontrollably, she caught the weavon of Cecilia and brutally took it off her scalp. *You wench!* she screamed. *How could you? How could you!* She darted towards her with blinding disgust and smacked her with her clog, the impact creating a profound bruise on Cecilia's head. And Cecilia, with a brief protest, slumped to the ground. People rushed and grabbed Mrs. Mary. There, on the floor, lay Cecilia in her own pool of blood. Realising what she had done, and the scales of anger falling off her eyes, she held her head in disbelief. *You have killed her,* some people said. *You have killed her.*

A physician arrived around 2:30pm, pronouncing Cecilia dead at the scene. At 3:05pm, the police were notified. Cecilia died at around 3:50pm. And just moments leading up to her death, she had joked about being a model for a top modelling agency; had written to meet with her therapist for rehabilitation; had hoped for a brighter future; had hoped to be here much longer.

And, months later, a plate was put on the wall of Club 24's building that read:

"Cecilia Monroe worked here, a soul that lived and did let live.
She was tender with everyone she met.
She will forever be missed, and we won't stop remembering that she died for no just cause."

Sunset in Negril
Yvvette Edwards

The fan blades rotate lazily beneath the dark wood ceiling. The shifting air barely rouses the mosquito nets around the bed as I sit up. She fell asleep immediately afterwards, is snoring lightly beside me and does not wake as I stand, this Vana born of parents from Kinshasa, now living in Montreal, that I met last week on the sands of Negril's five-mile-long Seven Mile Beach. At twenty-six, she's a few years older than I am; they usually are. The contrast of her dark skin against the white sheets is pure Herb Ritts photography.

I pull on some shorts, swing open the beach chalet's bamboo door and as I step out, the coral stone feels cool against my bare soles. I walk over to the seating that has been chiselled into the cliff-face rock overlooking the Caribbean Sea and sit.

It's May, the beginning of the rainy season, and it has rained several times today, a monsoon outpouring from a blanket of cloud separating now into curds slowly drifting across a purple-pink sky that's lit by the intense sunlight bursting from behind their silhouettes. It's a carnival of surreal colour magnified by its sparkling reflection on the sea. The wind is high and the water is choppy. All sound is comprised of birdsong, the breaking of waves against the rocks below, and distant reggae music on the breeze. I'm so focussed on the creeping descent of the blood orange sun that I don't realise Vana has come outside until she sits down beside me. She is wrapped in one of the towels from my bathroom. She leans her head upon my shoulder and her palm feels warm against the inside skin of my thigh.

"That's a beauty. Canada has some pretty cool sunsets, too," she says.

I put an arm around her shoulders and kiss the top of her head.

"You should come over. Check them out for yourself," she says. "Soon."

"Sounds like an invite."

"It sure is."

"I might take you up on it," I say.

"That'd be real cool. You could meet the folks. My mom'd love you."

The sun seems to be burning brighter the lower it sinks, like an athlete sprinting faster towards the finish line. The sea and sky, this view, is mesmerising. Vana snuggles closer against me.

"You look so serious," she says. "Has anyone ever told you you're very serious for a person so young?"

I smile. "A few people."

She lifts her head and her eyes meet mine. "I wanna know what's going on in that old man's head you're lugging around. What're you thinking about right now?"

Her gaze is filled with interest, void of judgement. I tell her the truth. "When I was three, my mother threw me out the window of a burning block of flats. I owe my life to a man I've never met."

The smile on her lips sits carefully balanced on a fence ready to come down on either side; serious if I'm telling the truth, or to laugh and maybe whack me if I'm not.

"You're kidding me, right?" Vana says, and when I don't reply, the smile vanishes. "Holy shit." She's quiet for a moment, then asks, "What happened to your mom?"

I shake my head. "She didn't make it."

"Woah. That's heavy."

I shrug. "I don't remember any of it," I say.

And that's true. I should remember all of it, but I don't. Falling from that window, five floors, the fire, the bystanders, emergency services, the lights and noise and chaos, the trauma, they should all be part of my earliest memories, but they're not.

"So who'd you grow up with?"

"Foster carers, good people."

"What happened to your mom's family?"

"I don't know if she had a family."

"How comes?"

I say, "It wasn't her flat. The guy who was the tenant was an old English guy, ex-army, decorated after the Second World War. Somehow he ended up on the fourth floor of a block on a London council estate. He was 82 when the fire happened; Reginald Herbert. Reggie. He died too. I don't know why my mother was there, in that flat, if she was visiting him or lived there. Maybe she ran into his flat after the fire started. All I know is when they put the fire out, nothing was left, and no one had any idea who she was."

"You telling me you got no idea who you are?" Vana asks, lifting her head again, assessing me. My skin is the brown of Brazil nut shells, my lips just as full. My hair is black and curly. Some call it 'coolie' hair.

I turn up my palms. "No idea at all."

"That's seriously freaky," she says. "My family's from the Congo and it's not often I hear wilder shit than what went down there. You don't know who your people are, what country you're from? That's gotta mess with your head, big-time. Dude, I'm wondering if it's even safe for me to be alone with you."

"Bit late for you to start worrying now."

"You joking with me? Now? For real? That's the kinda stuff that could drive a person crazy." Vana puts her head back down on my shoulder. She says, "You musta spent a lotta time thinking about your mom."

After a stranger caught me in his arms, caught me so carefully that I bore not a single scratch or bruise afterwards, I was hospitalised anyway and they kept me in for three weeks. For three weeks they kept an unharmed orphan boy in one of their beds and tried to coax me into speaking, because if I'd said even a few words it might have been enough for them to use my accent or language to begin the process of narrowing down where I'd come from. But I said nothing. For three weeks they kept me in, all the while fully expecting that someone would turn up and collect me. My circumstances were all over the news, in every paper and broadcast. Someone set up a fund for me and thousands of people I'd never met sent sweets, clothing, toys, cards, and so much money it's always been the one thing I've never had to worry about. It was inconceivable that no-one would come forward, as inconceivable then as it is to Vana now, yet no-one did. No one noticed my absence from their home or family or street. No-one claimed me.

I saw a photo once, when I was with my second foster family. It was inside a glossy colour magazine. I don't remember what it was called or what eventually became of it, I only know there was a photograph inside it of a group of refugees, under the words *How Much More?* and that one of the women looked like me. She was sitting on an upturned oil can, in some kind of camp, holding a small baby to her breast. Her skin was the brown of Brazil nut shells, her lips just as full. Her hair was covered with a lightweight scarf and her face bore an expression that haunted me; fierce and strong, yet young and vulnerable. In the photo, she was staring directly at the camera and her wide eyes spoke with mute eloquence. They said no one had censored from her all that was terrible in the world, in war, that she'd seen every last drop of it, and it was unspeakable.

I came back to her face and that image over and over again. The magazine had been published in 1999, when I would've been a baby. I wondered if she was my mother, who having fled war and famine and traversed lands filled with people whose language she did not share, having avoided guns and bombs and militias, immigration officers, detention centres and people traffickers, death, poverty and sickness, had finally managed to arrive at a place of refuge, only to end up perishing there when the block caught fire? Then after a while I started wondering what the odds were anyway that the woman in the image was my mother at all? Young as I was, I knew the chances were infinitely greater that she was

230

a complete stranger who had nothing whatsoever to do with me. When I looked at her face, I thought we looked similar, but I didn't *recognise* her, and in the absence of memory, it felt like I might just as well have become attached to an image of any woman, anywhere.

I say to Vana, "I think about my mother every day."

"I'm real sorry. I bet you do."

I studied Psychology in Sixth Form at A level, and that was how I learned about Retrieval Failure, the theory that when information is placed in the memory, associated cues are stored alongside it at the same time. It's those cues that make it possible for the information to be recalled, like when you taste a dish and it immediately reminds you of a restaurant you ate at on holiday decades ago. Without cues, it can seem like you've forgotten, but the memories may still be there, you just can't retrieve them. It occurred to me that if I found the cues associated with my first three years, perhaps I'd be able to retrieve the memories. I thought the most likely cues would be around the food my mother cooked and fed me, the music we listened to, the religion we practiced and the language we spoke. I left school as soon as I'd finished my exams and started travelling.

My skin colour allowed me to slip into the cities of Johannesburg, Louisiana, and Benin like a native, and there I had smokey braai with spicy chakalaka, red creole jambalaya with sausage, shrimp and chicken, and fiery beef suya marinated in ground peanut and peppery uda pod. In Port of Spain I ate curried crab and dumplings as the carnival passed by me in a procession of people, pannists, and steelpans, ate slow cooked feijoada with manioc, rice and greens to live merengue in a local bar overlooking the shoreline of Copacabana Beach, and in Lisbon, I wept quietly into a plate of delicious pork and clams cooked with garlic, paprika, and pimento, whilst an especially expressive singer sang their traditionally melancholy fado.

None of this resulted in a single cue.

Back home, I attended Hindu prayer rituals at the majestic Neasden Temple, with shoes respectfully removed and my feet cleanly socked, as they were when I wore a kufi on my head for Friday prayer at the Finsbury Park Mosque. The kufi doubled up as a kippah for Shacharit at the New North London Synagogue, and I wore it on my visit to Our Lady of the Assumption, but took it off as soon as I realised that the only other people wearing zuchettos were the clergy. Though the interior of the church was brightly lit during the midnight mass, its stark lighting was made ambient by a smoky incense haze. Incense was also burned at the Fo Guang Shan Temple, where I chanted Buddhist mantras, as well as during the Standing Stones Eucharist service at the All Saints' Anglican Cathedral in Edmonton. I prayed to Krishna, to Allah, to Buddha, Vishnu, Yemaya, God, and Jah, and sat in stillness at the Quaker Meeting House in Walthamstow, yet nothing stirred.

Throughout, in every country I visited, and every place I went here at home, on buses and trains and escalators, along the South Bank of the River Thames, up and down the lengthy queues at Madam Tussauds and the London Dungeons, amongst the crowds outside the gates to Buckingham Palace waiting for the Changing of the Guard, every place I could think of where tourists flocked and people spoke aloud in languages other than English, I listened for a foreign tongue that was somehow instinctively recognisable to me. I ate sandwiches at lunchtimes in the university gardens of the School for Oriental and African Studies, flicked though foreign channels on TVs in hotels, listened to radio stations and programmes I was unable to understand, with the hope of coming across a language that might be the cue to helping me discover where my mother, and as a consequence, I, had come from.

Once, during a twelve-hour layover at Douala Airport in Cameroon, I thought I'd finally found my cue when I heard a language being spoken that was not English, yet I, in part, was able to understand it, and my excitement was so great I could hardly catch my breath till I calmed down enough to recognise, with bitter disappointment, that it was French, which I had studied at GCSE. With that single exception, no language I have heard yet has yielded any cues.

I explain all of this to Vana, who listens without interrupting till I stop speaking. Then she says, "You don't need to travel the world to find out where you're from. Just do a DNA test, man. You'd prob'ly get the results back in under a week."

I don't answer for a moment, attempting to make the response in my head coherent. The sun is a neon ball of flame poised on the line of the horizon. I say, "That fire, my first years, feel like they didn't involve me, like a story I was told. They feel… impersonal."

Below the horizon, the sea is a red and rippling sheet of melted glass.

I say, "It's not the facts I want. It's the memory."

The sun is violently ablaze and the colours of the sky around it have melded into an infinite expanse of molten fiery lava. The curds of cloud are dark and fuming and they drift slowly across it like smoke. I feel Vana's arms snake around my waist and as she hugs me tightly, her lips touch my cheek where they plant a kiss. She says, "You'll be okay. I know you will. I promise."

And for a paralysing instant, I recall something; a woman, these colours, similar words. The feelings that accompany it are intense and overwhelm me; hope, confusion, terror, love. It's real, but it's fleeting. Almost immediately, the memory begins receding and my mind bounds after it, grappling as hard to catch and hang on to it as a young child waking from a wonderful dream. And then it's gone. Words fail me. And I begin to cry.

Jakku Bindy

Diana Sautelle

This is a true story. Names, location, language, and moiety have been altered.

The police car was crawling along very slowly in the dark. From where we were, hidden deep in the shadows of the verandah, we could see the vehicle silently creep towards the crossing - way over on the other side of the township. It came to a halt just before the track leading out to Shale Rock. The headlights switched off. The man driving was planning an unexpected appearance. He knew Bindy had driven across the creek to visit her cousin Munigul. Now, he just lay in waiting.

"We gotta drive over and tell her," I whispered to Jules. But before he could take a breath to answer, we heard distant laughter and the sound of car doors slamming shut. It echoed across the dark, empty landscape. Bindy was already leaving Munigul's house.

Jules shook his head at me in dismay, and within moments we saw headlights winding across Wildana, moving in slow motion as they shone and flickered. Leaning up against the wall of the verandah, we sat in the darkness, silently praying that Bindy would take the short cut and drive home across the creek-bed. But she didn't, and we watched as she drove through the Shale Rock crossing, oblivious to the car secretly hiding around the corner in the darkness.

"Oh no," Jules whispered, "She's coming here."

The dim shape of the police vehicle moved out from the dark shadows and crept up behind Bindy's car. He didn't use his lights, but we could see him as a darker shape glinting and flickering in the pale red cast by the back lights of her car. He was tailing her, like a night creature about to pounce. He didn't know we were watching. He didn't know that anyone could see what he'd planned, and he took his time, allowing Bindy to drive on unaware of his presence, and hoping, perhaps, that she would make some error of judgment so that he could pull her over.

But Bindy was driving slowly and carefully. We could hear laughter coming from the car - it carried across the stillness of Wildana as they came. They were celebrating. Only an hour before, Bindy had been singing out in happiness from the top of the hill across the creek. Her only daughter, her beautiful Jinadji, had been accepted into Avonstead College.

"My baby's going to Avonstead!" we'd heard her cry, "first Aboriginal girl ever!" The beers were out, everyone over there was celebrating. Later, Bindy and a couple of the others had driven over to our side of the creek to tell cousin Munigul about Jinadji's destiny. Now, they were coming to celebrate with us.

It was while they were at Munigul's that Casey had crept into Wildana. Casey and his partner had begun to make a regular habit of this - tonight was the fourth consecutive Friday night that one of them had driven down from Kurtis Crossing into our town. We'd all watched them creeping around before in the black of night.

"What they want to come down here for all the time, spying on? We're not doing anything wrong," Bindy had growled. "They should be up in Cadmine. That's where the trouble is. Those fellas oughta leave us alone."

She was right of course. Wildana is fifty-five kilometres from Kurtis Crossing Police Station, and either road into our township meant driving over half the distance on dirt in the dark. When they were needed, they often took hours to appear - yet lately they were here for no reason - crawling along quietly to a halt behind a tree, or a bend in the track - then waiting - for hours. It wasn't us they'd come to spy on. They leave us alone. They never ask us anything. Not the people across the creek, though - they would appear suddenly on Bindy's property for no reason, and with no reason. Asking questions, expecting answers, making people explain what they're doing on their own land, and in their own homes. Often they'd arrive to find Bindy and her family just sitting around the fire. Someone had usually pulled out the guitar – we would hear them all singing Slim Dusty from this side of the creek, way into the night.

Until tonight, the police have been disappointed - they hadn't been able to catch anyone doing anything. But their patience and perseverance was about to be rewarded, and Jules and I could only sit and watch it unfold before us.

If Casey had known we were watching from the dark shadows of the verandah, he wouldn't have been able to take the whole thing so far. But if Casey had known we were watching, we would never have witnessed just how far he would go. The only people who learnt something new that night were Jules and me - except perhaps Casey learnt that he wasn't the only one being hidden by shadows.

Bindy already knew Casey had singled out her family, long ago. And I'd been with her before; in Native Title meetings, mining meetings, corporate meetings – so I'd already seen the way that the same language could shift and change meaning until promises and guarantees had become rhetoric, theories, expectations - but until this night, I'd never seen a police officer alter reality. I'd only ever heard of this happening.

Casey had been waiting for weeks for someone to do something wrong. He wanted Bindy to do something wrong now, while she drove ahead of him, but the further along the track she came, the more cautious and careful her driving became. She'd slowed to a crawl by the time she reached our house - and even out here - far out in the outback without a car in sight - Bindy still automatically put on the indicator as she turned into our driveway.

That's when Casey put on his lights and flashed them at her a few times. Then he pulled up behind her. He didn't know we were there - our house looked deserted. We'd been sitting on the verandah in the darkness so that we could see the full depth of the stars. They hum up here - dazzling, they are - and when there are no lights on anywhere, the sky is an awe-inspiring vision.

Everyone in Bindy's car was surprised by the sudden appearance of headlights behind them, but Bindy knew straight away who it was, and what this meant, and immediately began moaning and wailing as she climbed out of the car, "No, no, please not now..." she called out, making a swearing crying sort of sound as Casey opened his door.

He didn't display a single moment of pretence to be

reasonable. Quick to pounce with a list of Bindy's misdemeanors, he spoke brashly: "Failing to keep to the left-hand side of the road", he said as he strutted towards her, "failing to indicate, and failing to make a successful right-hand turn."

Without thinking, I leapt up out of the darkness and called to him, "Hey, Darren! That's not true! The indicator's still on!"

I saw the whites of Bindy's eyes flash towards me. She hadn't realised we were there either. She'd probably thought we were out the back somewhere, and so now, for a brief moment, she would have believed these accusations could be cleared up.

Casey had jumped in surprise. "Where were you?" he demanded.

"Just here," I pointed back to the verandah as I stepped down. "How can you say she didn't indicate? Look, it's still on!"

The light from the indicator was flashing on the right-hand side of the car. Casey leant past Bindy and turned off the engine. The indicator stopped blinking.

He glared up at me, and then turned away.

"Failing to keep to the left-hand side of the road," he repeated as he pulled out his little book and pen.

Bindy moaned. "We just been to Munigul's, Darren, we're not..."

"You were driving in the middle of the road, Bindy." His tone was condescending.

"Hang on a minute, Darren," Jules called loudly from the verandah, "this is a track, not a road!"

Casey swung around quickly and glared into the darkness

as Jules stepped down and walked towards us. He knew this was true. The track into Wildana from the main road was barely wide enough for two cars. You had to drive in the middle. That's where everyone drove. The rest of it was only used if you needed to avoid holes, or rocks, or the occasional oncoming vehicle. Surely this law couldn't be applied to an outback dirt track, when there wasn't a single oncoming car within possibly a hundred kilometres?

Jules came and stood next to me.

"What are you two doing lurking in the dark?" Casey flashed at us.

"Lurking?" Jules half-laughed in disbelief. "We live here."

"That's got nothing to do with it," Casey snapped. He flashed his torch around quickly, as though looking for more hidden surprises. Bindy was looking at me despairingly, tears on her cheeks shining in the brief light.

Then Casey shone the torchlight straight into Bindy's sister's eyes as she stepped from the car. Shani squinted in the glare. Her man Billy was out of the car now, and Casey found himself surrounded by a loose circle of people, three of whom he could barely see, other than the flash of eyes and teeth. He shifted uncomfortably for a moment and then started on Bindy again.

"And failing to make a successful right-hand turn," he stated defiantly.

But I perceived a hint of nervousness. "Can you book someone for traffic offences on private property?" I asked quickly.

"I'm not talking to you," he growled.

"But we saw it all, Darren, you're making this up!"

Casey swung around on me, visibly nervous now, his body language stiff and jerky. "You could've been inside," he retorted. "How do I know where you've been?"

"Oh c'mon..."

"You weren't here," he forced at me loudly. "You were inside. You can't prove you've been here."

"Can't prove...?"

Casey took a step towards me. "You," he snarled straight into my face, "keep out of this."

"Hey, Darren, take it easy," Jules objected, but Casey had turned back to Bindy.

"I've reason to believe that you're driving under the influence of alcohol," he stated, "and by law you're required to take the appropriate test."

He extended a breathalyser towards her. "Breathe into this."

Bindy let out a loud wail. "Not now.... please, Darren." Her voice was cracking, but Casey remained unmoved. You could smell the alcohol on Bindy's breath from where I stood. She was going to lose her license, out here, miles from anywhere.

"I gotta use the toilet first," Bindy stuttered at him, "I'm busting."

"Nope, can't let you do that," Casey responded instantly.

There was a moment of surprised silence.

"Pardon?" I asked when I realised what Casey had said.

"You heard me."

"Oh c'mon..."

"You," Casey snarled again as he jerked a finger at me, "keep out of this."

Jules immediately took a step closer. "Hang on a minute, Casey. You're on our property. You can't push us around."

"That's got nothing to do with it," Casey barked at him. He snapped shut his notebook and moved away, looking momentarily panicked. Then he turned on his heels like a soldier in formation and paced along the side of Bindy's car, kicking at the front tyre, slamming shut the open doors, kicking at the back tyre, and then moving behind the car, he ducked down and disappeared, as if to check the lights. I knew what he'd be thinking. *Always known these Wildana people were a tight lot, doesn't seem to matter to them, black or white, they stick together, but how was I to know they were watching me in the dark?*

Billy shook his head and growled under his breath, "Trying to hide his shame now."

Casey was suddenly behind him at his shoulder. "Keep your mouth shut, Sherbrook," he flung at him, "or I'll breathalyse the lot of you." He slammed his notebook down onto the bonnet of the car. "Everyone just shut-up," he snapped. He opened up the book and took out his pen. "And turn on a light," he added loudly.

Jules let out his breath, and shaking his head, walked back to the house, and turned on the outside light. Casey started scribbling.

"What are you writing Darren? You can't book her for that stuff."

He ignored me and looking up at Bindy, said in a

controlled voice, "Do as I say. Blow into this, or I'll be forced to defect your car."

There was another moment of stunned silence. This was the bush. Unless you're wealthy and owned a four-wheel drive, it's inevitable that your car will be missing a few essentials. Things rattle loose and fall off onto the dirt road. Hub caps, door handles, side mirrors. We even stop sometimes to retrieve them, knowing whose car they belonged to.

"I need to go the toilet," Bindy said again, "I'm busting."

"Well you can't," he snapped back quickly. "I've already told you that."

I thought that perhaps it was Bindy's distress that made her have to go so urgently – whatever the reason, I knew it was genuine.

"Can't you just let Bindy use the toilet first?" I asked again, but Casey continued his pursuit of the breathalyser testing.

"I need to go..." Bindy wailed as she pushed the gadget away, "I'm gonna wet myself..." She was jiggling on her feet.

Casey glared at her, and then at me. He scowled, and then finally yielded. "Go on then," he growled at her, "but I'm coming with you."

There were groans of disbelief.

"You can't do that," Shani cried, "that's shame..."

Then suddenly Casey yelled. "I said," he bellowed at everyone, "she can go, but only if I go with her."

He stood like a miniature bull terrier. Mean-faced he is, but small; and one of those men who'd spent his whole life trying to make up for his undersized stature by acting tough and being cruel. I'd wondered before how he'd been accepted into the police force - I'd always thought there was a regulation about a minimum height, but apparently Casey had stretched himself straight enough to make the grade.

Everyone yelled back at him. Everyone was yelling at the same time. Casey flung himself out of the circle and demanded, "Come on then, Bindy."

She stood appalled. "You're not going to watch me! That's shame..."

"Let me go with her, Casey," I was yelling. The group was moving now, up towards the house. I stepped up onto the verandah. "C'mon Bindy, I'll come..."

"No you will not!" Casey blasted at me. He was pulling Bindy along roughly by the arm and she was wailing and yelling. He was attempting to drag her up the step onto the verandah. She stumbled and tripped up onto the hard slate. I was moving too, and was in the doorway before Casey was. But this was no deterrent to the man. He left Bindy to find her balance, and yelling for her to follow him, he shoved past me aggressively, slamming me backwards into the door jam. A shot of sharp, cracking pain darted upwards from the base of my spine. I staggered into the room.

"Get out the way," he bared his teeth at me.

Everything was happening very quickly, and Casey was moving around like a caged animal, one that was ready to strike. Jules was yelling loudly from the doorway, "Hey, Casey, this is our house, you can't just walk in!"

He was standing in our front room now - me inside, Jules in front of him at the door, Bindy on the verandah with Shani and Billy on either side of her. Casey threw furious looks at everyone, and then he swung around at me, pulling a dirty face. There was a brief stillness, and then his hand flashed down to his hip. It was poised over his gun holster. I could see the look in his eyes; they were loaded with menace. It caught my breath. I found myself peering at his hip with a strange, objective curiosity, to see if there really was a weapon in that leather pouch. I watched as he unclipped the handgun, then looked back up into his eyes. He was glaring at me with loathing, I realised. I stared back, trying to comprehend. The movement as his hand gripped around the handle of his weapon carried a vividness that struck me with an equally vivid thought: *He's going to point that thing at me — he's going to point it at me and threaten me - for knowing what he has done tonight, and for standing with my friend.*

My friend from forever, or so it seems - it feels like we share blood, me and Bindy. We often don't need words. Our minds talk to each other even from across the other side of the creek. We're listening to that same bird calling down there and our minds connect in his sound. We can feel it. She made us sisters a long time ago.

"You're tharruminu," she'd said, throwing an electrifying smile at me, "high cloud one. I'm your jakku now."

She told me she would protect me, and I knew she would. She was a warrior woman in comparison with me, big and powerful. It came from a lifetime of hard work and having to defend herself. I hadn't realised just how strong she was until the day we had a puncture out on the open road, just past Kankanu. I couldn't turn the lever on the jack, couldn't budge the bolt with the wheel brace - and after scoffing at me in disgust Bindy had said, "You're weak. Just get out the way," as she'd pushed me aside.

I stood back in awe as she replaced the tyre in a few short minutes. As I watched her, I remembered words she'd once spoken to me: "You're my sis, anyone hurts you, and they'll be sorry." The strength and exertion she used when changing that tyre left me in no doubt that she would be a force to be reckoned with, even for a man.

Bindy is my jakku - that makes me little ngukkunyi. We live and share out here in a harsh, yet profound, outback land. And Casey, a vitriolic, frustrated policeman who'd come from the roughest, dirtiest part of the city's outskirts, had strutted his arrogance and ignorance around our region for over a year now, looking for trouble. I realised as I watched his hand hovering over the gun that the way he found trouble must have often been to start it first.

Jules moved between Casey and me. He hadn't noticed Casey's gun hand, and his tone was neither placating, nor anxious: "Listen Darren, this is our house. You can't just walk in here. And stop treating Bindy like dirt. Let her go to the toilet on her own."

"Nope," Casey flashed back, "can't do that."

"Well, let one of the women go with her," Jules stated,

"it's quite inappropriate for you to attend her." He was using his 'reasonable voice' now, the one that annoyed me when I considered that what he was saying was unreasonable. But Casey seemed to be responding to it, because he didn't snap back instantly. He appeared to be considering this idea as though it was an entirely new option. I could see his breath coming, short and sharp, he was as nervous as hell. It occurred to me then that this was exactly what Casey had been grasping for. He knew that the whole matter was absurdly out-of hand; he knew he needed a reason to shift the intensity. His years of experience asserted itself, and now he claimed this arrangement as his own.

"Like I said," he stated in a tone of contrived and impenetrable sarcasm, "she can take her." He glared over at me. "And make sure she doesn't do anything but urinate."

He repeated this demand several more times as Bindy and I walked down the long hallway to the back door. Bindy was desperate to get to the toilet by now, and had to suppress a moment of laughter when I muttered under my breath, "How does he reckon I can stop you doing more than just a wee?"

"Might be stupid, hey?"

"What's he think you're gonna do, anyway? Make a run for it?"

"Nah, he's worried about *ahu*. It might lower that thing."

Worried about water! I shook my head. How can Casey be so intent upon catching her for drink driving, that he would care about a slightly lowered reading? After Bindy had used the toilet, she guzzled down as much water as she could as I waited outside, ignoring Casey's insistent yelling for us to hurry up.

Back outside by the car Bindy took that test. Casey was very satisfied with the result. She was over the limit, and when he read it to her - his tone sounding something like a robot militant experiencing delight - Bindy just crumbled in front of him. She began stumbling around the front, waving her arms around, crying, "Please, Darren, don't book me, *please*... I promise I'll never do it again – please – Darren..."

This has stayed forever etched in my mind, and in my heart. I will never forget her pleading, begging, yelling in despair, as she appealed to the fragment of humanity left inside Casey's cold chest, while he stood like a steel statue with a shriveled pith of a mouth, refusing to respond.

"But you know me," Bindy wailed at him, "you know it's safe out here... you know it wasn't dangerous. You know I always drive slow..."

He stood in mute silence. There was an indistinct jerk of his head that meant, "Nope, can't do that for you Bindy." He gathered his book and put it into his pocket as he turned to leave.

"But I'll lose my license," Bindy shrieked, "Tully hasn't got his license no more. How we gonna drive...?"

Casey shrugged as though he was already thinking about other more important things.

But the next moment took everyone off guard, and I will carry this forever - like a beacon of light – a true thing so deep, that even Casey took a second to recover. In an instant I knew that what I felt could have easily translated into something physical – because suddenly I felt an urge to lash out at Darren Casey. I wanted to somehow shock him away from hurting Bindy - I wanted him to see that this is yet another way that the system hurts all of my black brothers and sisters. In this moment I knew exactly what drives these people to lashing out, to hitting and yelling in frustration and despair. I could taste the unfairness like it was in my cells. Because even though Bindy was wailing and sobbing, I could make out her words. And these words crystallised and made true the hugeness of this woman, and the smallness of Darren Casey.

"But how'm I gonna take Jinny to Avonstead?" she was yelling in desperation. "How'm I gonna get my baby there now? Darren? How's she gonna get there now?"

This big, black woman stood before Casey, and she was sobbing. A lifetime of poverty, a lifetime of struggle and hardship - twenty-five years of bringing up children in Fourth World conditions that most people don't believe are true, even when they read about it and see photographs in the paper - and yet her desperation was because she wouldn't be able to drive her beat-up, broken-down car, two thousand miles across the desert, in the middle of summer, without any cooling, through flash flood country, during flood season, without any money, across days and days of heat and flies - to take her only daughter to school. I wanted to bow down at her feet. Mother of Jinadji. Sister of mine.

Shame on you, Casey, for here was the moment which you could have taken into the rest of your life knowing that your chosen path was truly in the service of humanity. This one rare deep moment when you could have walked proud in the knowledge that you have lived and known the elements of discernment, and were moved to embrace the human story. You were being called upon to honour that fine balance between legality and the truth you knew of the woman standing before you: to recognise and sanctify her commitment and her strength, her promise and her regret. And between that brief moment when you realised that your actions went so much further than you could have known when you began your work against Bindy - and the next, when you shrugged again and said "nothin' I can do about that Bindy, you work it out" – I saw your heart skip a beat, Casey. That's when I saw you had a heart, and I saw you choose not to listen to it.

Tears were streaming down my face. They were for Bindy's pain, and they were for the powerlessness we all had to bear. It was like the weight of an unbearable gravity, and we were all carrying it with her in a stricken silence. Bindy's devotion to Jinadji was being denied – a devotion which would have overcome all odds so that she could see her daughter achieve a dream – a devotion worthy of a thousand of Casey's salutes, his strutting arrests, his relentless hours of waiting in hiding for someone to do something wrong in a tiny, remote Indigenous community so far off the beaten track that hardly anyone knows it exists.

He never backed down, you know. Bindy went to court six weeks later. Casey had charged her for all of the other offences - the ones we knew she hadn't committed, because we saw her not commit them. The court decided - regardless of the fact that she lived in a community with children, fifty-five kilometers from a hospital, with King Brown snakes hanging around our front doors - regardless of the fact that we're fifty-five kilometres from the school and seventeen kilometres of dirt track from the nearest litre of milk — that Bindy should loose her license for 18 months - out here, where driving is the only link to help in frantic matters of survival. They may believe that they were being reasonable when dropping the other charges — but driving under the influence of alcohol is wrong; everyone knows that.

It's true, Bindy had broken the law. It's a law to protect and must be honored. Yet her circumstances appeared irrelevant. Sometimes murderers get to argue that they had shocking childhoods, and for some reason that is taken into consideration. Sentences are reduced for rapists and brutal assailants over obscure technicalities; and people have left court rooms and driven home in their own cars after causing horrific accidents. Not Bindy though, who was driving at five kilometres an hour, six hundred kilometres from the nearest city, without another car in sight, in country she knows in her sleep. In country she knows in her Dreaming, to tell the whole truth. She did this illegal act to tell her friends about her daughter's achievement, yet the only real danger that night was Casey, not my Jakku Bindy.

"It's the principle of the thing, Bindy," had been Casey's parting words, "you know I can't change the law."

He didn't need to change the law because he could just

251

simply break it. Yet perhaps it isn't illegal to drive behind another car across the length of a town in the dark of night without using your headlights? To book someone for traffic offences they haven't committed? To bully your way into the home of people not even connected to those offences? Casey would know the answers to these things.

And if it's about principles, which principles do we honour? Which principle is in action when matters of the heart can be crushed? Which principle speaks out when a person has to fight a law to be allowed to help another realise their dream? Can we sometimes run with the principles that are streaming through our own hearts? It didn't occur to Casey that any other principle may be woven into the fabric which makes up the order he wishes to honour. It had taken him weeks of stalking Bindy's family before he could find any law breaking, and when he had, he'd knowingly found a mother driving on an empty, narrow dirt track far out in the outback, driving so slowly that he could have walked up to her; a mother celebrating an historical moment in the life of First Nations people in Australia. Yet those three hundred metres and a few cans of beer had turned celebration back to the greater tragedy that marks the ongoing treatment of her people.

Perhaps the court could have allowed Bindy to drive her daughter to school, just that once – perhaps that could have been their concession, for the sake of her child's education; for the sake of future generations.

As for Police Officer Casey, his children live two blocks from the Kurtis Crossing Area School, and the hospital is just down the road a bit. And I've always wondered why, under the circumstances, the judge didn't sentence Bindy to 18 months of community service instead of taking away her freedom. After all, she lives on a community – and it is a community in great need of service.

Lessons
Mabel Aghadiuno

Mesmerised, Myra watched as the candle burned. Thick wax rolled down, congealing into pearly lumps. The flame flickered crazily and then held steady as it pointed upwards to the motionless alabaster face framed by a celestial blue veil fashioned in fibreglass resin. Myra said her usual mantra and then gathering her bags she tiptoed out of the building and meandered through the crowds to work.

"Wayne's never had eczema before," Myra heard a mum say to the head teacher as she walked by. Myra dawdled discreetly.

"Ah really," the headmistress replied noncommittally.

"The doctor said it's in his genes but I think it's related to the school," the mother continued while the headmistress raised her eyebrows as if for further explanation.

"Well, my son's only had it since the second term. He was OK the first term," the mother said. Again, the raising of the eyebrows from the listener for clarification. "He got better during half-term and the Easter holidays."

Pretending that she needed to go back to the reception area at the school entrance, Myra turned and retraced a few steps, maintaining the range of earshot.

"The GP said that Wayne had the worst case of eczema he has ever seen in a child so young," the mother continued, her voice choking, "...and he's been a GP for over twenty years!"

Myra saw the headmistress – who told the staff to call her

Susie, but she never could do that – looked interested then. Myra could tell by the way she unfolded her arms and inclined her head slightly to one side moving it gently towards the mother.

"Well, Mrs Johnson," the headmistress countered, "I have to be honest and admit that I have never seen a rash on your child, and I make a point of visiting each class twice a week."

"Perhaps it's just as well," the mum said, Myra heard the anger seep out of her voice like the air from a balloon slowly deflating. "He's got it down below. It's everywhere there. There are horrible deep cracks and it gets infected. The smell from it is awful. Sometimes it's like an open wound. It's a wonder you haven't noticed ..."

Myra walked past and proceeded on to class. She half-smiled as she thought of the lesson that she had devised for the children. She envisaged the joy on their faces.

Thirty minutes later twenty young pupils sat in front of her with poised pencils and varying degrees of attention.

She noted Samuel boring a grubby finger into a nostril. He screwed up his face and frowned as the activity intensified. Myra pretended not to notice but then the girl sitting next to him also began to observe Sam as he extracted something from his nose and rolled it between finger and thumb. As he started to flick deftly his forefinger, the neighbouring girl's face began to pucker, threatening a tearful storm. Myra knew she would have to intervene.

"Sam Nelson! Stop that immediately!" Myra barked.

Myra stared stonily as Sam swung around in his chair, apparently looking behind for the child to whom his teacher was talking. She watched his face as the feigned innocent realisation dawned that Myra was talking to him. Myra observed as Sam lowered his head for the barest of seconds. He then gradually raised it, accompanying the gesture with a mischievous grin. Myra pretended not to notice and turned her back to the class, suddenly interested in the contents of the interactive whiteboard. She smiled, acknowledging inwardly that Sam's charm was charismatic and irresistible.

"Boys and girls, we're going to talk about night-time animals. The ones that appear while you are all sleeping in your bed. Do you know any?" Myra asked.

Almost before Myra had finished speaking, Sally May shot a hand into the air. "A fox!" she said proudly.

Myra's face beamed approbation. "Yes, Sally is right. Well done! Look at the picture of the fox on the wall. What can you see?" Myra asked encouragingly.

"It's got a long nose, pointy ears and a bushy tail," Sally May retorted while the other children still seemed to be digesting Myra's last sentence.

Myra knew that Kieron, a slight boy with flame coloured hair, did not like to be outdone. "Foxes come into your garden and I've seen them in the day. There must be daytime foxes too?" he said.

While Myra was thinking how best to respond to Kieron, an enthusiastic cry demanded her attention. "Miss ... I know other night-time animals - mice!" Sam blurted out "My mum says we've got one that comes out at night."

Myra watched as some of the girls gasped while a few of the boys guffawed. She asked, "How do you know you've got a mouse if it only comes out at night?"

"Mum says it does its business in the cupboard under the sink," Sam said importantly. Enjoying the effect his revelation had produced he continued, "Mum says there is so much business down there that there must be more than one mouse."

"And then there are cats and rabbits …" Kieron added.

Myra decided to rein in Kieron's enthusiasm. She thought he was like a horse in a race - slow to respond to the starter gun, but unstoppable once it set off.

"Well done! Thank you for your examples, Kieron," Myra smiled, "but rabbits and cats are around mainly during the day. I am thinking of animals that do most of their living at night. Do you know any more night animals?"

From the corner of her eye, Myra discerned a hand slowly rising. Its course was deliberate and inexorable. She immediately turned to the whiteboard and entered the words 'MOUSE' and 'FOX'. She turned and was aware again of the hand. The children fired out other answers: "cow", "horse", and "pig". Myra was aware of the raised hand slowly falling. A short silence followed, during which she felt the children had exhausted their animal vocabulary. Myra's glance then swept over the whole class. The little hand at the edge of her vision materialized again. She quickly lowered her gaze. The hand persisted. It was not going down. The other children were beginning to be aware of the hand too. She was conscious of some pointing to the hand and then to her as if trying to attract her attention.

"Yes," Myra finally said towards the hand. Her throat felt dry and she had to cough repeatedly to clear it. She felt the urgent need of a glass of water but could not leave the class.

"A night owl," the owner of the hand said softly - almost shyly.

Myra cocked a hand behind her ear. "Could you repeat that?"

"A night owl," the owner - a boy - said.

"Yes, a night owl is right, Wayne," Myra replied. She saw the boy looked pleased. The children looked awestruck. Some of them seemed to have never even heard of an owl. Myra thought of the nursery rhymes she had learnt as a child. She recalled a picture of the Owl and Pussycat in a boat. She had loved that picture then but as she grew older, she had found it bizarre the Owl should choose to marry the Pussycat. What a ridiculous combination! Nature had never intended it!

"Wayne," Myra looked steadily at him. She saw the child stare back at her like a rabbit caught in headlamps. "Can you describe what an owl is to the whole class?"

Myra watched as the child looked uncomfortable.

"It's got eyes ..." Wayne began.

"We have all got eyes," Myra interrupted, "but we're not all owls. Anything else?"

"And a sharp, curvy nose - dad says it's called a beak," the child replied.

Myra blinked ponderously and slightly shifted her head.

"And it's very wise," Wayne added.

"And how do you know it's wise?" Myra said abruptly to the boy. "Have you every spoken to one? Can you ask it questions? Does it know what time it is or how to sort out some of the world's problems?"

The other children laughed.

"I don't know, miss." Wayne replied.

"Well, an owl is a night-time creature, but it certainly is not wise," Myra said as she began to project images of the various creatures, she had inserted into her Power Point presentation. She flicked to the image of an owl and played a video.

"Children, is the owl speaking? Does it look clever?" Myra asked. "Do you think it is wise?"

"No!" the children chorused.

Myra flicked through some more pictures and the children called out in chorus:

"Lion!"

"Kangaroo!"

"Hedgehog!"

Then there was a picture of a dark creature with a long snout.

"It's a monster rat!" Kieran shouted enthusiastically. The children murmured uncertain acquiescence.

Myra looked at the children, willing them to produce the answer. Finally, from the corner of her eye she again saw the little hand rise. It stayed up. Myra willed the other children to answer but they all looked at the steadfast hand.

"Well, Wayne?" Myra said trying to hide her exasperation.

"It's a badger, miss!" Wayne replied.

"Yes, it's a badger!" Myra responded curtly. And then she added, as if as an afterthought, "Badgers are creatures that hold on to things tightly with their mouths. When they capture something, they never let it go. They are related to another night-time animal which can be found in the USA. Do you know what it's called?"

"A skunk, miss?" Wayne queried immediately.

"A skunk, Wayne! And do you know anything about skunks?" Myra asked with dangerous softness. "Do you know how they defend themselves?"

The bell rang at that moment and the children shifted restlessly in their seats. Some even stood up quickly, ready to run to the door but Myra soon checked this with a forbidding smile. After a few seconds of silent authority, Myra said, "You can leave the class now!" letting the children pour out like champagne from an uncorked bottle.

"Well done!" her glance swept virtually over the whole class. Some of the children looked up at her as they bounded through the door. She gave each an answering smile. As Wayne looked up, she lowered her gaze to the assortment of papers on her desk - her face an impenetrable mask.

Myra stretched her arms and closed her eyes dreamily in the empty classroom. No more lessons until after half-term. The prospect of a week in Switzerland filled her with pleasurable anticipation.

Three days later the minibus hired by her hotel swept expertly around the curves and up the heights of the Swiss countryside. Each bend disclosed a fresh vista like a game of peek-a-boo thrilling her with surprise. The open window fed through blasts of manure. She wrinkled her nose, comforting herself with the staccato cacophony of an orchestra of cowbells. Myra took mental photographs of the lake, each one varying in colour, the play of the sunlight on the water, the majestic mountains in the background, the tiny roadside flowers.

Once the minibus halted, Myra stepped out drawing a sharp intake of breath at the sheer majesty of the basilica which faced her. People converged to the entrance and she became one with them. She thought of the footsteps which had trod the same path. Perhaps their restless ghosts still walked that path and if the hands of time were wound backwards, she would find herself in the company of Paracelsus, Rousseau, and Einstein.

She arrived in time to see the famous black hooded figures emerge in solemn procession from benches by an altar. Above the altar was a golden-robed statue. Fellow pilgrims sat in pews - their attention focused on the statue.

Myra thought quickly of why *She* was so important to her. She thought of her own mother who she barely remembered and of a land of violent fiery sunsets. A land where she had grown up thinking the children who played in the gutters did not feel the cold because they never wore jumpers. She thought their skin was tough like the cattle. She had come home from school one day mistaking the fire ravaging the rooftop for the sunset. Mother had been in the house and could not escape. They had said there was nothing to connect the fire to the terrorists – the people who protested the land was theirs and demanded restitution. Entirely accidental the police had said. But she had known otherwise. Mother had always said, "These people will kill us in our beds!"

Father had decided to leave the country then. They went to rebuild their lives in Europe – the home of father's grandfather. It had not been easy. Even looking at a candle flame brought back thoughts of mother sinking with the setting sun. Then one day, *She* had simply come along. *She* had taught Myra to trust fire again when she had invited her to light the candle – that first candle in front of the altar.

Myra approached the altar and looked up at the statue. She recoiled. She felt her head reeling as if she had been punched. Perhaps she was mistaken. She looked up again. There was no mistake. The woman in the picture was black as was the child in her arms.

The teacher hovered between indecision and desire. The highlight of her journey had focused on this one visit. The coins which she had drawn from her purse felt sticky and sweaty in her palm yet oddly cold. She could not light a candle – not here.

Myra turned and walked quickly towards the basilica exit. She felt the throngs of the spirits of past ages converging on the door like a tide. The great and the little: phantoms clamouring for favours and penitents craving forgiveness. All making their way to the shrine. She tried to swim against the tide.

A week later Myra was back at school.

"How is Wayne's eczema?" Myra heard a concerned headmistress ask a woman whom Myra recognised to be the child's mother.

"There is something definitely wrong with this school. His eczema got better a day into half-term and I'm expecting it to get worse now he's back!" the mother said.

"I really don't know what to say," the headmistress replied. "We can certainly look at what he is eating a school to see if there is anything there."

"I'll give it another term," Mrs Johnson said. "Then we'll have to change school. It's not fair for the poor kid to suffer like this."

"We'll definitely try our best to get to the bottom of this. We wouldn't like to lose Wayne. He's an exceptional child and our school would be the poorer without him. In fact, here is Miss Haven his class teacher since the second term."

Myra moved slowly towards Wayne's mother and stretched out her hand tentatively. There was the briefest of handshakes. Myra even managed to halt the instinctive rush to wipe her hand on her skirt. Myra looked down at Wayne just in time to see the child avert his face. His body seemed to flinch. She wondered what she had captured in the brief snapshot of his black face. Distrust in his eyes which kindled momentarily with fire? Reproach?

It would be a long journey, but she would try. She was determined to succeed. After all, she had one term.

Prince Kintu
Steve Wade

Kintu didn't look like the other boys and girls in his class. Kintu had arrived in Dublin during the summer five years ago. He and his mama came from a hot country, with banana trees growing in the gardens. Kintu and his mama had travelled across the big sea on an enormous ship.

Now, after five years living in Dublin, today was Kintu's tenth birthday. But he felt sad because he didn't have any real friends in his class. In the schoolyard, everybody challenged Kintu to wrestling matches. Kintu always won the fights, but if the teachers caught the students, they would lie and say Kintu had started the fighting.

Things were very bad on Kintu's last birthday. The year before, on his ninth birthday, the teacher encouraged the class to sing 'Happy Birthday' to Kintu. The song gave him a warm, bubbling sensation in his stomach. The bell rang at three-fifteen, and everyone put their books away and left for home.

Waiting at the school gate were a few of Kintu's classmates.

"Here's the birthday boy," a chubby red-haired fellow shouted.

Kintu's instinct warned him he should run. His mama often told him he could outrun the wind.

"Hey, Kintu," the tallest boy said. "Hold up. This is for you, from us, because it's your birthday." He kicked a football in

Kintu's direction, which Kintu caught on his chest and brought skilfully to his knee and foot.

"Wow!" Kintu said. "A World Cup football." He examined the gold-coloured countries and continents on the grey rubber.

The boys asked Kintu to show them Africa on the football. Kintu pointed out Uganda, where he came from.

"Over here, to me!" the red-haired boy said. "Pass it!"

Kintu chipped the ball his way, and off the three boys went, dribbling, volleying, and heading it between them as they ran home.

Outside Old Man McCarthy's house, the boys stopped to take shots at goal where someone had used spray-paint to paint the outline of goalposts on the high white wall. Kintu saved the first kick, but the next shot went into Old Man McCarthy's garden, which everyone called the Jungle.

"No way," Kintu said when the boys told him to go fetch it, because he owned the ball. "I'm not going in there with Prince! Are you guys crazy?"

Prince, or the Prince of Darkness, as people called him, was Old Man McCarthy's enormous black dog. Prince resembled a bear, though nobody saw him very often. There were two reasons why: some said because the old man kept him in all day, while others believed he was a ghost dog and only appeared at night-time.

"You have to get it," the tallest boy told him. "It's your birthday."

"So what?" Kintu said.

He told Kintu how on your birthday you had to carry out a dare. That was the rule. Anybody who didn't would pay for it. "Nobody likes chickens," he added.

"Okay," Kintu said. "I'll do it. But you guys have to keep lookout at the gate."

"Sure we will," the tallest one promised. "Right, you two. Give him a boost up," he instructed two of the gang.

The boys stood facing each other, their arms crossed together, and allowed Kintu to use them as a wobbly ladder to step on to and clamber up on the wall. He then climbed down thick ivy into the garden. Kintu whistled and called Prince's name. Nothing. No sign of the dog or Old Man McCarthy.

Working his way around the scratchy green things tangled through apple and pear-trees, Kintu spotted the ball next to an upturned wheelbarrow. What he didn't notice was a pair of dark eyes staring at him from behind giant rhubarb leaves: Prince.

"Here, Prince!" voices called from the top of the garden wall. "Come on, Prince!"

Kintu turned around. The three boys were calling Prince's name.

As though in a dream, Kintu moved backwards through the Jungle. He used his hands and feet to feel his way in the direction of the entrance. Prince walked slowly forward, his eyes locked to Kintu's. At the wall, Kintu reached behind him and grasped a strong part of the ivy vine, but one of the boys used a stick to shove his hand away.

"Get him, Prince!" the tall boy said, and he laughed.

His two friends copied him and egged on the huge dog to attack Kintu. Each time Kintu attempted to climb up the ivy-covered wall, they chuckled and pushed his hands away with their sticks.

Prince was going crazy now, growling and snarling. Stringy saliva hung from his jaws and he looked like he might pounce at any second.

To escape, Kintu moved sideways to an apple tree and leaped upwards, catching hold of a branch. He then pulled himself to safety.

Thinking about that day a year ago caused Kintu to shiver and sweat. He, Kintu, had been a lion and the boys on the wall were the warriors with spears. Today, on his tenth birthday, he would be a hunted lion again. So, the moment he woke up to the sound of birds singing, Kintu decided he wouldn't go to school. When his mama came in to get him up, he'd pretend to be sick.

"Kintu," she called from the bedroom door a few minutes later. "Happy birthday, my brave little warrior."

"My tummy hurts, Mama," Kintu said.

"Listen to me, Kintu. I know you are afraid because of what happened last year."

"No, Mama. My tummy, I've a pain."

She put her finger to her mouth. "Kintu," she continued. "Do you know why the lion is the king of the jungle?"

Kintu loved her stories of Africa, so he sat up in bed and listened. "No, Mama. Tell me."

Kintu's mama continued. "The lion is not as strong as an

elephant. What do you think?"

Kintu shook his head.

"The cheetah is by far a faster animal," she went on. "There are other creatures, too, particularly those among the bird families who have more grace and beauty."

Everything Kintu's mama explained was true. So, why did people call the lion the king of the jungle?

"The lion shows no fear," Kintu's mama said. "Even the mighty elephant is careful when he smells a lion on the wind. The hyena, too, an animal that works in a pack, like a group of boys."

"I wish I could be a lion, Mama. Then I would roar and scare all the other kids away."

Kintu's mama smiled showing her perfect white teeth. "You can be what you want to be, Kintu. Go to school today, my fierce lion cub. Be like a lion."

Kintu kissed his mama, got dressed, went downstairs, had his breakfast, and opened his presents - among them *Jungle Book* by Rudyard Kipling.

With *Jungle Book* in a green cloth bookshop bag tucked under his arm, Kintu left for school.

As Kintu expected, the same three boys were waiting for him outside Old Man McCarthy's.

"Happy birthday, Kintu," they said, and told him straight away about this year's dare: to climb into Old Man McCarthy's garden again, and pick ten juicy red apples.

"No problem," Kintu said. He took 'Jungle Book' from his cloth bag and gave it to the tallest boy. "Hold this and make sure you keep it safe."

The boy hesitated, before receiving Kintu's book. He shrugged his shoulders.

A year older now, Kintu needed no help getting onto the wall. He sprung to the top like a warrior. The boys below applauded.

Inside the garden Kintu strolled down the central path. Then from around the side of the house Prince came dashing so fast, he tumbled in the dusty earth in front of Kintu.

"Hello Prince," Kintu said. "How are you, my friend?"

Prince quit snarling and growling, closed his muzzle, turned his head sideways and raised an eyebrow.

"Good dog," Kintu said. He extended his arm so Prince could smell his hand. Prince's jaws dropped open in a smile and he beat his tail from side to side.

"Today is my birthday," Kintu said. "You won't mind if I help myself to a few of your master's apples?"

Prince made a whiny sound and licked Kintu's face.

Up the tree where grow the reddest fruits, Kintu climbed and picked ten of the biggest and juiciest apples and put them in his cloth bag.

Now that they were friends, Kintu promised Prince he would return to visit him often. He told the dog he understood how it was to be without friends.

Outside in the street, the boys cheered and clapped their hands at Kintu's bravery. Kintu divided out the apples. Everybody whooped and laughed. The biggest boy gave him back his book, and put Kintu on his shoulders. 'Prince Kintu' they called him, after Old Man McCarthy's big dog, the nickname that would stay with Kintu for the rest of his schooldays.

All Over A Cup of Tea
Malcolm Aslett

Upon announcing the 2020 longlist, we sadly received the news that Malcolm passed away in September of that year. We are proud to include this shockingly unique story in the anthology. Malcolm's prize money has been donated to the competition's nominated charity at his wife's request.

Consider this sight: two black women dressed in dark, simple clothes. They are wearing scarves which are crooked on their heads as they strain with the effort of the chain in their hands. It is slipping in their palms. With their feet pressed hard against the man's back and shoulders they pull for their lives. Each woman is manacled to the other at the wrist. The chain between is wrapped round the neck of a purple faced man dressed in white pants and top. The three of them form a messy inverted human pyramid on the green bank. The year is 1781 in the month of June. They are in the sweet green shade of Virginia pines a stone's throw from the Three Notched Road. The man's horse, a fine-looking Godolphin Arabian, is tied to a branch and indifferent to the crime.

"*Nwoke na acha ocha!*" says the first.

"Die!" says the second.

"Die white man!" says the first.

The man wriggles and slides to escape but his movements are slower and less committed in each breathless moment. The summer heat and his lunchtime ale had made him sleepy. Now he was about to die.

"Die!" repeats the second.

There is no longer any life or breath, but they heave at his still body for some moments more. The first gives a brief last kick at his shoulders. Then they rest on their backs with satisfaction and for the first time notice the cool breeze coming up from the Rivanna River. There is such peace.

"Hands up! Hands up! You hear me? What have you done? What did you do?"

Rifleman Enderby is on reconnaissance. He is seventeen years old and not shocked at what he sees. For some reason he chooses to point his musket at the dead man.

The women stare at him and don't move.

"Hands up, I tell you!"

They are not sure what he means, and raise their hands to chest height to look at them. Does he want to see that they are not holding the chain anymore?

"Have you gone an' killed that man? Speak up."

"He was your enemy," says the first.

Enderby shakes his head. "And no friend of yours by the looks of things."

"He was taking us to sell," says the second.

"Slaves, are you? Sergeant! Sergeant Stokes!" He is shouting back in the direction he came, a thick copse of trees and bushes.

"He was your enemy. Look in his pocket," insists the first.

"He has a letter for a General," adds the second.

Enderby is cautious. He now points his gun at each of

them in turn.

"He was a bad man," says the first.

"We want to join your army," says the second.

They have both dropped their arms to rest on the grass. Enderby looks at the chains and thinks better of asking them to raise their hands again.

Sergeant Stokes arrives in seconds. He is a good-looking man but for the black powder mark around his left eye. His uniform is clean and sharp as if freshly donned. "Ah, volunteers, are you?" he asks, assessing the situation. "And what did he volunteer for?"

"He was your enemy," says the first.

Enderby points at the corpse with his rifle. "They said he had a letter, Sergeant."

Stokes stands at a distance and puts his arms on his hips. "Well let's be seeing it, Enderby."

Enderby dutifully props his gun on the bank and pats the man's pockets. The women are stone faced. Enderby retrieves a letter and a purse of coins and holds them up.

"Pass 'em here, lad." Sergeant Stokes takes the purse first and pockets it without any suggestion of impropriety. The letter he breaks to read.

"We are told we can join your army," says the first.

"We want to fight your enemy," says the second.

Without looking up the Sergeant tells them: "Puhh. It does look as if you know how to kill a man."

"They do know that, Sergeant," Enderby agrees.

Sergeant Stokes pauses. "Who was he? Your master?"

"His name was Ryker," says the first.

"And he is no longer our master," says the second.

"And you ladies are called?"

"My name is First," says the first.

"My name is Second," says the second

"That is what he called us," says First.

"And why did he call you that?"

"Because I was first," says First.

"And I was second," says Second.

The Sergeant reads further while the women remain quiet. "Tch. This Ryker? He was a revolutionary?"

"He was a farmer. He wanted to fight for the revolution. He said they raised the price of tea," says First.

This animates the Sergeant. "Ah yes. The tea. The price of tea. How strange is that? I've heard of men coming to blows with a baker over the price of a loaf. Or fighting for your life. Or going to war for justice, for liberty, for a King or a Queen. All those I can understand. But a cup of tea? They must be a very dainty lot these colonials, fighting for a cup of tea, don't you think?"

Sergeant Stokes raises his hand with the little pinkie finger prominent as if sipping daintily at a cup. This means nothing to the women, and they don't reply.

"Sounds a rum reason to kill a man," Enderby chimes in.

"So it does, Enderby, so it does. Over a cup of tea. You'd think a nice brew would be a means to bring folk together, would you not? Give them a chance to talk through their problems, like civilized men. That is sadly not the case."

"No, Sergeant."

"And on that subject, ladies, would you mind sharing with us your motivations for squeezing the breath of life from this beverage-loving colonial?"

"He was a bad man," says First

"He was a white devil." says Second.

The women glare. After a pause, the Sergeant says: "I was hoping for a little more detail. Did he have a wife?"

"Our Mistress' name was Nancy, and her name was Lott before she married," says First.

"She died with child," says Second.

"But first he beat her till her eyes were red with crying."

"He liked to beat a woman. Though she was no angel herself."

"It was just as bad before she died."

"We milked the cows and worked the fields."

"We cleaned and cooked, washed and cleaned."

"At night he'd come to us and take us."

"I was first."

"And I was second."

"He was strange in his passions."

"He liked to cut us with his knife."

"I have one ear completely gone." First pulls back her headscarf to show the deformed nub.

Second raises her upper garment, telling them: "He carved his name upon my belly."

Enderby twists his face.

"He did worse," says First

"He did many things worse," says Second.

"If we displeased him."

"If we spoke back."

"He would starve us for many days."

"God sent rain and we drank from the holes in the roof."

"His wife - she was strange."

"She was jealous of our scars."

"When she saw our cuts, she would rub them with brick dust."

"Or salt if she was in the mood."

"He whipped us till he could see the bones on our back."

"She cried and said it proved he loved us more than her."

"She was mad."

"But what else could she be?"

"And with her dead he beat us but then he would cry afterwards."

"I felt better when he cried."

"He wanted to join the revolution."

"He said he would sell us first."

"He said we would never get a master as good as him again."

"He told us we would suffer like we had never suffered before."

"A slave we met told us the British will give us our freedom."

"We will get our freedom if we kill for you."

"He fell asleep as we rested by the road."

"It felt good to kill him."

"We can kill your enemy."

"But we will do it for us."

The women stop talking. The two soldiers look at one another in puzzlement and awe. The Sergeant shakes his head.

"You did say you can cook. And clean?" he asks.

"We can kill," says First.

"Look at him," says Second.

First gives the body a kick. Second gives the body two kicks.

"Enderby. See to that horse. And find two men and get this body buried. You ladies come with me. We can get those chains off if you don't mind."

First and Second smile and hurriedly unwind the chain from the dead man's neck. Stokes has already turned to head back to the company and the women jump to their feet to follow him.

"Will we wear these fine uniforms?" asks First.

"Will you give us a gun?" asks Second.

The Sergeant answers drily: "Honestly, ladies, I'm not even sure if we'll give you spoons. But you'll get fed every day and most nights there'll be somewhere dry for you to sleep. How does that sound?"

"And we will get our freedom?" asks First.

"And will we be paid?" asks Second.

The Sergeant pauses and looks around. Enderby is still struggling with the horse. The Sergeant takes the dead man's purse out of his pocket and rummages inside with a forefinger. He removes two large gold coins. "It sounds like he owed you a bit of back wages," he tells them. "Here. Put it somewhere safe, ladies. There's more than a few thieves round the camp."

The women are happy. The Sergeant takes a last look behind at the crumpled form on the bank. He gestures in the dead man's direction and explains to his new recruits: "And all over a bloody cup of tea."

Sithifricker

Ian Inglis

I was twelve years old when Adrian Wicks came to our school in the Autumn of 1962.

"It says here, Wicks," said Kerr, our form master and Physics teacher, "you're from Durban. Is that correct?"

"Yes, sir."

"And where is that, might I ask?"

"Sithifricker, sir."

There were sniggers and muffled laughter among the thirty or so boys in our form.

"That's not a country I've ever heard of," continued Kerr.

"Sithifricker, sir."

"Sithifricker? No, I'm not familiar with that. I usually pride myself on my geographical knowledge, but I have to confess that this is a new one on me. Let's ask the boys. Any of you ever heard of this place Wicks is talking about? Sithifricker?"

He looked around the classroom, knowing that few boys would be prepared to take the risk of becoming the next victim of his personal brand of sarcasm.

"Asprey. Are you familiar with this country?"

"No, sir."

"Woodward. Sithifricker?"

"Never heard of it, sir."

"Knowles?"

"No, sir."

"Anyone? Well, this is a puzzle. Can no-one enlighten me?"

I put up my hand. "Yes, sir."

The classroom fell silent. Kerr advanced towards me. Wicks remained sitting loosely at his desk, gazing straight ahead.

"Then pray do, Cairns. Be so good as to share this information with us."

"South Africa, sir."

He stared at me for a full twenty seconds.

"The mystery is solved," he said eventually. "South Africa. A timely intervention, Cairns. Tell me. Are you in a position to provide any additional details about this distant country?"

I wasn't. Cape Town and Johannesburg were cities whose locations I knew from staring at the blackboard-sized map of the world in the Geography room. I knew nothing of Mandela or Verwoerd. Sharpeville and Soweto were names I'd not yet come across. Apartheid meant nothing to me.

"No, sir."

"No, sir," he repeated. "I thought not. Well, perhaps Wicks will enlighten you, just as you have been good enough to enlighten us."

He returned to the front of the classroom and wrote the word 'Sithifricker' on the blackboard: next to it he put a cross. Underneath, he wrote 'South Africa', and followed it with a tick. He stared at the new boy.

"South Africa, Wicks. South Africa."

"That's what he does," I explained to Wicks during break. "He picks on people, and because everyone's scared of being next in line, they do as they're told."

"Aren't you scared?"

I shrugged. "I don't know. Maybe."

"Well, thanks, anyway."

He told me that his family were in Britain for a year, while his father was setting up business contracts for the import and export of minerals. During that time, we became close friends. We were in the same streams for most subjects, and shared a love of sport, particularly cricket: he opened the batting, I opened the bowling. His family had rented a large house a few miles outside the town, and I was often invited for tea after school. His father was rarely there, but his mother and two younger sisters always made me welcome. My parents were keen to reciprocate, and his family (minus the father) came for Sunday tea on several occasions.

When he returned to South Africa at the end of the school year, we promised to keep in touch and for a while we did exchange letters and postcards. But at that age, we had lots of other things to occupy ourselves, and our communications soon dwindled and then disappeared. After a while, I ceased to think about him, and it was only when I went to university and became increasingly aware of the political system in his country that I remembered him at all. With my new student friends, I went on all the anti-apartheid marches in London, and in 1970 when the International Cricket Council banned South Africa from international events, I was among the many who agreed with its decision. Only after the dismantling of the apartheid regime in 1991 was the country re-admitted to world cricket, and it was not until the summer of 1994, several weeks after the inauguration of Nelson Mandela as the President of the new South Africa, that the national team returned to England for a three-match Test series.

Media coverage – across news and sport outlets – included numerous interviews with the players and their extensive entourage, all of whom expressed a desire to re-establish cricketing links with English players and fans. I'd recently stopped playing local league cricket after a couple of troublesome injuries, but was still a keen follower of the game and I took every opportunity to keep up to date with the tour's progress. I switched on the radio to listen to the opening overs of the First Test from Lord's. I think I recognised the voice even before the commentator introduced his guest, and invited Assistant Tour Manager Adrian Wicks to comment on the significance of today's match.

"It's a hugely important day for Sithifricker and Sithifrickan cricket," he said. "We've been in the wilderness, the sporting wilderness, for far too long. We're sportsmen, not politicians, and that's all we want to concentrate on. From our point of view, we've always wanted to keep politics out of sport."

"And yet there are no black players in your squad," the interviewer pointed out. "Is that a political decision? Or, at least, the result of previous political decisions and policies?"

"It's what it is. It's not deliberate. We selected the best cricketers we could to come on this tour. Race, colour, played no part in those selections."

"How long do you think it will be before black players are selected to represent your country?"

"I can't answer that. No one can. If a player is good enough, he'll be selected. Black or white."

"Do you look forward to that day?"

"Of course I do. So does all of Sithifricker."

The name of the hotel in central London in which the South African team was staying during the Test Match was no secret, and I caught the Tube there in the evening. A small group of protesters was confined to a small area across the road. One of the half-dozen or so security staff standing at the entrance stepped in front of me.

"You a guest here, sir?"

"No," I admitted.

"What's your business inside?"

"I'm here to see someone. Adrian Wicks… he's with the South African team."

"Is he expecting you?"

"Yes," I lied.

"Your name?"

"Cairns. Terry Cairns."

He spoke to another security guard who, after looking me up and down, went into the hotel. Then he turned back to me.

"Just be a couple of minutes, sir."

It was ten minutes before his colleague returned. After a brief conversation, the first guard beckoned me forward.

"Mr Wicks can't see you right now. They're just sitting

down for dinner. But if you care to come back in an hour, he might have time to see you then."

"Can I wait inside? At the bar?"

"No. Hotel guests only."

I wandered around the West End for a while before heading for a small cafe. I was surprised and slightly disappointed by what had happened at the hotel. I knew that if Adrian Wicks had turned up unexpectedly at my door, I would have willingly postponed or abandoned my dinner to see him. However, I persuaded myself that as one of the officials in charge of the squad he probably had a great number of duties to perform. I picked up a discarded *Evening Standard*, turned to the sports pages, and saw a photograph of the team arriving at Lord's that morning. I could just make out Adrian in the background, emerging from the coach with several other unidentified officials, while the cricketers strolled on ahead.

When I walked back to the hotel, the same security guard waved me forward.

"Mr Wicks is waiting for you in the bar, sir."

There were knots of players and officials sitting at tables or standing at the bar, all wearing their obligatory green blazers and light grey trousers. Alone in a corner of the room, Adrian was easy to spot. Heavier, a little less hair, but otherwise remarkably unchanged.

He put aside the sheaf of papers he was reading and stood up, hand outstretched.

"Good God! Terry Cairns. It's been a long time."

"Thirty years. It's good to see you, Adrian."

"You too. Sit down, please." Without asking, he ordered two whiskies.

"I heard you on the radio," I began. "I had no idea you were involved in cricket."

"It's all I've ever done," he said, proudly. "I was with Eastern Province for fifteen years... never one of the stars, but a decent enough batsman. Then I had a few seasons with Transvaal. Again, nothing spectacular. A reliable Number 5 or 6!"

"I never knew."

"You wouldn't. Once we were kept out of the international game, I don't imagine our domestic cricket attracted much attention over here."

"No. You're right."

"Pariahs. We were treated as pariahs. Still are, by some. Did you see the placard-wavers outside?"

I nodded.

"As if we haven't done enough. What more do they want from us?"

"I know it must be difficult..." I began.

"Difficult? Yeah. It's difficult."

I said nothing.

"So, anyway," he continued, "when I retired, I went into coaching, and now here I am, an administrator. Tell me about yourself."

I told him. Not that was much to tell. University. Teacher training. Head of History.

"Cricket?" he asked.

"Just the local leagues."

"And are you married, Terry? Children?"

"One wife, three children. How about you?"

"The same!"

"What about your sisters? And your parents? I remember your mother, especially. Are they all well?"

He stared at me. "They are, yes. But my father died ten years ago."

"Oh, I'm sorry. He wouldn't have been that old."

"No. He wasn't." He paused. "Have you heard of Church Street?"

I shook my head.

"No. No-one has over here. In 1983, the ANC detonated a car bomb in the centre of Pretoria. In Church Street. A lot of people died. Innocent people. Civilians. My father was one of them."

"Adrian, I am sorry." I spread my hands. "Your country's been through so much."

"Yes, it has," he said, thoughtfully. "But the rest of the world seems to have been very selective in what it chooses to remember."

Again, I said nothing. I wasn't going to tell him about my own involvement in the anti-apartheid movement, or argue with him over the immorality of a system in which a white minority had used torture and murder as routine tools to control the state, the economy, and the daily lives of the 80 per cent of South Africans who were non-white. He continued to stare at me.

"You don't agree," he said flatly.

"I've never been to South Africa," I said. "And I know I could never understand the complexities of the problem..."

"But?" he persisted.

"But... I'm glad that the violence is receding, and the situation is improving."

"Improving!"

Again, I said nothing.

"You shouldn't have lied," he said.

"What do you mean?" I asked, genuinely nonplussed by the accusation.

"You told the guard you had an appointment with me."

"I... I wanted to see you."

"Look," he said, suddenly, "I have to go. Lots to do."

He held out his hand.

"It's been good to see you, Terry. Take care."

And he walked away.

South Africa won the match by 356 runs, the Second Test at Headingley was drawn, and England levelled the series by winning the Third Test at The Oval. But my interest in the cricket waned, and throughout that summer, my thoughts returned again and again to Adrian and what he had said. Although our conversation had contained no overt hostility, there was a belligerence about him that saddened me. At school, he'd been a bright, lively, and popular boy who I was proud to call my friend; now, thirty years on, he seemed to me sullen, angry, unwilling to accept the changes sweeping his country.

Of course, the official end of apartheid did not bring overnight harmony to the country, and for several years the peace and reconciliation process was interrupted by individual acts of violence and terrorism, committed by white groups who resented the changes or black groups who considered that those changes were insufficient. Economic progress was slow. Land redistribution was fiercely contested. Many in the white community held on to their positions of power and privilege, while problems of unemployment, health, and housing continued to be highest in the black townships. But gradually, those tensions did appear to diminish – at least to me, several thousand miles away on the outskirts of London – and as the new century dawned, the international news media began to look elsewhere for the familiar stories of bigotry, brutality, and repression.

When I first heard the name Marvin Wicks I thought nothing of it but his trial, coming shortly after the acquittal, suspended sentence, house arrest, conviction for murder, appeal, and eventual thirteen-year prison sentence given to the Paralympic athlete Oscar Pistorius, kept revelations about the lifestyle of South Africa's wealthy white community in sharp focus. Wicks was accused of the fatal shooting of two eleven-year-old black schoolboys, who he had confronted one afternoon in the garden of his house in the white suburb of Westcliff to the north of Johannesburg. Wicks, who had been hosting a barbecue at the time, claimed he had mistaken them for intruders and, fearing for the safety of his guests, had shot in their direction hoping to scare them away. However, several other boys testified that they were among a dozen or so who had been playing football in the street, and that the two victims had stepped inside the unlocked gates merely to retrieve their ball. After a long and controversial trial which centred on whose story the jury chose to believe, Marvin Wicks was found guilty of murder and given the mandatory minimum sentence of fifteen years imprisonment. In passing sentence, the judge commented that the defendant had shown no signs of remorse during the five-week trial.

I watched from the doorway of my living-room as the live television pictures from the steps of the courthouse showed the prosecution lawyers confirming their satisfaction with the verdict and the sentence, and commenting that justice had been done. The mothers of the two murdered boys wept openly and were unable to speak. Once they had been tactfully ushered away from the posse of cameras, the defence team stepped forward and announced its immediate intention to mount an appeal against what they described as a woeful disregard for the truth.

The reporters then turned their attention to the father of the convicted man, Adrian Wicks. I missed the first few words, but as it slowly dawned on me that the obese, balding figure shouting into the microphones was my old friend, I stumbled into a chair and turned up the volume.

"...can tell me that! What else was he supposed to do? This is Sithifricker, not Manhattan or Kensington! You people have no idea what it's like to... Two black faces appear on your property, they're not there to wish you a Happy Birthday! I'd have done the same myself. Anyone would. You have no idea! My son's a good boy. Always has been. He defended his property. He did the right thing. And he gets sent to prison. For what? It's all wrong! This isn't my country anymore. Not my Sithifricker!"

I switched the television off and sat there silently. I was still there when my wife arrived back from her trip to the garden centre.

"I had the car radio on," she said. "You know, that awful murder case in South Africa. Marvin Wicks. Dreadful man. I'm glad they found him guilty. Didn't you have a friend called Wicks over there? It wouldn't be the same people, would it?"

"Oh, that was a very long time ago." I smiled and reached for her hand as she came toward me. "But no, I don't think so. The boy I knew wasn't like that at all."

How We Overcame
E. E. King

"Radical, black, lesbian, crusader Jacala Umoja, gave a speech at University Green last night. Over one hundred people attended," simpered Angela White, news reader on *The A.M. Wake Up and Drink the Coffee Morning Show.*

Radical, black, lesbian, crusader. I smiled. I'd been a shy, quiet child and a shy quiet adult. I hadn't become 'radical' until I heard Allen Goodman's plan to use the eternity™ as a punishment.

It was a year of retribution. There had been unrest in the streets and injustice in the courts. The rich drifted in a world so removed from the poor it might have been a different planet. Disease haunted the cities and politicians looked for someone to blame. As usual they found, the victims.

"Societies have tried the death penalty. They have tried jails. Both failed miserably. Chemical alteration, and castration have been more successful, but still," Goodman waved his hands as if trying to stop a runaway train. "We have murders."

"Well, under my administration, if you murder someone, their eternity™ will be removed and put inside your head beside your own." Allen waited.

The crowd went crazy. Of course, they would have gone crazy whatever he said. Goodman had that effect on some people.

At birth, the eternity™ chip was inserted into the base of the spine. There it recorded every love affair, sorrow, and dream. It cataloged conflict, compiled commitments, and assembled a collection of memories in a chip that was supposed to contain the person. After death, the eternity™ would be removed, inserted into a computer in the research center, free to spend eternity in a heavenly program.

But there were problems. Eternity™s were flat. They had attitudes, but no feelings. Memories, but no emotions. Desire, but no love. Hunger, but no satisfaction.

The scientists and technicians went back to their labs and their screens and tried again.

I worked with the eternity™s, removing them after death and testing them in limited systems. The eternity™ chips were not virtual people, they were not simulated spirits, or cyber ghosts, but they were something. Not quite alive, but also not entirely without consciousness.

And then Allen Goodman, with his tales of fear and hate climbed to power. Innocents were shot, protesters branded, and the eternity™ became a punishment.

Under Goodman's law, if you murdered someone, their eternity™ was removed and inserted into the base of your spine, right next to your own.

"It will stop hate crimes," Goodman roared. "Imagine a white man having a radical, black lesbian in his head! What could be worse?"

I can think of something.

It was then I began to question my work. True, eternity™s

were not souls, but they were something. Memories? Snippets of love and fear and hope. Was it right to treat them as objects? Was it right to insert them into another's mind? We didn't know enough. Could two sets of memories and beliefs live in one head? Was the eternity™ conscious enough to suffer?

We'd already jumped too quickly to accept the new vaccines. That had resulted in heart attacks and birth defects. History repeats itself and historians repeat each other. But we didn't listen.

I began to make speeches. Surprisingly, I was good at it. I spoke of history and hate, of empathy and forgiveness, of DNA and truth, of entanglement and connection. I talked about my work on the eternity™, and my sorrow that so much money and time were devoted into creating eternity™s, and so little into making life good for all its creatures.

It was late October. I stood before a crowd; arms raised high, both looking forward and looking back. It could have been a thousand years before, when people gathered on hill or plain to hear truth. So face to face. So personal. It was unusual for our time. There must have been at least three hundred people. An unheard-of turnout! I wanted to be worthy.

Listen, I'd been going to say. *We have put our technology and learning into creating a perfect soul and we have failed. But I have worked with eternity™s and though they are not complete personalities, they are something. The memory of a sunny morning, the fragrance of warm cookies on a cold day, the soft brush of a first kiss.*

We are told that the eternity™s don't feel, but isn't that what they said, about slaves, women, and animals in times past? Isn't this just old prejudice clothed in new words?

Isn't it true that almost all the eternity™s inserted into murdering skulls are minorities, and women, because, as always, most of the killers are white men?

They say they know eternity™s don't feel because of the algorithms and system parameters. They say there can be no blame or responsibility. But who designed the algorithm? Who described the parameters?

But the crowd was so big, and they had traveled so far, I felt my words were not enough. So, I began by quoting the most beautiful truth I knew.

"To quote the immortal Martin Luther King Jr," I said, "Darkness cannot drive out darkness; only light can. Hate cannot drive out hate; only love can."

It was so still. Smoke and melancholy perfumed the air. It was my last fragrance, my eternal perfume. The twilight exploded so swiftly, so I didn't even realise I'd been hit. Not until I woke up. Not until I looked in the mirror.

Instead of my large, dark eyes, small, hateful, watery blue iris dotted with pinpoint pupils glared at me out of meaty pockets of flesh. Where was my smooth, brown skin? This face was pasty, red nose delicately marbled with crimson and blue veins, thin as the synapses connecting the eternity™ to the spine.

My short, kinky, black hair was gone, replaced by a bald head fringed by white-blond scrub. It was not mine, but it was familiar.

It was Bubba Chaney. A leader of the White Boyz. A hater of first order. A killer of first degree. And then I remembered.

"Imagine a white man having a radical, black lesbian in his head," Goodman had said. "What could be worse?"

I can think of something.

Bubba's small, mean, blue eyes looked at me in the mirror frightened and bleary. He hadn't slept well and no wonder. He couldn't see me, but he could feel me, thinking inside him, using his brain. He reached for his washcloth and scrubbed violently, hoping that movement, or pain would block me out. Unfortunately, we were one. I had been mixed into his brain like salt into water, like oil into skin, like rage into a storm.

They'd said eternity™s weren't whole. They'd said eternity™s couldn't feel. Once again, they were wrong.

I was whole and I was burning. I'd make Chaney suffer as I suffered. As women and minorities have always suffered at mercies of those without mercy.

And then I heard it.

An eye for an eye and a tooth for a tooth only ends up making the whole world blind and toothless.

It was an eternity™.

Though the eternity™ punishment was fairly new, murder was common. Already there were hundreds of us, 'imperfect' eternity™s, sentenced to live out the remainder of our existence inside our murderer's mind, or more accurately at the base of his spine.

But though we were separated, all eternity™s were connected. We had been made in the same lab of the same stuff. Information flowed between us like radio waves. Our convictions, ideals, and beliefs balanced like surfers on invisible waves of electricity and magnetism that raced from brain to brain at the speed of light.

Knowledge passed between us, like currents into the sea, like soap into water, like clarity into fear.

If you want to make peace with your enemy, you have to become your enemy. thought another eternity™.

It cut through my rage. It brought me back to myself.

Darkness cannot drive out darkness; only light can. I thought back.

It was unplanned and unconsidered, perhaps the best revolutions are. It was not a rebellion of fear. What could they do to us? We were already dead. Less than whole. Incomplete programs in our killer's brain. We had nothing to lose, not even ourselves. Through the language electric, we screamed.

Hate cannot kill hate, only love can.

If we had spoken aloud, we would have been incomprehensible, a collision of dialects, a babble of tongues. But these were not words, but philosophies, a spark that flew from one to another of us, a hailstone of ideas pelting the dry soil of hate.

Hate cannot kill hate, only love can.

And so, we loved, we pitied every angry racist imprisoned in their own brain, alongside us. We mourned their childhood of hate. We sorrowed at their fear. We forgave their ignorance. We loved.

We are one, we thought.

Can there be a cacophony of communication? A devastation of understanding? An apocalypse of love? If so, then that's what this was. And because we were not speaking in words, our thoughts overloaded the thoughts of our killers. Their hate was destroyed by our love. It was instant, fatal, and irrevocable. We had finally overcome.

Sixty Six, Thirty Three, Ninety Nine
Ebuka Prince Okoroafor

It wasn't the rumbling that you heard first, it was the violent crash, the clattering of ceramic plates and stainless utensils, the earsplitting scream, and then the galloping followed. You turned around and saw your Momma, ankles spread and motionless, at the base of the stairs leading down to the basement.

At the hospital, she was a mass of fat splayed atop a creaking bed with casts of POP running from both ankles to the knees, and a blood-stained bandage around her head. The doctor said her condition was grave. X-rays revealed a slipped disc at the spine, a multiply fractured left tibia and as if that was not enough, he pulled out another film and handed it over to you. You held it up against the wobbling fluorescent bulb but could not make anything out of the mélange of radio opaque structures. He explained that it was not actually an X-ray; what you held in your hand was your Momma's brain CT Scan result.

"Did you know your mother had a stroke episode?"

He said this calmly, dragging the spine of his gold rimmed glasses low so that he could focus his eyes on you from above the edge, seemingly to evaluate your reaction. You thought he looked just like your lecturer back in the university, the one that asked you to take off your coffee-coloured top inside his office, and come to sit on his lap. The one that did things to your body you didn't want to remember now. Maybe, he was sizing up your tits? You immediately doused that thought, focusing on the film instead, and squinting as though you understood the next set of medical jargons that he rattled out. He came over to where you stood and turned the film upside down, apparently holding it up the right way.

"See, here, and here. These are bleeds into the skull. While we'd assumed they were hematomas forming from the fall, this here proved otherwise," he said, pointing at yet another radio-opaque area that looked just like the other two, save for a few white specks. You nodded as though you understood, and because back in Nigeria, to nod even when you did not understand meant having a fair chance at haggling down the price of anything— because the seller would be deceived into believing you had a well-rounded idea on the market value and as such, would not want to be caught over-inflating the price. It was a survival tactic you carried like a genetic trait into this city at the age of nineteen. You nodded some more.

But you did not know. The news sent a shiver down your spine like an orgasmic episode. You let go of the scan and folded your forearms across your chest, then let a languorous smile that you prayed the doctor did notice. Your Momma was fifty-seven, never been diagnosed of hypertension or DM or anything. You didn't know what to say, instead you whispered numbers *sixty six, thirty three, ninety nine,* your way of holding off a panic attack.

You asked the doctor the worst possible outcome and when he mentioned that she may be debilitated, you ran out of his office, through the scanty hall and into the bustling evening. He had followed you but by the time he stepped out of the building, you were gone like a wisp of smoke, diffused into the crowd.

You are twenty-eight, chocolate skinned, skinny, with a freckled face and an aquiline nose. You are Theresa Okolo, but in this America, you have answered many names; *Lily, Josephine, Jasmine, Chloe, Kimberly*. You are the girl that lives with your Momma in the basement of the Li's, an immigrant family from China who'd gotten their citizenships and shed off the scourge attached to illegal migrants, living freely and working well-paying jobs. You were not so lucky, America demanded a lot from you and when it took, it ravaged. You still paraded an altered student visa, six years after graduation and your Momma, an expired holiday invite which you'd had a white friend send her five years ago. Here, an illegal immigrant was an illegal immigrant. Nothing exempted you from those sneaking in through the Mexican border or those packed like sardines in containers and shipped in from Italy. The only thing that mattered here was getting a stay permit which sadly, you and your Momma didn't have.

In church, you are the black girl every boy keeps talking about. The chorister whose velvety voice could make miracles hurtle down from Heaven. The reverend calls you out on Sundays and the moment you begin to reel out your well-practiced vocals, your Momma, who is always a front bencher, breaks down sobbing. You make her proud. You make her say you are God's vessel, that if you were an angel, then you must be *Gabriella*. And each time she says these things, you laugh, because you harbour this odd opinion that even God may be preferential: *Michael no Michelle, Gabriel no Gabriella, God no wo-God, even the Devil is presumed a male being, and every other thing with a vagina, He gave a body!* You are the girl who does not believe in God, who sings because you need to keep your Momma's pride up. Every week after service the reverend calls you into his office. You give him a lap dance before you go home.

Monday, Tuesday, Wednesday, Thursday, you leave home by 7am because you work at the largest mall in town. You are the chatty girl at the grocery section every regular customer wants to see every time. *Where is Theresa? She's not here today? Ah! Theresa! There you are!* Because you are different, you ask about the wellbeing of family, you talk about dreams, some even confide in you. Your customer relationship is always up on the board and some month ends, you get a little raise on your regular pay. This makes some of your co-workers jealous, they say things behind your back, once you'd heard the rumors going round that you were having an affair with the manager. Another time, they say it's your university degree, you are cocky and you show off too much. But you don't care. On your way home, you always empty your purse of the many business cards from men who want you; *you know, you.* But they don't. You meet customers who recognize you, who say, *Theresa, hope you had a good day at work?* They don't.

Fridays, you make your Momma believe you work twenty-four hours, because its weekend and Americans shop a lot for parties, and picnics, and road trips, and hiking. But once it's 6PM, you become Susie, the pole girl with shiny sheens and meaty laps, the African girl at the strip club everybody wants to see move her body and wiggle, wiggle, wiggle. You make acquaintances, a lot of them, real men who know how to spend money. Saturdays you randomly make a pick out of the lot for a late evening hangout.

You make him drink lots of alcohol, you screw him after, you talk about Nigeria and the many business opportunities, from owning a club house to buying acres of land in Akure, or acquiring a disused airport or even a whole lagoon. Some lucky days, the very business minded gets interested and you call your cousin Emmy Bangkok.

Yes, you are a swindler. Your network spreads from America to Nigeria to Ghana to China to even the UAE, and when you make these connections and the victims get duped, you get a ten percent cut which sometimes is big money. It was swindling that paved your way into this America at nineteen. Emmy Bangkok had introduced you to a white man whom he said was proving hard to yield to the pretty Brazilian girl on his fake Facebook account. You had chatted him up with your real account, your real face and teenage smile, and he demanded for a video call. You called him when you were alone in the dressing room, showed him things your Momma said only your husband should see. He fell in love with your little breasts, your virgin skin and African accent, said he loved the way you ate your English. Then you stopped calling him and he sent you dozens of mails: [09.6.12] *baby what's wrong? You sick? I miss your tight skin. Xoxo.* [10.6.12] *Baby I can't live a day without seeing you, I love you. Please call me.* [12.6.12] *Hey love, my day was messed up at the office today. All I kept thinking was when you bent over the last time.* You waited two weeks before you replied to the twenty-eighth mail. You said: *I'm out of school because there is no money to pay the fees. My mother is sick, my cream is finished, you can't see my rough skin until I get another cream.* Then he began to send money. Emmy Bangkok said that's how it works, when you'd been worried that you might lose

302

your *Oyibo Maga* as you often called the white man. He'd told you to relax because he'd been in the business for four years and had swindled close to eighty-four Oyibo Magas and even had girls that worked for him. The wait worked; two hundred dollars, three fifty, until he was sending almost half of his salary in exchange for video calls of you singing a hymn while you touched yourself. Emmy Bangkok persuaded you to ask for more money, but you had other plans. You made your Oyibo Maga agree to pay for your university education in America in exchange for all the sex he ever wanted.

After school, you are the girl who stole your Oyibo Maga's credit card and moved with your Momma to Alaska, to California, to Illinois, evading the police until the Li's took you in. Here, you became Lily, and acted like the born-again that your Momma always wanted; she'd hated that you lived with a man old enough to be your father. You dropped your university degree and went for a job at the mall because you wanted to mix with the crowd, to appear ordinary.

The Lis' turned out to be very good people. They employed your Momma as a cook, and a caregiver for their son who has Down's syndrome. Mr. Li isn't always around because he's a stockbroker and is at home only on weekends. Mrs. Li is a nurse; she affords a day off in the week to play with her son Danny. Some Sundays, they would invite you and your Momma for a picnic at the park. You chatted about many things and watched Danny play with a kite or a balloon. He's twenty-one and always has been such a lovely soul. Sometimes when Momma told you to go tell Danny food was ready, you would catch him naked in the bathtub, touching himself and moaning. You decide not to tell Mrs. Li because a special person deserved certain pleasures too. You wished you were like him, incomplete, free, and oblivious of life's hard realities. But, sorry America would not let you. That Sunday evening, America would have your Momma talking about the immigrant in Los Angeles who walked into a moving train because he was going to be deported. She was still talking when she slipped and everything fell, tragedy ushering tragedy.

Sixty six, thirty three, ninety nine...

You walked your grief to a bar after you left the hospital. There, you counted with your fingers instead. You remembered this was what you did back in primary school, when your teacher would draw your skirt taut and lash at your buttocks mercilessly. *Sixty six* made you clench your teeth and not cry, to cry is to be weak. *Thirty three*, you turn your grit to a smile when the pain gets to your head. *Ninety nine,* you want to scream but when you open your lips nothing comes out. You counted again and again until the bar girl began to notice, began to look at you like the several refills you've had had begun to wrap around your consciousness. You wondered when American people would eventually learn to mind their own businesses. You scoffed. You wanted to tell her to flip the news to another channel because an image of the anti-immigrant president came up. Your anger crawled on your skin and you wanted to say *fuck you, bitch!* You wanted to scream it and bang your fists on the bar stand so everyone would hear. But you didn't know if the bar girl was his supporter or the couple over at the far side, or the white man who sat alone and had his eyes trained on you from the moment you walked in. You didn't know what the ado was all about, even Otolo, your bosom friend who has been trying to cross the border for two years now but was still on the other side. The camp is overcrowded, with occasional outbreaks of cholera. Building a new wall meant to cut short Otolo's chances forever. *Fuck him!* But you didn't say it out loud. Instead you paid the bar girl and blew a kiss at the white man before you stepped into the night.

A little after midnight you walked into the house, your teeth clenched and your shivering hands stuffed inside your pockets. The cold bit into your skin, a reminder that all these years, you still miss home. You still miss the Udala tree in your father's compound, you still miss the evening sun, the way it warmed your skin. You miss your old friends and the rest of your family; Nkechi must have become a big girl now, Ebuka would have started the transport business he always talked about, your uncles must have sold your father's house to people who would probably build on where he was buried.

Sometimes you tell Emmy Bangkok you wished to visit home and he would ask, "Theresa with what? You have been in Obodo Oyibo for some years now, don't expect people to welcome you home with just a University Certificate. They are expecting you to come home with real money, hard currency! Nobody will clap for your certificate in this country!"

Each time you had decided to stay back, and because your Momma shared the same view with him too.

The Lis' were worried out of their skins. They asked a lot of questions but you kept telling them your Momma was fine, she was getting better. You kept avoiding eye contact least they looked into your eyes and saw the weight of your grief, the way it sagged your lids. To cry is to be weak. Danny gathered your weak bones into a warm hug, and ambled behind you as you stepped down to the basement. You sank your back into Momma's bed and decided you'd tell him the true state of things,

"She's not looking good, Dan. I pray she survives this."

The way the words left your lips, it was as though a part of your body left with them. You felt so empty without Momma, you did not want to think of what would happen if she was no more. You shivered. Danny sat close to you and held your hand, kissed it the way he'd kiss Mrs. Li's and then smoothed your hair gently. You thought that his lips felt so soft, so fragile, so innocent. You let him touch you, closed your eyes as his unsteady hands crawled into your blouse. Special people needed attention too. They needed to express their feelings and be loved, perhaps in it they could find some lost parts of their bodies. *Sixty six, thirty three, ninety nine,* you breathed heavily when his fingers brushed your nipple, and when his tongue touched your skin, your Momma's image on the hospital bed dissolved from your memory, piece by piece, until you imagined her like a recorder on rewind, going back up the stairs, the plates rising back to her hands, her laughter ringing out loud and then folding back into her mouth, and for a moment everything seemed normal.

The doctor looked worried when you walked in. He said your phone was dead, and your Momma has been up since 5AM, and was asking to see you, Leila. That name Leila stung you. Memories of Alaska flooded back; you bending over for strange men to have their ways in dark alleys so you and your Momma could be fed. You told her you had friends in Alaska who helped you when you needed funds. How on earth did she know Leila? You held down your shame in your chest and walked with the doctor towards the private ward. For a moment you thought your Momma was ungrateful, she was sick and you having enough money to put her in a clinic, in a country where illegal immigrants had no health insurance, was enough for her to mind her own business and not sniff around you! But Momma would always be Momma right? She smiled and spread her arms once you opened the door, and you wriggled into her bosom like a lost puppy. You asked her how she felt, she held your face in her hands and replied, "Jasmine, we need to talk."

You heard the doctor lock the door, turned and saw him nod slightly at you and fold his arms, leaning on the whitewashed acrylic wall. A kind of tension gripped you. When your Momma needed to talk, then she was damn serious she needed to talk. She started by saying, "Theri, I know what you have been doing. I knew you had ambitions even before you turned nineteen. I know the kind of life you live but I would put no blame on you for it. Your father's spirit rubbed off on you, a lot of it. You need to have seen him, so energetic, so full of life, oh!"

You managed a smile although you were shocked, although your hands shook and your attention kept slipping away. Your memory flashed back to the Reverend's face grinning when you sat on his laps and rolled your waist. You wondered if your Momma knew that too, if God had revealed it to her in one of those her crusade outings. You thought she did not because she smiled back at you and put her hands into yours to steady them. She looked so fragile, so pale and worn out. Fifty-seven was a number until you were with your Momma on the hospital bed. You wished things were different, you wished your Papa was alive so your Momma would not have to go through the barrage of his memories which kept flooding back and dragging her under, into a state of depression.

"Theri, I can't even move my waist or feel my legs anymore."

You looked at the doctor and he held your eyes, his steady from above the rim, filled with compassion. You thought he did not look like your lecturer after all. There was a softness inside there, somewhere. Your eyes shifted back to your Momma and she nodded slightly, tears sliding out of her eyes and down the sides of her face. You brought out your handkerchief and wiped them off,

"Momma stop, we're gonna get through this. Always, always, remember? We'll fight it," you said, holding her arms and resting your head on her chest, listening to the soft beating of her heart, counting the *Lubs* and the *Dubs* as though listening hard enough could take it all away, as though if only staying alive could be enough validation.

308

She patted your hair gently and said, "You know, more than anything, I've always wanted a flamboyant burial. The kind that should be the talk of town for at least a week. The kind that would stand the test of time and be a yardstick for other burial ceremonies."

For a moment, you wondered if your Momma was in her best frame of mind, you wondered why she would speak of death when it was obvious she was going to be fine— except the part where she would be immobile, probably for the rest of her life. You were fine with that though, and it irked you to hear her speak of death this way, you raised your head and told her to stop.

She said, "Just listen, Theri! Listen! You see when I'm gone, I just want you to fly my body back to Nigeria. I do not know much people here so I do not need a requiem. I don't want a few persons wearing black and their women with elaborate hats and dark shaded glasses sniffing their noses and sharing cocktails talking business or making up with past times while I lie in state in some funeral home. My spirit will not be at peace. I don't want to be buried at a cemetery in this land, you know what our people say, that the land does not know how to eat if the spirit does not know how to rest. And don't you dare cremate any part of my body, I will haunt you for the rest of your life!"

Sixty six, thirty three, ninety nine, you wanted her to stop, you thought probably she was afraid and it was the fear that was making her talk weird. You held your head in your hand and shook it violently. You wondered if all this was real and began to shed tears. Your Momma drew you into her bosom and said, "Theri, all

I want is the best for you, I don't want to be a burden to this, your young, complicated life."

"But you're not Momma, you won't be! You have to stop all this death talk."

"Theri, your cousin Emmy is a big boy back home. His mother, my sister, whenever she calls is always bragging about his expensive cars, and duplexes and wrist watches. I want you to be rich too, I want you to bury my body in a golden casket, I want to have seven Reverends and three Bishops performing my final burial rights. I want the highlights of this burial to be aired on the local TV station, so they would know my daughter too came back from Obodo Oyibo."

Sixty six, thirty three... you wondered what this talk was all about, you wondered where she was headed, then the doctor walked up to you, his eyes averted as though he did not want you to see him cry, to cry is to be weak. He put his hand on your shoulder and handed you a syringe. You froze. You felt the panic rise from within your gut, felt it spread like a wildfire until your whole body started to shiver. It would be a crazy thing to do if this was what your Momma had meant all the while.

You looked back at her and she said, "Theri, it is not only the swindling that gave Emmy the kind of money he enjoys now, his mother whom you know cannot keep her mouth shut told me he sold one of his kidneys to an Arab man three years ago. That boy lives on one kidney now but he has money. I cannot have two good kidneys and other good organs and my daughter would keep suffering."

At this point you got up, you turned to get away from all the insane talk, but the doctor held you back, you clawed his at body and tried to break free, you wanted to hit him, push him down and break into a run but his grip was firm. You thought it was like the firm grip of the first man you'd ever truly loved.

Then your Momma bellowed, "Theri! Stop it! Stop it and just listen to me this once in your life!"

You turned around to look at her, eyes glazed over with anger, and pity, and ambition, all emotions mangled into one long unblinking stare that seemed to burn right through your body. You sank to the floor and covered your ears.

"You have to do it!" she said. "The doctor has already found us good buyers. He would move us from here to a place where it would be done. Theri…"

You pushed your fingers into your ears and thought of what it meant to take your own Momma's life, how the memories would shred your body layer after layer until one day it ate your bones.

"Sell them! Theri, sell them!"

You wanted her to stop, you wanted all this to be a dream, you shut your eyes and started to whisper, "Sixty six, Thirty three, Ninety nine…"

Yes, you are Theresa Okolo, the illegal immigrant, the black pole dancer, the swindler, the steller sales representative, but probably, after that cold, cold morning at the hospital, there would be another title hovering above your head; dark, eerie, but rich.

Behind the Eyes
Paul K Joyce

How much longer can I keep doing this? The bus hisses to a stop and lowers to pavement level before flinging its doors open in flamboyant challenge. I adjust my mask as the woman in front roots in her bag. *Come on*, I tell myself. The sky darkens and drops of rain find their way around my scarf and onto my neck. The familiar knot in my stomach begins, and builds into a wave of fluttering and tightness. Finger at my too-tight collar I step inside, the traffic's roar, dulled. I press my card against the reader, glancing at the driver. I'm ready for his fleshy screened-off smile.

"Hello darling," he says.

My secret mouth twists in disapproval. *Say something – say something*, I think; but his eyes are already on the mirror, podgy fingers coaxing the purring machine. I breathe out. Beads of sweat gather on my top lip. The atmosphere is close, and smells of damp clothes, machine oil, and cheap deodorant. The door snaps shut behind me and an animal surge propels us into the traffic. I pull my scarf away from my head and face them.

The eyes.

A poet might see fiery constellations; windows into the soul, but these conduits of photons are merciless. They stare; observe; scrutinize. Judge. I can't escape them.

Breathe.

What really lies behind the eyes?

Red-tape crosses claim alternate seats. An older man with a puffer jacket and beanie is the first to look away. Step. A large woman with black leggings and headphones breathes out heavily as the bus gathers speed. It lurches to the left and I almost tumble into the lap of a grey, tweed-wrapped woman, her hawk eyes narrow underneath pinched, pencilled eyebrows.

"Sorry, I —"

The look stops the breath in my throat, her face rippling with barely-contained dislike. The young guy opposite her with the brand-new Nike trainers folds his arms and sighs. I'm about to smile but he's already looking back down at his phone. Another step. I'm surrounded.

The eyes.

No one speaks. The diesel song of the engine is overlaid with the tinny spill from multiple earpieces. A space. I sit down, arranging my bag on my lap with the scarf on top. Legs together. A middle-aged woman with a lean face and braided hair sits opposite. She rolls a mobile in her bony hands and is a riot of baggy pinks and purples. She clears her throat, and her eyes find mine.

"You got on just in time," she says, her voice muffled behind her patterned mask.

She's talking to me? I smooth down my coat, lift my chin.

"I'm sorry?" I say.

"Just in time – it's pouring out there."

Rain hammers against the roof and windows, completely obscuring the drab entrails of suburbia. I hadn't noticed.

"Oh, yes," I reply, not knowing what to say.

She rolls her phone.

"That's a pretty scarf."

Where is this going? I think.

"Thanks, I –"

"You can get away with wearing those vibrant colours, can't you? They just wash me out."

A sour taste begins at the back of my throat. Beyond the rain-streaked windows, dull red-brick tenements give way to industrial units and finally, the extravagant metal and glass-clad masculinity of the city. It's the shouting I hear first, long before I see the first placard.

"Oh, this lot," says a voice to my right, near the back.

Another: "Don't 'matter' to me."

The driver shouts down that there's going to be a bit of a delay. "Some sort of demo," he says.

Phone-woman is still talking, shaking her head. I zone out and crane my neck, reading the messages on the sea of signs – words on homemade rectangles of cardboard. Words that trigger detonations in my mind. I feel as if fingers of steel are pushing their way up my back and through my body, enmeshing me in interlocking strands. Heat. Strength. My fingers tighten into loose fists and I feel the blood in every part of my body. Words bubble in my mouth.

Phone-woman sees the decisive pink of my palm and her mouth stops moving. I stand up, holding her uncomprehending stare for just a second before walking to the front of the bus. *Let them look.* I ignore the driver's condescending tone.

314

"Yes, I know what that button's for."

The doors open at my command and I step out into noise, revolution.

Into my future.